GRACELAND
CEMETERY

GRACELAND CEMETERY

CHICAGO STORIES, SYMBOLS, AND SECRETS

ADAM SELZER

3 FIELDS BOOKS
An imprint of the University of Illinois Press

3 Fields Books is an imprint of
the University of Illinois Press.

Library of Congress Cataloging-in-Publication Data
Names: Selzer, Adam, author.
Title: Graceland Cemetery: Chicago stories, symbols,
    and secrets / Adam Selzer.
Other titles: Chicago stories, symbols, and secrets
Description: [Champaign, Illinois]: 3 Fields Books, an
    imprint of the University of Illinois Press, [2022] |
    Includes bibliographical references and index.
Identifiers: LCCN 2022002587 (print) | LCCN
    2022002588 (ebook) | ISBN 9780252086502
    (paperback) | ISBN 9780252053429 (ebook)
Subjects: LCSH: Graceland Cemetery (Chicago, Ill.)—
    Tours. | Chicago (Ill.)—Biography—Anecdotes. |
    Chicago (Ill.)—History—Anecdotes.
Classification: LCC F548.612.G72 S45 2022 (print) |
    LCC F548.612.G72 (ebook) | DDC 977.3/11—dc23/
    eng/20220126
LC record available at https://lccn.loc.gov/2022002587
LC ebook record available at https://lccn.loc.gov/2022002588

Contents

Acknowledgments

Thanks to the Effing Chicago crew: Mandy Piotrowski, Leyla Royale, Patti Swanson, and Ben Archer. The Whiskey and a Cookie Crew: Patti Vasquez, Esmeralda Leon, Elliott Serrano, and Scott Stantis. To the internet's Chicago History Avengers, including but not limited to Robert Loerzel, Bill Savage, Jeff Nichols, Mary Jo Hoag, Luigi D'Napla, Liz Garibay, Scott Prizzini, Mark Jacob, Shermann Thomas, Robert Lerch, Liam Ford, and JJ Tindall.

To my agent, Adrienne Rosado, and my family.

Special thanks to the Graceland staff for being so accommodating with my research requests. And to the coyotes.

Extra special thanks to The Mysterians.

The Origins of Graceland Cemetery

During Thomas Barbour Bryan's time in Chicago, there was hardly a week that he wasn't in the papers for something or another. An 1848 Harvard grad who spoke half a dozen languages, Bryan built railroads, erected concert halls, founded the suburb of Elmhurst, ran for mayor more than once, and rubbed elbows with the famous and infamous. The son of an abolitionist Virginia politician (and, by some accounts, a grand nephew of Daniel Boone), he served as a pallbearer for Abraham Lincoln,[1] and during the last months of the Civil War he organized the Great Northwestern Sanitary Fair, which became a sort of victory lap for the just-won struggle. When General Grant made a speech at the fair—his first public speech—Bryan introduced him onstage.[2]

In the 1880s Bryan had an office in William Le Baron Jenney's Home Insurance Building, the first modern "steel frame" skyscraper. In the early 1890s, he was Vice President and Commissioner at Large for the World's Fair and Columbian Exposition, traveling the world and meeting with people such as the Pope to promote the interests of the upcoming Fair.[3]

And in the middle of his Columbian Exposition work, he sold a 51 percent interest in a copier machine company to H. H. Holmes, the murderous "Devil in the White City," who paid him with a $7000 promissory note. Bryan never got a cent in cash, making him one of Holmes' biggest individual swindling victims.[4] He is probably the only person who knew both Abraham Lincoln and H. H. Holmes.

And, in the midst of all these exploits, he somehow made time to found Graceland Cemetery.

• • •

When Chicago first began to grow from a mudhole into a metropolis in the 1830s, most American cities still relied on overcrowded churchyards for burials. In 1822, when a man was hired to cover New York's Trinity Churchyard with quicklime, he wrote that "the stench was so offensive as to cause several of my laborers to cascade (vomit) freely."[5] Across the Atlantic, a London Sanitary Commission investigating burial grounds in 1839 found horrifying scenes everywhere they went: bones scattered about, limbs protruding from overcrowded graves, open pits of gunk and effluvia, and stenches beyond description.[6]

Chicago had first attempted to set up better cemeteries in 1835, setting aside plats of land on the north side, near where the Water Tower is now, and on the south side, near the present site of Chinatown. Another is known to have existed around the spot where the Merchandise Mart now stands. None of these remained in the "outskirts" for long, though, and as the city expanded these burial grounds were quickly abandoned in favor of a hundred-acre tract further north that became "City Cemetery."

The formation of City Cemetery lined up temporally with the growth of "garden cemeteries" in the western world. Beside the problem of overcrowded churchyards, large cities were dealing with a distinct lack of green space—public parks were so rare as to be practically unknown as of 1831. In that year, Mount Auburn Cemetery was founded in Cambridge, Massachusetts, which provided both an uncrowded burial ground and a green space for recreation. Other garden cemeteries, such as Brooklyn's Green-Wood, quickly followed, and these large spaces became popular retreats for city dwellers.

However, City Cemetery was by no account an attractive place. Besides being close enough to the drinking water to be disastrous for sanitation, there was little attention given to groundskeeping or landscaping. Dr. A. J. Baxter, who was in the habit of robbing the graves there so his medical students would have cadavers to dissect, cheerfully recalled it as "a dismal, neglected place . . . usually ankle-deep in sand."[7] Dewitt Cregier was even more explicit, stating that in City Cemetery, "There was nothing but sand and sand. . . . After a wind storm the bleak shore looked positively grewsome [sic]. At the low places the coffins, sometimes showing half their contents, would be exposed."[8]

In 1855, Thomas and Jennie Bryan's five-year-old son, Daniel Page Bryan, was buried in the City Cemetery, and Thomas found the place "in a condition sad to behold," in addition to being terribly expensive. "The neglected and actually repulsive condition of the cemetery," he wrote, "induced my search of land for a rural burying ground, more remote from and more worthy of the city."[9]

Bryan threw himself into studying the nascent art of cemetery management and making plans. His project was shelved for a while when the opening of Rosehill Cemetery was announced, but when the Rosehill company offered to make Bryan their president in 1858, it only renewed his enthusiasm for starting a cemetery himself. After a couple of years of working with landscape designers, purchasing land from the heirs of Justin Butterfield, and battling with neighbors who didn't want a cemetery in their backyards, the first burial at Graceland took place in April 1860 when Daniel Page Bryan was reinterred in a new grave. The formal dedication was in late August of that year, with Bryan as president and his great friend, the artist G. P. A. Healy, as treasurer.[10]

Throughout the 1860s and early 1870s, thousands of bodies from City Cemetery were moved to Graceland and Rosehill as the old City Cemetery grounds were converted to Lincoln Park. Some prominent people started building new monuments to themselves in Graceland, often long before they were needed. Soon, as all garden cemeteries strove to be, Graceland was at once a park, an open air museum, and an art gallery.

By the turn of the 20th century, it was such a popular place that it had

Thomas B. Bryan—Digital Library of Illinois

Bryan was also known for his comic poetry. Little of it survives, but one anecdote states that in boarding school, he was subject to some ritual in which he was spanked with a ruler until he could come up with an epigram. Mid-spanking, he asked "Why does this resemble an epigram? (Because) an epigram is defined to be wit regulated by rule, and, like a bee, with a sting in the tail." Source: Dean, C. *The World's Fair City* privately published, 1892.

to be closed to all but ticket holders on Sundays and holidays for a time, as lot owners were afraid it had become too much of a "pleasure ground."[11]

Though much of the landscape remains the way it was carved out by glaciers thousands of years ago, the grounds and layout have changed some over the years. A former alternate entrance on Buena Avenue was removed, and a second pond, Lake Hazelmere, was filled in. A section known as "The Grotto" became a row of vaults. As the 20th century progressed and social trends moved away from using cemeteries as places of leisure, the cemetery fell into periods of neglect, but by the turn of the 21st century it had been revived and restored back to much of its 19th-century landscaping and ideals.[12]

But nature continues to alter the land. The 2020 "derecho" wind storm uprooted more than 50 trees in the cemetery and led to weeks of closure to clean up the mess. Graceland's associate director, Jensen Allen, told

There's music in bells, e'en though without chimes,
And harmony dwells in thoughts without rhymes,
The bird that on wing, was caught in my net,
Ne'er striveth to sing, but why the regret?
Her melody's best, whose mate hath ne'er heard
Shrill notes in their nest, my bonnie, "Jay Bird."

A poem written by Thomas to his wife, Jenny Byrd Page Bryan (above), when she expressed regret at not being able to sing. This 1856 portrait of her by their friend (and Graceland treasurer) G. P. A. Healy is in the Smithsonian. Healy painted many Graceland residents, though many of the portraits are now lost. Source: Hill, Josephine, *A Souvenir of World's Fair Women*, The Blocher Co., Chicago, 1892.

Time Out that "it looked like a dinosaur came through and had a temper tantrum."[13] New trees have been planted, but many won't reach maturity for decades.

Though early records make it difficult to ascertain the total number of interments, most estimates today hover around the vicinity of 175,000. Though perhaps best known for its many architects, there are also famous athletes, artists, politicians, and business leaders whose names are still known today, and countless people who were famous in their day but haven't had anything written about them since their epitaphs were carved.

And, of course, there are countless others whose names were never widely known at all, but whose stories *should* have been a part of local history, if not world history. Short biographies and obituaries often simply give little more than a list of what they owned, who they gave birth to, and perhaps what clubs they joined. It's easy to forget, but good to remember, that the people here were once alive, and that there was more to their lives than business transactions and weddings. Most everyone here who lived long enough played games, told jokes, sang songs, pulled pranks, fell in love, fell out of love, got diarrhea, pursued hobbies, and landed in trouble. And, though they can be hard to find, sometimes the stories survive.

About This Book

I've attempted to tell as many of these forgotten stories as I could and to show how the lives of the people interred here intersected with each other and with history.

Cemetery books are commonly divided into categories ("Politicians," "Captains of Industry," and so forth), but many people here don't fit into any particular category, and others fit into more than one. Therefore, I've chosen to arrange the book "Choose Your Own Adventure" style—a selection of different walks, with stories organized by geography. Five "stations" are marked out, and from each station there are two different "walks" taking you to the next station.

In some cases, less attention than might be expected has been paid to famous people whose names remain familiar. I wanted to use as much space as possible for people whose stories can't be found as easily, so many of those who have been the subject of several biographies and articles are given less-detailed biographies here.

While my years as a tour guide at the cemetery gave me a head start, I tried to research as many new people as I could for the book. Some stories were found by simply looking up names on random headstones or browsing the interment books for interesting causes of death (the youngest people listed as dying of "old age" are in their early fifties). Often, while researching one person, I'd find mentions of other interesting people, find out they were at Graceland as well, and start researching them, too.

Naturally, with over 175,000 interments, I couldn't cover everyone. By no means is this a complete book, or the most comprehensive biography possible of anyone here—just an ice breaker. Taken as a whole, these stories at Graceland present a unique lens through which to view American history. And there's always more to find.

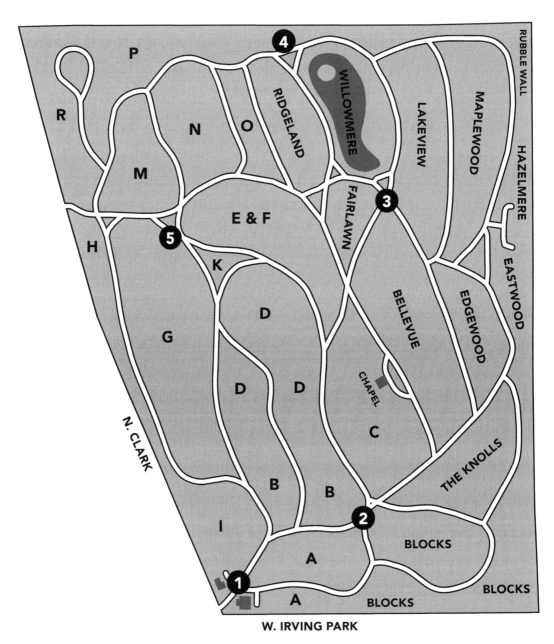

P

R

N

O

RIDGELAND

WILLOWMERE

LAKEVIEW

MAPLEWOOD

RUBBLE WALL

M

HAZELMERE

H

E & F

FAIRLAWN

5

K

EASTWOOD

D

BELLEVUE

EDGEWOOD

G

N. CLARK

D

D

CHAPEL

C

3

THE KNOLLS

B

B

2

I

BLOCKS

A

BLOCKS

1

A

BLOCKS

BLOCKS

W. IRVING PARK

Map of Graceland Cemetery

GRACELAND
CEMETERY

THE CEMETERY ENTRANCE

Col. Webb's Hidden Monument

"These volunteer quartermasters would ruin forty governments if they had rope."

—William Webb on aspiring war profiteers, quoted in letter of David Stuart to *Chicago Tribune*

Upon entering Graceland at the main gates, you'll face a small section of flowers and bushes, flanked by the office to the right and a waiting room to the left. Behind the greenery in the center, it's easy to miss a single large gravestone featuring faded military insignia. Like many stones of its era, it's now illegible, but it was once a showpiece for the cemetery.

There were fewer than a hundred burials—mostly removals from City Cemetery—at Graceland in 1860; burials started in earnest the next year, which lines its growth up neatly with the beginning of the Civil War. In April of 1862 came the Battle of Shiloh, which was not only the bloodiest battle in American history up to that point, but the first Civil War battle to claim the lives of a significant number of Chicago soldiers. While the city celebrated the Union victory, a meeting was held to determine what was to be done with the remains of local soldiers who were being returned.[1]

Privately owned cemeteries were a new sort of business in those days, and people were sometimes skeptical about them and their motives. In late 1862, the *Tribune* criticized both Graceland and Rosehill, saying that "the companies are . . . just as purely associations for money making as any other within our knowledge."[2]

They weren't totally wrong—both cemeteries *were* businesses, no matter how pure their motives. And there may have been something in Bryan's nature that made cemetery ownership particularly suited to him: he was a collector. Newspapers are full of stories of his buying such treasures as the original courthouse bell,[3] a chair made from the timbers of Fort Dearborn,[4] the handwritten draft of the Emancipation Proclamation,[5] and other curios and relics. In running a cemetery, he was, in a way, collecting people. It would have been unseemly to say so, but surely neither cemetery wanted the other to get *all* of the prominent people. At the meeting, Bryan graciously offered several plots in Graceland for the Chicago veterans.[6]

But Rosehill Cemetery had already set aside a prominent section for soldiers nearly a year before,[7] and the city chose to continue using that spot for the Shiloh dead.

However, there was one soldier, **William A. Webb (1827–1861)**, whose remains had been reposing in the Graceland vault all winter. Three days after Bryan's offer was rejected, Webb's body was taken from the vault to be buried in the large plot, donated by Bryan, at the very front of the cemetery.[8]

William Webb had served as quartermaster in Chicago before been sent to Warsaw, Missouri, as a colonel in the 42nd Illinois Infantry in the fall of 1861. On November 1st, the regiment was ordered to march to Springfield, Missouri, with so little notice that they didn't even have time to pack up their tents. Despite the physical torture of sleeping outside in the cold November air, they made the ninety-seven-mile hike in under three days—and then had to march right back five days later, when Springfield was evacuated.

The 42nd went without decent shelter for fifteen days, and the lack of warmth, sanitation, and nutrition took their toll; Colonel Webb died of typhoid fever on December 24. A committee of soldiers issued a statement praising him as a gallant leader, telling his friends that "(We) crave of them the sad privilege of mingling with their sorrow a soldier's tear."[9] Though a few articles from months before had noted that Webb was an excellent speaker when he made brief remarks at ceremonies, they had never transcribed what he said. Perhaps they thought there would be time for him to make speeches later.

Bryan may have intended the triangular plat near the entrance to be a soldiers' lot, but in the end only Webb would be buried there. His monument, paid for by his fellow soldiers, would be pointed out by reporters on Decoration Day as a landmark of the cemetery for years,[10] but over time Webb's name faded, both from public memory and from the gravestone itself.

■ ■ ■

When one faces the landscaping in front of Webb's grave, the cemetery office, designed by Holabird and Roche (page 108), is on the right. Between Webb's grave and the office, are two paths: one leading northwest into the heart of the cemetery (Route 1-A) and one leading west parallel to the southern wall (1-B) (1-B may be converted from a paved road to a grass path in the 2020s).

For **Route 1-A,** turn to page 5.

For **Route 1-B**, turn to page 35.

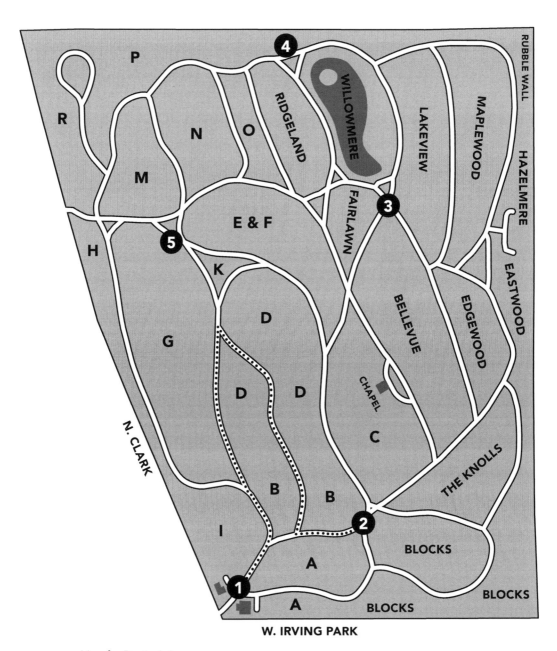

Map for Route 1-A

ROUTE 1-A

Walk up the road; on the right you will pass a marker to policeman **Jacob Wolf (1821–1890)** and a small red stone for **Anton Lassich (1903–1957)**, the musically inclined may hum the notes carved into the stone, which are a portion of Brahms' Lullaby.

Just past the marker for grocer **Godfrey Jacob (1824–1912)** on the right find the small marker notable for its "Real Daughter" plaque.

Elizabeth Ely Gridley Butler: Daughter of the Revolution

> "My father, Theodore Gridley . . . was in the engagement at Bunker Hill. . . . My mother accompanied him from Clinton, N.Y. to be present and assist in the laying of the cornerstone of the Bunker Hill monument. . . . I have also a gold spoon that each 'real daughter' is entitled to."
> —Elizabeth Gridley-Butler, "Another 'Real Daughter'"

The "real daughter" plaque on the headstone for **Elizabeth Ely Gridley Butler (1826–1921)** comes from the Daughters of the American Revolution and indicates that her father fought in the Revolutionary War. The dates on the stone suggest an interesting story, as the youngest of the Revolutionary soldiers would have been rather old to be having children in 1826.

Elizabeth's father, Theodore Gridley, enlisted in Washington's army in May, 1775 and served at least through December. He was nearly 60 when he married his third wife, **Amy Ely Gridley (1776–1876)**, in 1817. When the Bunker Hill monument was built in 1825, he and Amy journeyed to Boston to hear Daniel Webster give a speech at the dedication.[1] Theodore died a year later while Amy was pregnant with their only child, Elizabeth;[2] he is buried in Oneida, New York.

For Amy to carry a baby to term and survive at the age of 50 was a remarkable feat in and of itself, particularly in 1826. But she not only survived, she lived another half century, moving to Chicago in 1854. As of 1868 she was getting $96 a year as a widow's pension.[3] An 1875 profile of Amy in the *Tribune* identified her as the oldest woman in Chicago and took care to note that "Unlike the conventional old lady, she does not smoke a pipe or require much attention."[4]

However, she had never fully recovered mentally from the night she spent in a cabbage patch fleeing from the Great Chicago Fire: "Her only occupation for the past year," the reporter wrote, "has been rumpling handkerchiefs, from which she seems to derive considerable amusement."[5] Amy died the next year, just shy of her 100th birthday, and is buried in the plot.[6]

Her daughter, Elizabeth, studied for a time at the Young Ladies Domestic Seminary at Clinton, a member of one of the first classes there to be racially integrated.[7] Though only Elizabeth has a marker, there are many family graves in the plot.[8]

• • •

On the other side of the road is a boulder for the Malcom Family. Among the many people buried in the plot was **Robert Malcom (1803–1871)**, who died October 9, 1871, as the Great Chicago Fire was engulfing the city. He didn't die from the fire, but from dropsy. It's a curious fact to consider: even as the city burned, the world kept turning, and people continued to die of the same ailments that afflicted them every other day. The Graceland interment book shows deaths from the days of the fire due to tuberculosis, typhoid fever, cholera, and cancer,[9] and it was said that as many as eight babies were born during the fire to mothers fleeing the flames in the old City Cemetery.[10]

Only a couple of victims of the fire were buried at Graceland in the immediate aftermath; a monument in Section R for **Jacob Wolf (1832–1871)** bears the epitaph "Burned in Chicago Fire." The other marked "Fire" grave is just behind Malcolm: **Horace P. Dewey (1818–1871)**, whose modest twin-arch family monument is a few spaces back and to the left (and facing the opposite direction). Dewey, a widowed insurance man, died after a daring attempt to jump from a third-story window to the roof of the building next door.[11] His marker calls him a "Hero of the Great Chicago Fire." Dewey's wife, **Mary A Dewey (1824–1866)**, has a matching marker denoting her "A Natural Born Artist of Early Chicago." Horace and Mary's daughter, **Jennie B. Dewey (c1860–1945)**, orphaned at 11 years of age after the fire, became a schoolteacher and was buried with her parents when she died nearly 75 years after the death of her father.[12]

The Dewey Marker

• • •

Just to the right of the Malcom boulder is a section of graves with the name Aiken, including a large, faded one for Captain Hector Aiken, which is mostly illegible after years of wear.

Captain Hector Aiken

"Last night, as I was crawling over the field (wounded), I saw men moving around, and knew what they were after, so I took my meerschaum pipe, a present from my friends when I left home, and a $10 gold piece, and hid them where they would not be likely to look for them. The first fellow was satisfied with my pocketbook; the next took my soft hat and threw me this hard one, which did me good service in the heat as a fan. He took my sword, belt and pistol."
—Hector Aiken, "The Late Captain Aiken"

Shortly after the Emancipation Proclamation went into effect in 1863, the first regiments of Black soldiers were recruited—a hugely controversial move at first, though most Union supporters got used to it quickly enough. These regiments were dangerous to join—the Confederacy refused to treat Black troops the same as other soldiers, and rather than taking them prisoner when captured, they would often enslave or murder them. The white officers of these units, too, expected that in the event of their capture, the Confederates would treat them without mercy.

Among those who took on this additional level of risk was **Captain Hector Aiken (1839–1864)**. The son of business man **Edward H. Aiken (1801–1870)**, Hector could probably have used his family connections and wealth to avoid service. But he left school to join the army, and after serving as a private in Chicago's famous Board of Trade Battery he was made one of the white officers of the U.S. 29th Colored Regiment, the Black regiment formed of Illinois soldiers.[13]

After briefly being stationed at the White House in June of 1864, the 29th ended up in Petersburg, Virginia. At the time, the *Tribune* wrote that "Among the host of noble young men that represent the loyal patriotism of Chicago in the army, there is not one more promising, none more cool, brave and determined than is Capt. Aiken. He will be heard from hereafter."[14]

That summer, amid the long and tedious trench war in Petersburg came the Battle of the Crater. Washington Roebling (who would soon take over for his father in engineering the Brooklyn Bridge) worked to dig a tunnel under a Confederate fort and blow it up from beneath. The ensuing attack was a disaster for the Union; captured Black and white troops were marched up and down the streets of Petersburg, Virginia, to stoke racial resentment, the sort of public humiliation that would be a war crime today.

Aiken, having been wounded in the fight, was left on the battlefield to die. According to a report issued days later, "The enemy refused a flag of truce and (Aiken) was compelled to lie upon the field in the broiling sun, all day Saturday and Sunday. Sometime during Sunday night he managed to drag himself over to our lines, (where) he was taken to a hospital and suffered amputation. He lingered along in great agony for several days until death put an end to his sufferings."[15]

He was 24 years old. His sad story would be retold in Chicago for years.[16]

■ ■ ■

Beyond Aiken is a fork in the road that frames the triangular Williams family plot, with its towering pillar topped by a statue marking the grave of grocer and financier **Eli Williams (1799–1881)**. Veer left at the fork, proceeding north up Graceland Avenue. To the right, you'll see a white marker for Helen A. Carter, marked "Mamma's Grave."

Mamma's Grave: The Carter Plot

"Use the name of Mrs. Leslie Carter? Why, sir, I will make
it a by-word throughout the world! I will put it on bill-
boards and on fence posts! I will be Mrs. Leslie Carter,
the actress, former wife of Mr. Leslie Carter of Chicago
society. Tell that to the family!"

—Attributed to Caroline "Mrs. Leslie" Carter,
   "Tragedies of the Stage"

Helen Leslie Carter (1830–1861) was 20 when she married **James Carter
(1817–1873)**, a successful Galena merchant. By 1860, the couple was living
in Chicago with four children, and James' occupation was simply listed in
the census as "gentleman."[17] Helen died of apoplexy in 1862, leaving four
children.[18]

Among those in the plot is James and Helen's oldest son, **Leslie Carter
(1851–1908)**. As an adult Leslie served as director of St. Luke's Hospital,
but he achieved particular notoriety when his wife, Caroline, divorced him
in 1889. The trial—in which each accused the other of misbehavior—was so
scandalous and packed with details of their sex life that by some accounts
only men over 35 were allowed in the courtroom. Newspapers all over the
country reported on the proceedings in great detail (though they only hinted
at the more sordid bits), and some said that Caroline *must* have been the
guilty party simply because she was willing to *talk* about some of the things
that came up (even though the judge had ordered her to do so against her
objections).[19]

The sneering reporters said Caroline lacked "the qualifications of a good
actor,"[20] but Caroline proved them wrong: when the judge ruled against her,
and she was left without alimony or support, she used the national notoriety
the trial brought her to launch an acting career that lasted for half a century,
long after Leslie died and the case had faded from memory. Using "Mrs. Leslie
Carter" as a stage name, she was successful on Broadway, moved into silent
films, and was still playing "matron" roles in westerns in the 1930s. She was
the subject of a 1940 biopic, *The Lady with Red Hair*, and a 2006 biography
by Craig Clinton. She is buried in Ohio.

■ ■ ■

Just north of Carter on the left side of the road is a handsome marker featuring a relief sculpture in profile of the plot occupant, John A. Huck.

John Huck's Missing Tunnels

"Certainly I remember the (Huck) tunnels. When we were kids we played in them all the time, and believe me, we got many a scolding and spanking for going into them. We thought they were our discovery and tried to keep them a secret from the adults, but it didn't work."
—Marie Planendon, "When the Gold Coast Was a Brewery"

Most of the brewery **John Huck (1818–1878)** owned was destroyed by the Great Chicago Fire of 1871, and, though he lived another seven years, Huck never really rebuilt the business.[21] His son, Louis, was a hugely successful brewer in his own right (page 247).

But John's name would come back into the press every few decades because of the mile or so of brick tunnels he dug under the Gold Coast in the 1850s as a cool place to age his beer in the summer time. Sneaking into the old "Huck Tunnels" to play cops and robbers became a rite of passage for local children in the decades after the Great Chicago Fire, but parents were so afraid that *real* robbers were hiding in them that they had them closed off around the turn of the 20th century.

Today, though the tunnels are still presumably there, no one is entirely sure just *where*, making them one of the most tantalizing mysteries of the Gold Coast. They were apparently last seen in the 1920s when the Ambassador Hotel was under construction at State and Goethe.[22]

■ ■ ■

Back on the right side of the road, just north of the Carter plot, is an old white monument topped by a fireman's helmet.

John Butler Dickey and the *Other* Great Chicago Fire

"The upsetting of a lamp, the ashes carelessly knocked out of a pipe, the torch of an incendiary, or any of the numberless causes by which originate fires, may light just such another flame tomorrow."
—"Reorganization of the Fire Department," *Chicago Tribune, 1857*

On October 19, 1857, a fire broke out in the Loop. Rumor had it that a "dissolute" woman had set fire to a man's apartment when he didn't pay "the price of her shame,"[23] but this was only one of several theories as to the origin of the blaze.

The fire spread to become the worst the young city had even seen, destroying a number of buildings and claiming the lives of more than 20 people. Among these was **John Butler Dickey (1832–1857)**, described in the press as 25 years old and "a young man of excellent character."[24] He had been the foreman of the Liberty Hose Company, a volunteer fire department, and was crushed to death when the burning walls of Hempstead's Store on Lake Street came down. John High (page 243) also perished in the blaze.

As of 1857, volunteer companies were still the city's only formal defense against fire, and they would induce men to help by offering free whisky. The day after the 1857 fire, with the ruins still smoldering, the *Tribune* wrote, "We do not forget the fact that these firemen sacrificed their lives . . . when we say that the department never more clearly manifested its inefficiency, its want of discipline, and general worthlessness than in the disastrous conflagration yesterday. . . . Where there is whisky, good sense is not."[25]

Dickey's funeral was held at his parents' house on Monroe Street, and he was interred at the old City Cemetery. He and a few family members were moved to Graceland in 1866. One of John's sisters in the plot, **Zenana Scott Dickey (1836–1917)**, was widely reported at the time of her death to have been one of six women who were among Lincoln's honorary pallbearers at his Chicago funeral in 1865.[26]

▪ ▪ ▪

Continue the path. On the left will be an obelisk for **W. R. Loomis (1819–1894)**, a realtor and spokesman for Dr. Horne's Electro-Magnetic Belt, which he claimed had cured his rheumatism.[27] Just before Western Avenue will be a gray obelisk marked "O. Morrison."

The Morrisons: Pioneers and Eccentrics

"Sick hell! I'm just as [expletive deleted] spry as I was twenty years ago, and I'll be just as spry the same twenty years from now. I just (had) a [expletive deleted] bad spell on the other day . . . so I'm just staying around the house, except when I want a drink of whisky or a shave."
—Captain Edward W. Morrison, "-!!**!!_*!——* !!!-**-!!!**!!"

In January of 1834, a correspondent of the *New York American* became perhaps the first New Yorker to marvel in print about just how *cold* Chicago was. With temperatures dipping near -30F, he wrote that his usual letter to the paper was delayed because "It has been almost impossible, notwithstand-

An early map showing the "elephant trunk" bend in the river that Morrison worked to eliminate.

ing the large fire kept up by an attentive landlord, to prevent the ink from freezing while using it."[28] In those days part of the loop was still a forest, and when the weather warmed up enough for anyone to venture into it, fragments of a man's body were found; he had likely frozen to death and been devoured by wolves.[29] It was likely this body that early Chicago historians were referring to when they credited **Orsemus Morrison (1805–1864)**, the city's "high constable," as performing the city's first autopsy on a body found in the "stretch of woods" at Washington and LaSalle.[30]

When Morrison came to town in 1833 after working on the Erie Canal, the Chicago River didn't flow right into the lake parallel to the current Wacker Drive as it does today; it bent sharply south down what is now Michigan Avenue and joined the lake a few blocks south at Madison Street. Morrison got the contract to dredge the mouth of the River, removing the "elephant trunk" curve and moving the harbor to the place where it's been ever since. This was an important step in turning the waterway—which some early maps called a "creek"—into the river as we know it and turning the harbor into a busy and desirable port.[31]

An early biographical entry calls Orsemus "a terror to evil-doers,"[32] and others call him a "practical abolitionist," which implies that he worked on the Underground Railroad.[33]

An "E. W." stone marks James' wildly eccentric nephew, **Captain Edward W. Morrison (1836–1929)**, a man once referred to in the press as "the most eloquent blasphemer this side of Brimstone Junction."[34] At the age of 80, Captain Morrison's skill at swearing amazed reporters. One *Tribune* article about him ran under the headline ""-!!**!!_*!—* !!!-**-!!!**!!."[35]

As a young man, Edward ran away to become a sailor, but after some 30 years at sea, he inherited a large estate from his father, and seemed to get right down to the business of spending it as lavishly as possible. He was known by name to every bartender and cabdriver in the loop.[36] Stories circulated of him giving cabbies tips in the form of thousand-dollar bills and casually dropping $50,000 to pay for damages to a bar someone told him he had wrecked in a drunken stupor the night before.[37]

Being as casual with fifty grand as he was with fifty cents, however, made him an easy target for con artists; it was entirely possible that he was just taking peoples' word for it when they told him he'd wrecked their bar during a night he didn't remember. In 1916, his relatives began fighting to stop his spending in court, and most of his money was tied up, leading the press to call him "The Millionless Millionaire."[38]

· · ·

Just after passing Western Ave., you will see an older white monument topped by a pillar. The name "Manierre" is legible on the base, marking the grave of another "practical abolitionist" whose activities in that field are better documented than Orsemus Morrison's.

George Manierre:
The Abolitionist Judge

> "In 1860 I was with my father in the Wigwam . . . where we saw Lincoln nominated. I remember in the early days hearing Stephen A. Douglas speaking from the porch of the Tremont House; also going with my father to the Metropolitan Block to hear Frederick Douglass, the negro, make a speech soon after he had escaped from slavery."
>
> —George Manierre Jr., "A History of the Manierre Family in Early Chicago"

Born in Connecticut, **George Manierre Sr. (1817–1863)** began his career as a poet. After moving to Manhattan as a teenager, it is said that he wrote verse that was published in the *New York Mirror*. None of Manierre's poems could be identified in the *Mirror*, which seldom gave individual bylines, but one note from the editor in 1833, may have referred to him when it said a sonnet submitted by "G.M." was "neither bad nor good."[39] In any case, poetry was not a reliable way of making a living, so Manierre worked a day job as a law clerk.[40]

Upon moving to Chicago in 1835 he became part of a tight-knit group of abolitionist lawyers, along with James H. Collins (page 61). E. C. Larned (page 192), and his own clerk, L. C. P. Freer (page 59). His house at Michigan and Jackson was sometimes used as a stop on the Underground Railroad. His son, George Jr., remembered his father and his mother, **Ann Hamilton Manierre (1823–1900)**, dressing escapees in new suits of clothes in the back of the kitchen.[41]

Manierre's most famous contribution to the antislavery cause came in 1851, shortly after the Fugitive Slave Law was enacted. In June of that year, a Chicago man named Moses Johnson was claimed by an enslaver. Under the new law, this was incredibly easy: a southerner could see a Black man with a distinctive scar in Chicago, go back to his home state and swear out a warrant describing a man with such a scar, then return to Chicago and claim that man as his property.[42]

Manierre and E. C. Larned (page 192) defended Johnson in court, arguing that he didn't fit the description of the "copper colored" man for whom the slave catcher had a warrant.[43] The debate over exactly how Johnson's skin should be described was degrading and descended into absurdity, but it worked: the judge ruled that Moses Johnson was the wrong man. The technique became a useful strategy for other abolitionist lawyers throughout the country.[44]

After a career as a judge, presiding over nearly all of the most notable murder trials of the 1850s, Manierre succumbed to typhoid fever at the age of 46. An early biography described his as "A life that rose to the zenith of its splendid powers in Chicago and then was blotted out as a star from the sky."[45]

● ● ●

To the right of Manierre you will see the pyramidal monument to the Sanger family. **James Y. Sanger (1814–1867)** started a construction business in Chicago after building the first small railroad in California;[46] the black rhyolite monument and bronze statue were designed in 1907 by George R. Dean.[47] James had a daughter, Hattie, who is buried elsewhere in the cemetery beside her husband, George Pullman (page 120).

Across the road from Manierre and Sanger is an obelisk for **Martin O. Walker (1809–1874)**, who was known as the "Stagecoach King in the Northwest."[48] His obelisk lists several family burials from well before Graceland was founded, including one for a **Livonia Walker (1811–1815)** (presumably Martin O's sister). Records seem to indicate that she really is buried there, having been moved in 1866 along with the other pre-1860 bodies in the plot, which would likely make her the earliest-dying person to be buried at Graceland. But Martin didn't move to Illinois until 1838, making it seem highly unlikely that the body is truly here.

The Sanger monument

North of Walker is a marker for sign painter **Benjamin Franklin Chase (1830–1900)**, to the right of which is an unmarked space that is the burial spot of Graceland founder Thomas B. Bryan's five-year-old son, **Daniel Page Bryan (c1850–1855)**. Daniel was moved here in 1890, after having originally been buried in what is now the Eli Williams plot (page 8).[49] (Thomas Bryan himself is buried in Washington, D.C., but a new cenotaph for him was added near the entrance in 2020.)

Just up the road on the right is the gothic obelisk for **Henry Witbeck (1813–1891)**, a lumber man.[50] Behind Witbeck and a bit to the left is a large obelisk, often covered in ivy, featuring relief portraits and marked "Brainard."

Dr. Daniel Brainard:
The "Count" of Rush University

"We are very proud of our city, and if you want to get into the good graces of any Chicago man or woman, you have nothing else to do but tell them it is a nice place."
—Dr. Daniel Brainard, *Dr. Brainard's Address Before the American Dental Association*

In September of 1835, **Dr. Daniel Brainard (1812–1866)** arrived in Chicago on a pony, having traveled all the way from Pennsylvania, and decided to stop there and set up a medical practice simply because he'd run out of money to travel further.[51]

He became famous as a surgeon. In 1848 when he used chloroform to sedate a woman who was having a cancerous growth removed from her right breast, the newspaper *Gem of the Prairie* remarked that he was "One of the most skillful surgeons in the country, and every day (he) adds to his celebrity."[52]

Within a few years, Brainard would become the founder and first president of Rush University, where his regal demeanor led students to call him "The Count" (a term that would have seemed less ghoulish a generation before *Dracula* was written).[53] When he wasn't teaching, he found time to travel to Paris to study venomous snakes (he developed an iodine injection as a snake bite cure)[54] and to get involved in politics as a "free soil" Democrat.[55] During the Civil War he made numerous rousing speeches at Bryan Hall.[56]

In 1866, Brainard was staying at the Sherman House hotel when he was struck by one of the young city's periodic cholera outbreaks. "He had just returned from Europe," wrote the *Tribune*. "He came home to fall a victim to the destroyer, which had but a few weeks preceded him."[57] He was one of dozens of victims of the 1866 outbreak to be buried at Graceland; there are entire pages in the interment book from that October where nearly every burial is a cholera death.[58]

■ ■ ■

From the Brainard obelisk, walk several yards north, passing by the rough-hewn stone for grain dealer **Adolph Gertsenberg (1860–1941)**. To the left of the gray obelisk for businessman **Charles W. Cook (1832–1900)**, who was in the stone business, find the small marker for George Fergus.

George H. Fergus and
the Chicago Zouaves

"Dearborn School was erected in 1845. It was a two
story and attic brick building. Corporal punishment?
Yes, indeed—it flourished. I used to get licked almost
every day on general principles."
—George H. Fergus, "Talk of Old Times"

In Adam Goodheart's epic *1861: The Civil War Awakening*, he notes that in
the 1850s "volunteering for military service was more like joining a weekly
bowling league than in enlisting in the army as we know it." Much of the
drilling was done on weekends through a haze of booze and what we'd now
call "male bonding." These local militia groups, envisioned by the founding
fathers as the country's only standing army, hadn't been called into service
since the War of 1812, so there was little reason to take this sort of soldiering
entirely seriously.[59]

The United States Zouaves of Chicago were a different sort of militia. Their
leader, a dashing young man named Elmer Ellsworth, dressed his cadets in
the flamboyant outfits of French Zouaves, with eye-catching caps and flaming
red harem pants. He enforced a strict code of conduct, worked them to the
bone, and turned them into a crack team whose drills seem to have resembled
acrobatic routines—modern writers almost invariably compare them to Cirque
de Soleil. His cadets, including **George H. Fergus (1840–1911)**, idolized him.
Soon, the rest of the country would, as well.[60]

In the Summer of 1860, in the shadow of a presidential election and rumors of Civil War, the Zouaves embarked on a national tour and captured the
country's imagination. President Buchanan sang their praises and suggested
that they'd be useful against "a foreign enemy."[61]

At one tour stop, the drill ground was particularly wide, and Fergus and
another cadet ended up so far away from Ellsworth that they couldn't hear
his commands and missed a cue. Ellsworth joked to the audience that they'd
be "stripped and sent home." After the demonstration, as Ellsworth dealt
with a crowd of admirers, Fergus and the other man approached him in their
underwear, saluted, and asked for clothing and train tickets home. Ellsworth
chuckled and said they could stay; decades later a reporter said that "Fergus
laughs heartily over the incident now, though it was serious enough then."[62]

The last stop on the tour was Springfield, Illinois, where then-candidate
Abraham Lincoln was so impressed that he induced Ellsworth to join his law
office when the tour ended, and then to personally accompany him to Washington D.C. when he was elected president months later. When the war broke

out, Ellsworth raised a new company of "Fire Zouaves," consisting largely of New York firefighters, but also including some veterans from his old touring group—including Fergus.[63]

In May of 1861, with the new regiment assigned to guard Lincoln personally in Washington, Ellsworth saw a Confederate flag flying from the roof of a hotel across the river in Alexandria, Virginia, and decided to impress Lincoln by taking a group over and capturing it. Fergus was part of the team, and was stationed outside of the hotel when Ellsworth, having successfully retrieved the flag from the roof, was murdered by the hotel's proprietor. He helped row the body—and the treasonous flag stained with his blood—back across the Potomac to D.C.[64]

Ellsworth was the first Union officer to die, and his murder galvanized the nation. Streets, towns, and children were named after him. Thousands enlisted in the army specifically to avenge Ellsworth's murder, and cries of "Remember Ellsworth!" were heard at several early battles.[65] A funeral march, "Ellsworth's Requiem" by A. J. Vaas, would be a familiar melody at funerals and Memorial Day services for some time.

Though he'd be forgotten by the next generation, no Chicagoan who remembered 1861 ever forgot about Colonel Ellsworth, and George H. Fergus retold the story of that night in Alexandria for the rest of his life.[66]

Born in 1840, Fergus was one of the generation of Chicagoans who were born into the pioneer town and grew up along with it. His father, **Robert Fergus (1815–1897)**, a printer, had published the city's first business directory.[67] The Scottish Robert came to Chicago in 1839;[68] he was killed crossing railroad tracks during a blinding storm in 1897.[69] His own space is not marked.

After the war, George joined his father in running the printing house, where their prize possession was a printing press reputedly once used by the poet Robert Burns.[70] By the time he was middle-aged, George seemed to exist in a haze of nostalgia; newspapers from the late 19th century are full of letters he wrote comparing fires, storms, horse shows, and other events of the day to similar ones that he remembered from the city's early days, an era only a tiny fraction of the city's exploding population had seen firsthand. Eventually he shifted the focus of the printing company almost entirely to local history and filled the office with his collection of historical letters and manuscripts.[71] He died after a long illness in 1911.

■ ■ ■

Just a bit north of Fergus, and bit closer to the road, is the large obelisk marked "Newberry."

The Newberrys and the Legend of the Barrel

"If I were obliged to earn my living I might make a name for myself that will last, but situated as I am, it is more than likely that I shall live a comfortable life and die and be forgotten."
—Julia Newberry, *Julia Newberry's Diary*

Though stories of **Walter Loomis Newberry (1804–1868)**, a real estate millionaire, tend to paint him as a cold and serious man, his daughter Julia remembered him as a kind soul with whom she wrote mildly naughty limericks when she was only six. One she remembered went:

> *There was an old man named Grundy*
> *who whipped all his boys every Monday.*
> *So all through the week*
> *unable to speak*
> *they only had rest on a Sunday*

He encouraged his daughters to be independent and free spirits, often telling Julia to "Be someone, July."[72] She took the advice to heart; as a young woman she traveled the world, writing in her diary about adventures such as the time in Egypt when she "visited two harems and drank coffee and smoked with the ladies."[73] When she died of a throat infection in Rome at 23, she was buried there at Cimitero Acattolico, near the markers of poets Keats and Shelley, whose work she loved.[74]

Walter's other daughter, **Mary Louise Newberry (1845–1874)**, is interred in the family plot beneath the obelisk, having died of tuberculosis at 28. She took a very active role in managing her family's financial affairs after her father's death, once writing a trustee of the estate that "You must have discovered by this time that I am very tenacious of my rights, the few that I have!"[75]

Mary was deeply suspicious that the men who seemed interested in her or Julia were just after their money; she personally put a stop to the attentions paid to Julia by a grand-nephew of Napoleon and may have herself turned down a proposal from General Philip Sheridan. Her paranoia was probably well-founded but got on Julia's nerves. "I have never enjoyed myself more than I have during the last four weeks," Julia once wrote. "Sister has been fully occupied and I always enjoy myself so much more when she is thinking about something else."[76] Mary Drummond (page 188) remembered young Mary as "a veritable Goody Two-Shoes."[77]

BURIED IN A BARREL.
HOW MILLIONAIRE NEWBERRY OF CHICAGO, WHO DIED AT SEA, WAS INTERRED IN GRACELAND CEMETERY.

The *Police Gazette* illustration

In 1885, a curious story began to circulate in the press: that when Walter had died at sea in 1868, his body had been preserved in a barrel of rum, and was now buried, still in the barrel, at Graceland.

Newberry had taken ill and died en route to Paris; one passenger remembered that Walter had been wandering incoherently, asking for his horses to be prepared for a ride. Though this suggests a clear health issue, and he was only 64, the cause of death was declared to be "old age."[78]

The normal custom in that situation was to bury the body at sea, but the story went that a passenger who knew the family insisted that Mr. Newberry's remains be preserved for a proper funeral. Hence, the body was placed in a barrel of rum, sent back to the States on the next ship to leave Le Havre, and then arrived by train in Chicago under cover of night, where a man was waiting with a wagon and several friends to sneak the remains into Graceland. "The barrel was rolled out of the dray and into the hole and the earth closed over the body of the millionaire," one paper wrote. "Surely there never was such an end to such a life. Lowly at the beginning; harsh and autocratic in its prime; at the very end lowly and alcoholic. To be enshrouded in rum, he, the most abstemious of men."[79]

The story was published in papers all over the country. The *National Police Gazette* (a Victorian "lad" magazine) even carried a hilarious drawing of mustachioed men in top hats rolling the barrel into the grave. Chicago papers did what they could to fact-check the story; it was quickly determined that Newberry had, indeed, died onboard the steamer *Periere* in late 1868, and several passengers confirmed he had not been buried at sea, but placed in a barrel.[80] But the U.S. Consul at Le Havre said that he'd had the remains taken from the barrel and put in a proper casket.[81]

After his wife, **Julia Clapp Newberry (1818–1885)**, died there were no remaining direct heirs, and a large portion of the estate was used to found the Newberry Research Library, which now houses an impressive collection of manuscripts, including those of Graceland residents Kenneth Sawyer Goodman (page 147) and Matt Rizzo (page 172). The library recently digitized the original copy of Julia Newberry's diary, which was a surprise hit when it was published in 1933, sixty years after her death.

. . .

Return to the road and head north, passing the monument to box company owner **Douglas M Goodwillie (1843–1884)**, on the right. On the other side of the road is the Dodge plot, including an older marker for **Lizzie Coombs Dodge (c1843–1866)**, whose epitaph, "Died of Cholera," marks her as a victim of the October 1866 epidemic.

Further up the road on the left, with a row of colorful underground vaults looming behind it, is a white gothic marker for baker **Joseph M. Dake (1812–1869)**. (The vaults are covered on page 226.)

Proceed a few feet beyond Dake to the next bend in the road, then take the sharp right turn and begin heading south. On your left you will see a white marble statue of a girl encased in a glass box, one of Graceland's most famous and mysterious monuments.

Inez Briggs (alias Inez Clarke) (1873–1880): The Girl in Glass

"From the hint of a smile perched on her lips to the incredible detail in her attire, the statue of Inez Clark (Briggs) is mesmerizing. Visitors who stand in front of her final resting place often discover small piles of coins and trinkets left for her by others, and upon leaving, many are drawn to find out more about the seemingly mysterious death of the sweet-faced little girl."
—Lindsay Currie

The haunting statue of the young girl named on the base as "Inez, daughter of John and Mary Clarke," has captured imaginations for years, inspiring ghost stories, children's books, and urban legends.

Some of the stories have simply grown to fill the void in what we know about Inez, as details about her are scarce. In 2009, after stories circulated that "Inez Clarke" wasn't even a real person at all, researcher John Binder determined that her real name was **Inez Briggs (1873–1880)** ("Clarke" was

Inez

the name of her mother's second husband).[82] Her mother's divorce records provide more data, giving few details about Inez herself, but a great many about the tumultuous family life that went on around her.

Inez's grandmother **Jane Aruseo Mclure Rothrock (1836–1893)** was only about 15 years old when she gave birth to her first son, Philander.[83] Five years later came a daughter, **Mary Cora McClure (later Mary Briggs, then Mary**

Clarke)[84] **(1856–1912)**. Jane's husband, Amos McClure, moved the family from Maine to Michigan sometime in the late 1850s and volunteered for the First Michigan Cavalry in the Civil War. He was discharged for disability in 1864,[85] and it appears that he died soon after (Jane applied for a widow's pension late that year,[86] and he has a military gravestone in Grand Ledge, Michigan).

> Files at Graceland call Inez "Amos Briggs," which briefly led to claims that Inez never existed. It was more likely simply the result of someone mis-reading paperwork when she was interred. That Inez's maternal grandfather was named Amos may be a clue or may be nothing at all.

At some point the widowed Jane was engaged to another Union army veteran, **David Rothrock (1833–1897)**, and she, Philander, and Mary moved to Chicago, where Jane and David were married in May of 1872.[87] On September 24th of that year, 16-year-old Mary was married to Wilbur Briggs in a ceremony at the Rothrocks' home on Center Street (now Armitage Ave).[88] The couple remained living with Mary's mother and stepfather after baby Inez was born a year later.[89]

Divorce records from 1876 paint an unpleasant portrait of Wilbur. According to Mary, "It was his constant habit to go off upon 'sprees' and return home in drunken, intoxicated conditions, and to remain in such condition for days and sometimes weeks at a time." By the time Inez was a year old, Wilbur was barely working; Mary later told the court that "He would go to work and come home in the middle of the day and go off and get drunk and remain so."[90]

Weeks before their second anniversary, Mary begged Wilbur to give up drinking. He became enraged, announced that he was leaving, and took off, never to be heard from again.[91]

Two years later, Mary initiated a divorce. Wilbur's whereabouts were now unknown; rumors held that he was living in San Francisco and drinking more than ever, but letters sent to him there (with no specific address) came back marked "Return to Sender."[92] Newspaper ads failed to get his attention.[93]

Jane Rothrock (who usually went by "Jenny") backed her daughter's claims. "(Wilbur) would drink sometimes for weeks at a time," she told the court. When asked who was taking care of Inez, Jane said, "I have always and can still."[94]

Mary was granted the divorce, as well as "the care, custody control and education of the said child Inez, without any interference on the part of the defendant."[95] What became of Wilbur is not known.

Unmentioned in the divorce proceedings was Inez's baby brother, **Dilbert Briggs (1876)**, who had died of cholera infantum (a disease now thought to have been malaria) just two months before the divorce suit was launched.[96] It may have made the divorce impossible if Dilbert had survived; since Wilbur disappeared in September, 1874, and Dilbert was born in February, 1876, Wilbur could not have been the father, which was bound to complicate proceedings in court, where Mary would be asked questions such as "did you do the best you could to make his home happy," as well as whether she had children, and how many. But when Dilbert died, the path became clearer. When the court asked if she had any children, Mary merely said, "I have one."[97]

Mary and Inez probably kept living with the Rothrocks and Mary's brother Philander, though Mary herself doesn't seem to appear on the 1880 census. The date on which she married bookkeeper **John Newton Clarke (1839–1910)** is not known, but was probably shortly before Inez died of diphtheria in 1880.[98] In a letter to the cemetery shortly after Inez's death, Mary calls herself "Mrs. John Clarke" but signs her name as "Mary Briggs," indicating that she wasn't quite used to her new last name at the time.

A family plot was purchased at Graceland jointly by John Clarke and David Rothrock days after Inez's death, and baby Dilbert was moved from a section of single graves to be buried beside his sister.[99] The statue was made by Andrew Gagel, a sculptor whose advertisements in trade magazines said he could create "anything from a marble crucifix to a life-size portrait."[100] The small headstone to the right, with a now-worn lamb, is Dilbert's.

When Inez died, Mary was pregnant with another daughter, who would be named Beatrice. As an adult Beatrice moved to Los Angeles, and Mary joined her there after John Clarke died in 1910. When Mary died of gallstones in 1912, her remains were returned to Chicago; she is buried in front of Inez and Dilbert.[101]

Beatrice's own daughter, born in 1919, was named Inez, presumably after the half-sister she never knew.

■ ■ ■

Behind Inez and a bit further west, note the statue of an angel pointing upward. It's a memorial to **Tuthill King (1804–1886)**, who arrived in Chicago in 1834 and prospered in real estate. At the age of 81, he married Sarah Bell, who was 36 years his junior (and was said to look younger still). He told people that he suffered from chronic bronchitis and only wanted to marry Sarah because her previous husband had been a druggist, so she knew a bit about medicine and could take care of him. But they honeymooned like any other couple.[102]

The marriage caused a bit of objection among King's daughters, and even more so when he died 10 weeks after the wedding. There was some question as to his sanity at the time of his marriage, and, more importantly, at the time of his writing his will. The court case over his estate dragged on for years.[103]

• • •

Returning to the path, heading south, on the left you'll see a marker for lawyer **Lewis H. Davis (1833–1908)**, and an enclosed plot containing a tall shaft for the family of sugar planter **Daniel Thompson (1824–1900)**. A bit behind Thompson is a faded white monument, topped by what appears to be a small rendering of a draped bed, to one of Graceland's first—and lesser-known—architects, **Max Hjortsberg (1826–1880)**, who worked mainly on the design of railroads, including the Pullman car works.[104]

Barriers for Family Plots

It's uncommon to see dividers blocking off family plots at Graceland. From the beginning, the cemetery had strict rules that dividers be small, and eventually disallowed them altogether. Most of those that existed were removed over the years. Dividers and walls around family plots were falling out of fashion by the 1860s. It's common to hear that this was because people believed they were "undemocratic," and equally common to hear that it had more to do with groundskeepers disliking them.

However, an 1864 article in the *Tribune* praised Graceland's strict policy against walls over a few inches high and took the former view. "This is a wise provision, morally as well as for the sake of ocular symmetry," they wrote. "The graveyard is the last place for the exhibition of that exclusiveness . . . Death levels all distinctions. How absurd, then, the practice of attempting to indicate their perpetuation in the tomb."[105]

Continue down the path, veering to the right beyond the boulder for railroad and bridge builder **William B. Howard** (1832–1898), and by the William McCormick plot on the right, which is covered in this book as the end point of route 5-A (page 244).

Past them on the road is a tall white marker with faces carved onto two sides, standing alone in an otherwise empty expanse, for **Elbridge G. Hall**

(1815–1877). Hall was a partner in the firm of Hall and Kimbark Hardware—and married to **Elizabeth Kimbark Hall (1821–1866)**, of the Kimbark Family (whose plot is directly south of the Hall plot).

Proceeding along, on the left you will see a grave marked "H. Samuels" (contractor **Hugh Samuels (c1832–1910)**. Take a left off the road and pass the stone marked "D. W. Gale" (dry goods merchant **Daniel W. Gale (1822–1896)** and you'll find a plot bounded on the left by an illegible, eroded white marker (a monument to **George Stowell**, a baby who died in 1869), plus three nameless markers reading "Mother," "Father," and "Sister," and two small, but legible, markers for **John Stowell (1841–1914)** and **Amelia Farnham Stowell (1836–1906)** on the right.[106] One empty space in the plot was the location of a now-missing monument to Amelia's brother, Daniel Farnham.

Daniel R. Farnham: Graceland's Shiloh Victim

> "Well did (the) people know that Chicago was largely represented in the ranks of the Federal troops engaged in the severe and bloody battle that had been fought (at Shiloh). Pale faces and tearful eyes surrounded the bulletin board at the Tribune office all the day, and there was an intensity of feeling pervading the entire community in regard to the result that no previous battle of the war had brought out."
>
> —"Aid for the Wounded," *Chicago Tribune*

Though the city didn't take Thomas Bryan's offer of plots for soldiers killed at the Battle of Shiloh (page 1), a month later he donated an entire family plot to **Amelia Dowd Farnham (1808–1883)**, whose son, **Daniel Farnham (1834–1862)**, had been shot through the heart in the battle.[107] Daniel had been a grocery clerk before the war.[108]

At his burial, the Literary Union donated a marble monument reading "Daniel R. Farnham, private in Company A, Chicago Light Artillery; killed in battle at Shiloh, April 6, 1862, aged 28 years, 2 months and 7 days. This monument is erected under the auspices of the Chicago Literary Union, of which he was a member, as a token of his many virtues. He was a patriot, a soldier, and a Christian."[109]

It must have been a large monument just to have room for an epitaph like that. An 1864 article states that it was "a shaft, memorable as having cast its shadow over the remains of (Senator) Douglas,"[110] a particularly odd thing to mention without elaborating. Perhaps the shaft was among the temporary markers used to mark Douglas' south-side grave after his 1861 death, during the long process when his monument was being constructed.

In any case, the monument itself is a mystery, not only because of its unclear connection to Douglas, but because it no longer exists. Being made of marble, it probably simply eroded and fell apart, a victim to Chicago winters, and was removed long ago.

. . .

Proceeding south on the path, on the right will be a statue of an angel in mourning, alongside a few faded memorials. The angel is for **Eliza Scott Campbell (1818–1874)**, the wife of **Benjamin H. Campbell (1814–1891)**, a millionaire businessman who served as U.S. Marshall under President Grant. Benjamin's disappearance in late 1890 was a national story; he was eventually found to have drowned in the river.[111] Though politely ruled accidental, the death was likely a suicide. The date of death on his stone, 1889, is incorrect, based on both news accounts and the lot record.

Across the road, past several rows of markers, you'll see the back of the mound covering the Stevens mausoleum (page 58). If you walk to the top of the mound, there'll be a patch of grass with one worn monument in the shape of a partially draped tree stump on which the name "Hosmer" can be faintly discerned.

Ann Hosmer:
An "Intolerant" Abolitionist

"The day of the election (of 1864) was much dreaded by all; rumors were that the city would be burned . . . Those were days of great anxiety, and I felt we were living on a volcano ready to burst any moment."
—Ann Hosmer, "Reminiscences of Sanitary Work and Incidents Connected with the War for the Union"

With the Civil War raging, Graceland founder Thomas Bryan built a Soldier's Home where sick and furloughed soldiers could enjoy some measure of comfort in Chicago. For funds, he sold facsimiles of the manuscript of the Emancipation Proclamation, which he'd purchased. The Lincoln-hating *Chicago Times* approved of the Soldier's Home but disapproved of them using the Proclamation for funds, thus "politicizing" the institution.[112] Editor Wilbur F. Storey had called the Proclamation the most wicked deed in history.[113]

Ann P. Hosmer (1811–1892), a manager at the home, was once referred to in the press as "The Florence Nightingale of the North."[114] During the war, she made numerous trips to army camps and hospitals. When she was home in Chicago, she spent several days a week at the Soldiers Home, often staying the night, and once raising the ire of the *Times* in the process.

When a *Times* reporter came to the Soldiers Home inquiring about his son, Hosmer asked, "Can it be that you have a son in the Union army and write for the *Times*? I would sooner have my right hand cut off than write for a paper that denounces our government." The man sheepishly said that he only wrote commercial reports, not their political screeds.[115]

When word of the encounter got back to the *Times* office, Storey fired off an editorial attacking the "intolerance" of abolitionists as seen in the person of Mrs. Hosmer. "The case is one deserving more than a passing notice," he wrote, "[for] the details furnish evidence of the way in which even a noble charity . . . may be abused when engineered by abolition monomaniacs."[116] She offered to resign, but Bryan wouldn't hear of it.

Oliver E. Hosmer (c1809–1879), Ann's husband, published a reply of his own, stating "my first impression was to seek the blackguard who wrote (the article) and administer to him a severe castigation, but calling to mind the adage 'he who handles pitch soils his fingers,' I concluded to keep my hands off from such a dirty lump of clay."[117]

After the war, Ann wrote a memoir of her war experiences. The handwritten pages tell a few particularly thrilling stories, such as the time she was captured by rebels and held prisoner. She and a small crew escaped and found shelter in a small hut in the mountains near Chattanooga owned by a British woman. This hostess seemed to be a neutral party in the war, but overnight it became clear to Hosmer that the woman planned to rob them, and possibly even to murder them.[118]

To scare the woman off without letting on that she was suspicious, Ann began to brag about her abilities as a sharpshooter. "I descanted freely on the merits of my pistol," she wrote, "and my skills in using it, (and that I had) practiced in a Pistol gallery (which was literally true some thirty years before) and could shoot with precision . . . [I told her I] would not hesitate to blow anyone's brains out that molested me." In reality, she had no gun at all, but her boasting successfully convinced the woman that she was dangerous, and the party made their getaway unharmed in the morning.[119]

Ann and Oliver are both buried in the plot, though their spaces aren't marked. The marker is for Ann's son, **Major Charles H. Hosmer (c1840–1867)**, a former member of Ellsworth's Zouaves (page 17) who went on to fight with the 1st U.S. Infantry in the Siege of Vicksburg. He survived the battle, but contracted tuberculosis while stationed in New Orleans and died from the disease in 1867.[120]

Between the Hosmer plot and the road is a larger marker for paper company president **Charles Mather Smith (1831–1912)** and his wife, **Sara Rozet Smith (1839–1903)**. Their daughter, Mary Rozet Smith, was a cofounder of Hull House and lifelong partner of Jane Addams; though cremated at Graceland, Mary's ashes were scattered in Lake Michigan.[121]

From Smith's grave, walk a few feet south. Next to the vault-style gravestone of **Elizabeth Dawson Hill (1822–1909)** is a smaller marker, flush with the ground, for baseball fanatic **Scott Bram (1955–2005)**, which features the epitaph "Couldn't Wait for the Cubs to Win It." His obituary describes him as a "lonely south side Cub fan" and notes that he played for and coached several Hyde Park amateur teams.[122] Cubs souvenirs are frequently left on his grave.

A little south of Bram is the Perkins lot, including **Dwight H. Perkins (1867–1941)**, an architect whose designs include Lane Tech High School, Café Brauer, and the Lion House at the Lincoln Park Zoo.

Return to the road and proceed south. When it reaches a fork, veer to the left. Directly in front of you on the south side of the road will be the obelisk to the Wilmarth family.

Mary Wilmarth: An Activist Socialite

> "No one could have looked at Mrs. H.M. Wilmarth walking (in the Suffragists' Parade) . . . umbrellaless in the driving downpours, unmindful of her 81 years, and not felt a thrill."
> —Madame X (Caroline Kirkland), "Chicago's June Weather Spoils Garden Parties"

In 1915, police stormed a meeting of the unemployed at Hull House, the settlement house founded by Jane Addams nearly 30 years before. Lucy Parsons, a widow of the Haymarket Anarchists (see the John Altgeld entry, page 155), was a featured speaker that night, and the scene became a riot. Six women branded as dangerous radicals were arrested and taken to jail, but they were quickly released when **Mary Wilmarth (1837–1919)**, a longtime Hull House supporter, signed $1000 bonds for each of them.[123]

Mary had wed **Henry Wilmarth (1836–1885)**, a banker, in 1861. Their house was one of few left standing in the loop after the Great Chicago Fire in 1871; later she leased the land on which it stood for the new Congress Hotel, moving into the hotel herself permanently after it was built.[124]

Mary was associated with nearly every social reform movement that flourished in the city in the half-century following the Civil War. She was one of the early supporters of Jane Addams and was particularly close with Hull House cofounder Ellen Starr Gates, at times serving as her main source of financial support.

All the while, though, she maintained a position in the upper echelons of high society. She was a founding member of The Fortnightly Club, Gilded Age Chicago's most exclusive club for women, among many other clubs and organizations. She died in 1919, barely missing the chance to see her dream realized when the 20th amendment gave women the vote the next year.[125]

■ ■ ■

A bit behind the Wilmarth monument, and a little to the left, is a white monument on which the name "Carpenter" is clearly visible at the bottom.

Philo Carpenter: Pharmacist and Abolitionist

"I didn't vote for (Andrew Jackson). I saw him once when I was in Washington. He was a plain-spoken sort of a man with a brusque sort of a way. Carter Harrison (page 219) makes me think of him."

—Philo Carpenter, "Topographical Legends"

In 1832, **Philo Carpenter (1805–1886)** heard a tip that the muddy village of Chicago was a good place for a young man to make a name for himself, and he arrived in town via canoe that July. General Winfield Scott had just arrived there with his troops from the Black Hawk War, and they had brought a cholera epidemic with them.[126]

Having studied to be a doctor for a time before deciding to train as an apothecary instead, Carpenter rolled up his sleeves and got to work helping out with the sick, sometimes resorting to blood-letting to treat patients.[127] He even saved one man who was not quite dead from premature burial.[128]

By the end of that summer, with the epidemic in retreat and the soldiers gone, the village had gone back to business as usual, and Carpenter, losing no time, had established the first pharmacy in town. During times of outbreaks, he worked as both druggist and physician, fearlessly tending to patients with contagious diseases whose spread no one truly understood at the time. One boarder in his house noted years later that Carpenter must have lived a charmed life never to catch any of them himself.[129]

In 1834, he married **Ann Thompson Carpenter (1806–1866)**, and the newlyweds rode through town in the first "one horse shay" the city had ever seen. It was said that "(Though Ann was) in perfect sympathy with her husband in every work of reform, she was ever fearful that his zeal should find some hasty utterance that would wound the feelings of another. He was a person of strong conviction; she, of deep sympathies."[130]

Philo Carpenter

Philo's "works of reform" included being a founding member of the city's antislavery society; among his real estate holdings was said to be a timber farm where he employed refugees who'd arrived in town via the Underground Railroad.[131] When the time was right, he would accompany them by night to vessels bound for Canada. By the time slavery was abolished it was said that he'd assisted as many as 200, none of whom were ever recaptured.[132]

Returning to the road, only a few feet to the East on the right-hand side will be a marker with military insignia for Joseph Scott.

Joseph R. Scott: The First Zouave

"He was the soul of honor. Good-bye, brave Joe Scott,
the youngest of your rank, and none braver!"
—Rev. Thomas M. Eddy, "Another Gallant
Soldier Gone"

A self-taught military scholar, **Joseph R. Scott (1838–1863)** was the original founder of the famous Chicago Zouaves drill team (page 17). Though he turned leadership over to the magnetic Ellsworth in 1858, Scott remained with the group for their famous tour and can be easily identified next to Ellsworth in contemporary sketches.[133]

When the Civil War broke out in 1861, Scott enlisted in the 19th Illinois Infantry, where his status as Ellsworth's old second-in-command lent him considerable status. At 23, he became the youngest colonel in state history.[134]

The 19th was in Tennessee in late 1862, fighting The Battle of Stone River. As Confederates attacked the Union's left flank, Brigadier General Negley rode to the front and shouted "Who will save the left?" Scott immediately shouted back "The 19th Illinois!" and led his troops into action. The exchange between Negley and Scott became something of a catch phrase, even inspiring the song "Who'll Save the Left" by Chicago songwriter George Frederick Root (who was best known for "The Battle Cry of Freedom").[135]

But Scott was badly wounded in the battle and sent home to Chicago to recover. Six months later, he was thrown from a carriage and the wounds re-opened, this time proving fatal.[136]

A band played "Ellsworth's Requiem" at his funeral, and when his marker was added (several years later),[137] his famous exchange with General Negley was carved into the stone.

■ ■ ■

Proceed further east on the road. On the left will be a headless statue for transportation executive **Captain Jonathan Tuttle (1818–1878)**. On the right will be matching tall gothic monuments for grain merchant **Hiram Wheeler (1809–1892)** and transportation baron **Franklin Parmalee (1816–1904)**. In 1853 Franklin founded the Chicago Omnibus Line, the city's first bus service, which began with six horse-drawn busses.[138] Franklin's daughter was married to Hiram's son a few years before the plots were purchased.

Between the two, you'll see a memorial boulder set well back from the road, beside which is a very old gravestone shaped like a cradle. The boulder is for **Conrad Sulzer (1807–1873)**, the first nonnative settler of what would eventually be the town, and then the neighborhood, of Lakeview. After studying medicine in his native Switzerland, Sulzer came to Chicago and made his home at what is now Clark and Montrose. His land was purchased by Grace-land Cemetery in 1863, and is now Section R, in the northwest corner.[139]

Next to his stone, which was added in the 1950s, notice the "cradle" style grave of his four-year-old son, **Conrad Sulzer Jr. (c1837–1841)**, who died of dropsy.[140] Curiously, the internment book notes that cradle grave was removed "from Sulzer's garden" in 1860, not from City Cemetery, so its original location would have been within the current boundaries of the cemetery. From a certain point of view, this makes it a Graceland grave that predates Daniel Page Bryan, the first official interment (page 15), by nearly 20 years.

■ ■ ■

The fork in the road at the bottom of the hill, marked on the right by the massive Sherman obelisk, is Station 2. Turn to page 53.

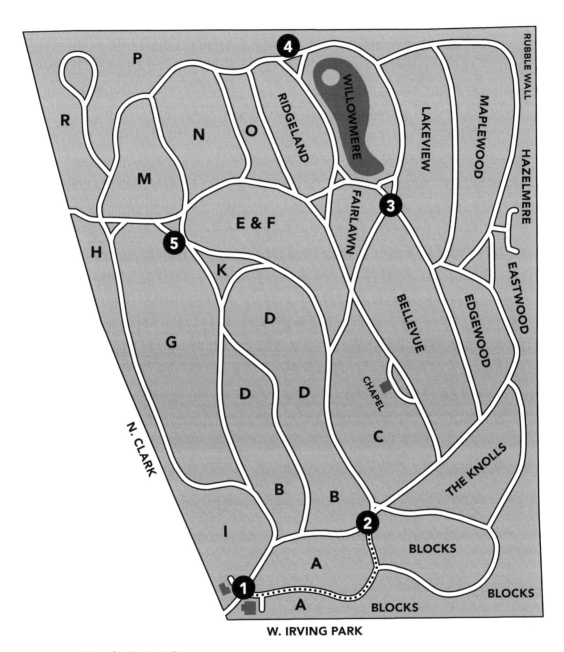

Map for Route 1-B

ROUTE 1-B

From the cemetery entrance, turn onto the road on the far right, which runs parallel to the south wall. (It is paved as of 2022, but may soon be replaced with a grass path.)

Walking along the path, the first plot you're likely to notice is one on the left that features a carved portrait of its occupant, **Charles Moessinger (1826–1880)**, a stone carver.

Further along on the left will be the large Rehm plot.

Jacob Rehm and the Whisky Ring

> "Some time in 1872 some of the distillers complained that others were running crooked. . . . [I] finally made an arrangement with Mr. Irwin by which Miller & Reid could run crooked for $500 per month."
> —Jacob Rehm, "Hush Money"

In 1886, a *Tribune* reporter described the long and varied career of **Jacob Rehm (1828–1915)** with awe: "Wood cutter, butcher boy, politician, constable, policeman, Street Commissioner, Deputy Superintendent of Police for 'steen years, street railroad magnate . . . is it not an example for the American schoolboy?"[1] He politely left out Rehm's stint in prison for his role in one of his era's biggest corruption scandals.

Rehm came to Chicago as a child around 1840. By the 1860s he was splitting his time between brewing, politics, and work for the police department, serving as superintendent from 1866–1868, and again in 1873–1875. In the 1870s, he was involved in the Chicago branch of the "Whisky Ring," in which brewers and public officials defrauded the government out of millions of dollars in whisky taxes. The ring stretched into high places—right into the pockets of officials in the Grant administration. Rehm was considered the organizer of the ring in Chicago; in one account, "it [had] been utterly impossible, since the spring of 1872, for any one engaged in the business of distilling to prosecute it without paying contributions to Mr. Jacob Rehm."[2]

Rehm turned informer when the scandal broke, and by doing so received only a six-month sentence.[3] President Grant issued a pardon after he completed three months, and the former police chief emerged, somehow, with his reputation more or less intact.[4] When he closed his career by selling his stake in a railway company for nearly half a million dollars, a Washington paper marveled at the sum and said "It pays to be chief of police—in Chicago."[5]

. . .

On the right hand side as you proceed further east down the path, note a red granite elongated triangular structure atop a gray stone altar for **John E. Wilkins (1826–1889)** and his brother, **Francis Wilkins (1833–1874)**, both of whom served as British consuls in Chicago, where their duties included stopping British citizens from being drafted, keeping Black Canadian citizens from being enslaved, and, after the Great Fire of 1871, persuading the British government to donate thousands of library books. They were also thought to be terribly corrupt, with one British journalist writing, "It is impossible to fix the precise amount of fees arbitrarily levied upon the (British) public by the Wilkins family at Chicago. They are doubtless enormous, but Messrs. John Edward [and] Francis . . . render no account to any living mortal."[6] But if they were corrupt, the people of Chicago didn't seem to care. It was Queen Victoria's problem, not Chicago's.

Proceed down the road. In the plot on the left with the large "Otis" marker is an art deco cross for **Philo Adams Otis (1846–1930)**, who was a choirmaster, historian, and author who used to organize hymn-singing parties to "combat the jazz spirit and youthful cynicism of modern boys and girls."[7]

But Otis did have his wild days . . . in a way. In 1890, he entered two bay geldings in a horse show. When the first and second prizes were given to other people, it was reported that "Mr. Philo A. Otis and Mr. Charles Lawrence Easton said something softly under their mustaches and drove madly out."[8]

Walk off the road, passing the Otis cross and into the section. Just beyond the marker for retail grocer **George Sommer (1825–1914)** is a gray rectangular stone, flush to the ground, for the only confirmed Revolutionary War soldier buried in Chicago.

Merrick's grave

Noah Merrick: Chicago's Only Confirmed Revolutionary War Veteran Burial

> "My father, Noah Merrick, enlisted as a private during the Revolutionary War from Monson, Mass. at time of enlistment being quite young. Up to the fire of 1871 I had his military history . . . (but now) I have no means of finding the regiment, date, or length of service. Will you kindly furnish a copy of such?"
> —Charles C. Merrick, Letter to the Adjutant General, U.S. Army, 1893

Born in Monson, Massachusetts, in 1760, **Noah Merrick (1760–1847 or 1849)**[9] is likely the earliest person born at Graceland.

In July 1779, he volunteered for a six-week enlistment in Colonel Elisha Porter's regiment in the Revolutionary War, traveling 65 miles from home to serve under Captain Joshua Shaw in New London, Connecticut. Most of the company was mustered out August 27th, and Noah was home by September.[10] So far as is known, the regiment saw no action, but this makes Noah the only undisputed Revolutionary War veteran to be buried in the city of Chicago.

After his service, Noah and his first wife had three children together; upon his wife's death in 1811, he married a widow, Eunice Clark-Shepard, who was busy with three children of her own. After Eunice's death, 64-year-old Noah married her daughter, **Delphia Shepard Merrick (1797–1864)**, who had been 14 or 15 when Noah became her stepfather and was now 26.[11] They had two sons together.[12]

Exactly why Noah, Delphia, and their sons moved to Chemung, Illinois, near the Wisconsin border, is not recorded, but it may well have been to get away from gossiping neighbors. Though the age difference between them wasn't *that* unusual at the time, the fact that Noah's young bride had previously been his teenage stepdaughter might have been a bit more scandalous. In the tiny town of Chemung, no one knew that part of their history.

Noah died of an apoplectic fit in 1849;[13] when Delphia died in Chicago and was buried at Graceland in 1864, Noah was disinterred from a nameless country cemetery and laid to rest beside her.[14] Their son, Charles, purchased the plot.[15]

Noah and Delphia's marriage was not officially recorded—one can just picture a justice of the peace looking at the situation and not wanting any part of it—which is fortunate for researchers, because Delphia's difficulties in proving she was legally his widow left a paper trail that provides proof of Noah's status as a veteran. Delphia and her sons had always believed that Noah served the entire length of the war, but records were found for only the one brief enlistment. She spent her declining years trying to work with L. F. Bingham, the same attorney who worked with Amy Gridley (page 5), to get a widow's pension. Since the marriage wasn't legally recorded, the pension wasn't granted.[16]

However, the associated paperwork confirms Noah's service, however brief, beyond a reasonable doubt. He may have served further enlistments later—his son claimed in 1893 that he'd had a complete history of his service that was destroyed in the Great Chicago Fire[17]—but records back up only the first, and it's more likely that he simply *told* his wife and children exaggerated stories about his service in his old age. After all, it had all happened nearly 20 years before Delphia was even born, and they would have had to take his word for it.

Though his war service is verifiable, and mentioned in his son's 1893 obituary,[18] somehow Noah's status as a Revolutionary veteran buried in Chicago escaped the city's notice until 2020, when the data was uncovered during research for this book. He doesn't appear in any listings or indexes of Chicago veteran burials (most likely because he was initially buried in McHenry Country, not Cook), and the grave was unmarked for decades; a widowed daughter-in-law, Emma Merrick, had the simple marker bearing only names and dates for Noah and Delphia placed in 1917. The next year she sold the remaining spaces in the plot to be used for single graves.[19]

There's something almost charming about the whole story—we finally have a verified Revolutionary War grave in Chicago, but he served only a few uneventful weeks and then married a woman who had been his teenage stepdaughter and apparently spent his later years telling tall tales about his service to his children. He's really a very "Second City" sort of war hero to have. But it's true that when his country called, he answered.

And it *was* an awfully long commute.

While there are confirmed revolutionary graves in the suburbs, there are only two other possible ones in Chicago, and neither can be confirmed:

Rosehill Cemetery has a military grave for a William DuVol, but nothing is known of him besides the fact that an earlier gravestone called him a "soldier of the revolution." When people first became interested in the grave in the 1950s, Rosehill said they had no records about him—even a year of death—at all. The grave had presumably been moved from the old City Cemetery, and there was no data about his age or even his date of death.[20] Records have never been found to verify any detail of his life, death, or service; notably, the gravestone doesn't specify *which* revolution he was a soldier of. It may have been the French Revolution or even some sort of metaphorical revolution.

Better known, but even more dubious, is the story of David Kennison, who has a memorial boulder in Lincoln Park (the old City Cemetery, from which he was never moved). At the time of his death in 1852, Kennison claimed to be 115 years old and the last surviving participant of the Boston Tea Party. People who fact-checked his story in the 20th century found that he was decades younger than he claimed, and likely didn't serve in the Revolution at all (though some believe he may have). A note in his pension file says not to listen to a word he says.[21]

However, multiple accounts of abolition and free soil meetings attended by Graceland residents such as Isaac Newton Arnold, L. C. P. Freer, and Daniel Brainard in the late 1840s mention that Kennison was there too, making fiery antislavery speeches.[22][23] So, while he was certainly a bit of a con man, at least he used his powers for good.

. . .

Return to the path. Just east of the Otis plot is the worn monument to **Jason Gurley (1807–1865)**, a Chicago pioneer who managed the Mansion House hotel in the 1830s and built Metropolitan Hall, a concert venue, in the 1850s.

Following the road as it bends sharply left, you'll see the large Celtic cross memorial to **Reverend William Fawcett (1842–1901)**, who preached that the image of God as a divine father, not "a judge severe," was "an offspring of an effeminate imagination and an opiate for depraved humanity."[24] He died in 1901 after eating bad canned salmon while traveling to Canada to dedicate a new church.[25]

· · ·

Continue North on the Path as it curves. Just before the fork in the road (stay left), on the ground you will see a gravestone composed of six individual squares with foliage growing between them.

William Le Baron Jenney and the First Skyscraper

"No apology is needed for any effort, however feeble,
to improve the taste for art."
—W. L. B. Jenney, *Principles and Practice of Architecture*

Legend has it that **Elizabeth Jenney (1848–1898)** should get some of the credit for the development of modern skyscrapers, of which her husband, **William Le Baron Jenney (1832–1907)**, is sometimes credited as the inventor. Earlier skyscrapers had heavy, load-bearing walls, which made it impossible for them to climb particularly high by modern standards; the Monadnock Building on Dearborn needed walls nearly six feet thick at the base to go over ten stories. According to an oft-repeated story, one day William noticed that Elizabeth was stacking heavy books on top of a bird cage, saw that the cage wasn't collapsing, and came up with the idea for steel frame construction, in which walls are essentially draped over a steel skeleton, allowing for much lighter and taller buildings. He went on to use the technique for The Home Insurance Building, a LaSalle Street edifice often credited with being the first steel-frame skyscraper.[26]

In addition to his development of the skyscraper, William worked on the landscape architecture for Graceland itself. Elizabeth was buried in the plot upon her death in 1898, and when William died in 1907, his ashes were scattered here. The memorial to him, with a design evoking a steel frame, was added a century later thanks to efforts led by Graceland trustee John Notz.[27]

. . .

Continuing north, it is impossible to miss the imposing specter of "Eternal Silence," the large statue of a man in a hooded robe.

Eternal Silence

Henry Graves and the Statue of Death

> "This monument I desire to be made as substantial and imposing in appearance as the sum set aside for its erection will permit."
> —Henry Graves, Last Will and Testament

No one who has seen *Eternal Silence*, the statue Lorado Taft built for the Graves family plot, has ever forgotten it. It is one of two monuments (the other being Inez Briggs, page 21) that I include on every walking tour.

The plaque on the back of the statue says that **Henry Graves (1821–1907)** came to Chicago with his father, **Dexter Graves (1789–1844)**, in 1831 on a schooner called *The Telegraph* with Captain Naper. However, in 1905, Henry recalled that three weeks after leaving Ashtabula, Ohio, the schooner had gotten only as far as Detroit, and Dexter, fed up with the cramped conditions, bought a horse and wagon and drove his family the rest of the way. They beat the schooner to Chicago and lived in the then-vacant Fort Dearborn, staying on when the other twelve families who'd been aboard went on to Naperville.[28]

In 1834, Dexter built a hotel on Lake Street, The Mansion House, which is notable for being the site of the city's first public entertainment by a professional actor: a performance by one Mr. Bowers, who ate fire, dipped his fingers in melted lead, and then performed a ventriloquist act and did magic tricks. Admission was fifty cents.[29] Though this performance was referred to many times by early historians, so far as can be determined it was the only performance Mr. Bowers ever gave that attracted any notice. Later the hotel was sold to Jason Gurley (page 40).

Dexter, his wife **Olive Graves (approx. 1791–1849)**, and three of their children had died by the time Graceland was founded. They were initially buried in City Cemetery, and moved to Graceland in 1873, a fairly late date for removals.[30]

Henry made his fortune in race horses. "I was always crazy about horses," he said, "and made my money by buying a horse that looked to be good, training it up so it could go a pretty good pace, and then selling it . . . For years I attended every race meet of any importance that was held in Illinois, and my horses were known all over the West. I enjoyed life in my own way, never mixing up in politics, and have seen the city grow from nothing to what it is now."[31]

In his will, Henry left funds for two statues to be built in Washington Park: one of George Washington, and one of Ike Cook, a race horse that reportedly earned him half a million dollars.[32] When Washington Park built their own statue of Washington, the will was amended to add the money to the fund for his own family monument, which now came to $250,000—several million today.[33]

Graves had envisioned a granite mausoleum to be placed on his lot "to cover the remains of those hereinbefore mentioned, and to contain a room with suitable inscriptions stating names of the parties buried underneath . . . said monument shall be open for the inspection of the public on the first Sunday in each of the months of May, June, July, August, and September in each year and on all public holidays." He specified that he wanted the most "substantial and imposing" monument money could buy.[34]

For whatever reason, the executors of his estate didn't build the mausoleum he requested, but he certainly got a substantial and imposing monument. Lorado Taft, one of the most prominent sculptors of the day, was hired to craft the statue known as *Eternal Silence*. Its grim visage attracted a great deal of notice even when it was new; the magazine *Art and Progress* called it "an unusually impressive conception, reminiscent in general feeling of Saint-Gaudens' mysterious figure (built for the grave of Marian Adams in Washington D.C.). It breathes the same spirit of awe and carries the suggestion of the unknown life beyond."[35]

How much the executors *spent* on the monument is not known, nor is what became of the rest of the money, since it probably couldn't have been nearly $250,000. A bronze statue of Marcus Daly built by Augustus St. Gaudens, a sculptor of similar reputation, was built in Montana the same year as Eternal Silence and cost only $25,000.[36]

Often known as "The Statue of Death" (though the figure is probably supposed to be Father Time), it soon became the subject of urban legends. Honestly, one would be disappointed in the city if it didn't. Rumors held that it was impossible to take a photograph of it that remained in focus (a legend that died out with the rise of digital cameras), or that if you looked it in the eye you would see your own death.

. . .

The Southeast Blocks

Behind *Eternal Silence* is a large expanse of what appears to be empty space. In fact, though the space looks largely empty, it is almost full. Though most of the cemetery was broken into lots that each had room for several burials, the "blocks" in the southeast portion are mostly single spaces that were sold to people who wanted only a small monument, or none at all.

Much of the area was added to the cemetery grounds in the early 1880s. At the time, monuments themselves were going out of fashion; *The Modern Cemetery*, a trade magazine, frequently praised Graceland for its landscaping, but still maintained that "even at Graceland there are too many stones."[37] This new section would follow the trend of the day and maintain a "prairie" look.

A few people in this section:

Henry Harris

In 1867, the police knocked on the door of a Monroe Street building described by the *Chicago Republican* as a "swindling den." **Henry Harris (c1830–1867)** was reportedly there to have his fortune told prior to his upcoming wedding. Though not suspected of any crimes himself, Harris was clearly terrified of the police; when they knocked, he jumped out of a second-story window and ran.[38]

It's quite likely that Harris, a Black man born in North Carolina around 1830, had been escaping slavery when he came to Chicago five years earlier. Though slavery was over by 1867, one can imagine he might have maintained an instinctive fear of authorities.

Harris ran until he collapsed, at which point officer Reuben Slayton grabbed him and began beating him about the head. Slayton's own testimony conceded that Harris was cooperative after he was caught but admitted that he'd continued hitting him. "I kicked at the prisoner with the side of my foot . . . in the pit of the knee. I think I slapped him also in the face."[39] Other witnesses described Slayton being considerably rougher."[40]

Harris died that night in a jail cell. The coroner ruled that it was because of a heart condition, made worse by the stress of the chase, but the press suggested he was "scared to death" by Slayton. The interment book at Graceland gives Harris' cause of death as "over-exertion and brutality of policeman."[41]

The *Tribune* said that a man who behaved as Slayton had no more belonged on the police force than a burglar belonged on the Supreme Court. But Slayton was given just a 30-day suspension[42] and remained on the force for more than 20 more years, including arresting (and nearly shooting) Adolph Fischer, one of the Haymarket suspects (page 155).[43] Harris is in Block A, space 142.

George Driver

The old courthouse and jail were badly damaged by the Great Chicago Fire, but the jail section was still in good enough shape to remain in use while a new one was slowly built. In 1873, **George Driver (c1828–1873)** became the last man executed in the loop before the new jail was opened in River North. Driver had murdered his ex-wife in a drunken rage the year before. On the scaffold, he said, "Give up drink—all liquor. You see where I am standing now."[44] He was buried in Block 6, Space 108, only hours after his execution.[45]

Maria Thomas

Maria Reynolds Thomas (c 1828–1878) was the first wife of John W. E. Thomas, the first Black state legislator in Illinois. John was born enslaved in Alabama, but was taught to read by his enslaver, and under the shadow of the Civil War worked to illegally teach others. In 1864 he married South Carolina–born Maria, who is said to have been a member of the Catawba tribe. The two moved to Chicago in 1869, where John opened a school and Maria ran a grocery store.[46]

In 1878, while John was in the midst of an election, Maria collapsed after an event at Farwell Hall and died of heart trouble.[47] Maria is in Block 4, Space 1271; John is buried in Oak Woods Cemetery.

Horace Jackson and William Gill: Freedom Fighters

> "No class of people on this earth are to me more hopeful, so far as moral good is concerned, than these ex-slaves of Kentucky."
> —Rev. John G. Fee, "City Brevities"

In the far back area are the graves of two members of the 116th United States Colored Troops.

Kentucky was in a peculiar position during the Civil War—it was a border state, remaining loyal to the Union even though it was not a free state. Even early in the war, though, it was evident that times were changing there. The rabidly anti-Lincoln *Chicago Times* noted as early as 1862, "That the rebellion has put (slavery) in rapid course of extinction in the Border states . . . is plain to the dullest comprehension."[48]

The Emancipation Proclamation that went into effect in 1863 did not affect enslaved people in border states, only those in Confederate territory occupied by the Union army. The government offered up to $300 in compensation for enslaved people who were let go to join the army, and a great many enslavers saw that this was likely their last chance to get any sort of compensation at all. By the end of 1864, they were likely to get only about $15 from the sale of a human being.[49]

Grand Army of the Republic, John Brown Post 50. No names are given, but it may well have included both Jackson and Gill.

As such, an enslaver from Garrard County, Kentucky, allowed **William Gill (1836–1913)**, to join the 116th United States Colored Troops,[50] and one from Fayette allowed several of the people he enslaved to join the same unit, including **Horace Jackson (c1846–1912)**.[51] (Jackson did not know his birthday; later records give different years.)[52]

The 116th was organized in early summer, 1864, at Camp Nelson, Kentucky. Though many Kentuckians claimed that slavery in their state was not as cruel as it was in the deep south, Reverend John Gregg Fee found that 60 percent of the first recruits had "marks of cruelty" on their bodies.[53]

In September of 1864, the 116th defended their camp against an attack by confederate troops commanded by future Ku Klux Klan founder Nathan Bedford Forrest. The next month they were sent to Virginia, and from then on fought alongside the Illinois-based 29th U.S.C.T. In 1865 the 116th and 29th were both involved in the final push against Robert E. Lee's army in Appomattox, and there is an excellent chance that both Jackson and Gill were nearby when Lee surrendered.[54]

After the war, both Gill and Jackson found their way to Chicago, perhaps because of their connection to soldiers in the 29th. Jackson worked as a janitor,[55] and Gill as a sexton for a church.[56] The two men likely knew each other; they were neighbors, and both were probably members of the John Brown Post of the Grand Army of the Republic.

CLAIM OF

FOR THE COMPENSATION OF SLAVE NAMED

I, *George M. Sutton* a loyal citizen, and a resident of *Lexington*, County of *Fayette*, State of Kentucky, hereby claim compensation, under the provisions of Section 24, act approved February 24, 1864, and section 2, act approved July, 28, 1866, for my slave *Horace Jackson*, enlisted *July 11th*, 1864, at *Camp Nelson Ky*, by *Capt A G Kemp* in the *114th* regiment U. S. Colored Troops, Co. *F*; certificate of which enlistment, and a descriptive list, as required, accompany this application. That I did not acquire said slave subsequent to said enlistment, but had a valid title to him at the date of said enlistment, and previous thereto: I having acquired my title to him and my ownership over him as follows, to-wit: *Born my Slave, and raised on my farm*

Jackson's military records include this compensation form that his enslaver filled out.

Few anecdotes about their lives survive, but Jackson did have one recorded adventure late in life: while working as a janitor in 1901, he accidentally shot a police officer in the shoulder while firing a pistol at a burglar. Though arrested, Jackson seems (almost miraculously) to have been released;[57] one report says that the bullet only blew a hole in the policeman's coat.[58] Upon his death more than a decade later, the *Chicago Defender* called Jackson "one of Chicago's most highly respected citizens."[59]

Jackson's Mississippi-born wife, **Florence Jackson McCall (c1863–1945)**, was also likely enslaved at birth. She survived Horace by more than three decades and remarried, but was buried in a spot beside him when she died in 1945; they had purchased two adjacent single plots years before.

■ ■ ■

Across the path from Eternal Silence, *the Kinzie family headstones climb up the hill.*

The Kinzie Family Plot

> "I have a family and have been impoverished by my tak-
> ing an active part in the late contest (The War of 1812).
> I have suffered much in the loss of property; and pray
> that something might be done for me to enable me to
> make a comfortable living."
> —John Kinzie to President Monroe, 1817 (a letter
>   that historian James Ryan Haydon described as "a
>   transparent and amiable fraud")

John Kinzie (1763–1828) is in his fourth grave. He was initially buried near his house upon his death in 1828 and then moved to the cemetery near Chicago Avenue in 1835; he was then moved to City Cemetery in 1842.[60] When one of his sons died in 1865, a new plot was purchased at Graceland, and the elder John was moved there, along with nearly a dozen other family members, nine of whom are identified only as "Kinzie," with no other data, in the cemetery records—likely infant children or grandchildren of John. Overall, the Kinzie family plot contains nearly 50 graves, many of which aren't marked.

Born in 1763, John Kinzie was one of the first handful of people known to have settled permanently in the Chicago area. In 1812, Kinzie was made the "sutler" for Fort Dearborn—essentially a shopkeeper from whom the soldiers at the fort were required to buy most of their goods. As sutlers could charge whatever they pleased, it was a plum gig (and one he got by being the son-in-law of an officer).[61] He made a lot of enemies in the area, including fort interpreter Jean Lalime, whom Kinzie eventually killed in what has variously been described as self-defense, a drunken brawl, or a "perfect assassination."[62]

The fort was burned to the ground after the Battle of Fort Dearborn in 1812, but Kinzie and his family escaped unharmed, and returned to Chicago in 1816 when the Fort was rebuilt. After much pleading, Kinzie was appointed Indian Agent to the Lakes in 1818.[63]

It was absolutely overstating things for early historians to call him the "founder of Chicago," but for a number of reasons, the story endured for decades. For one thing, when historians began to accuse Kinzie of corruption, murder, enslavement, and treason, it simply fit many people's image of the kind of person Chicago *would* have as a founder.[64]

Alexander Wolcott (1790–1830), who married John's daughter Ellen, was the first private medical doctor in Chicago. Wolcott died in 1830 and is buried in front of John (Ellen remarried and is buried in Detroit).

One of John's sons, **Robert Allen Kinzie (1810–1873)** (who is in the front row of graves) was appointed paymaster in the Union army by Abraham Lincoln. His wife, **Gwinthlean Kinzie (1818–1894)** (buried to the right of Robert), is the niece of the artist Whistler's famous mother. Their son, **Walter H. Kinzie**

(1858–1909), was a professional baseball player whose career included a stint for the Chicago White Stockings in 1884. He retired with a career batting average of .132.[65]

Major **John H. Kinzie (1803–1865),** another son of the elder John, is second from the right in the back row of graves. Of all the dozen or so people moved to the plot from City Cemetery in 1865, he had been there the shortest amount of time, having died only months before the removal. One of the city's first trustees, he, too, served as a paymaster during the war.[66]

> "The canoe balanced a moment—then yielded—and quick as thought, the dogs, furniture, and lady were in the deepest of the water. . . . my husband insisted on my putting on dry shoes and socks, and (must I confess it) drinking a little brandy, to obviate the effects of my ice bath."
>
> —Juliette Kinzie, recalling her journey to Chicago.

The major's wife, author **Juliette Magill Kinzie (1806–1870),** is buried to his right. Sometimes referred to as Chicago's first historian, her books *Narrative of the Massacre at Chicago* and *Wau Bun: The 'Early Day' in the North West* form some of the earliest published accounts of the city's days as a prairie outpost. After a period in which she was often maligned as an unreliable historian, she's now being reevaluated as one of the city's "forgotten founders." She was the subject of a 2019 biography, *The World of Juliette Kinzie* by Ann Durkin Keating, which covers everything from the nascent days of Chicago society to the great amusement John H. and Juliette got from their pet parrot, Polly.[67]

One of John H. and Juliette's sons, **John H. Kinzie Jr. (1838–1862),** was killed while serving aboard the ironclad Union gunboat *Mound City* in 1862 and is buried in front of his parents. He appears to have been a leading participant in the "Wide Awake" rally of October 1860, in which 10,000 "Wide Awakes," a para-military organization supporting Lincoln's election, marched peacefully through the city with torches.[68]

Another son, **Arthur Magill Kinzie (1839–1902),** is buried in front of his grandfather. In the war he served as an aide-de-camp to his uncle, General David Hunter (who was married to Maria Kinzie, the elder John's daughter; the Hunters are buried in New Jersey). Hunter was perhaps the most outspoken abolitionist of the early Civil War generals, and in early 1862 issued an order that slaves in any territory he took over were "forever free."[69]

As this came before the Emancipation Proclamation, it's hard to overstate how shocking Hunter's order was at the time; the *Chicago Times* called it "the most startling event of the war," and, being a pro-slavery paper, called Hunter "The Emperor of the Asses."[70] The order was quickly nullified, but Lincoln

Named graves in the Kinzie plot: 1. John Kinzie 2. Alexander Wolcott 3. Arthur Magill Kinzie 4. John H. Kinzie 5. Juliette Kinzie 6. John H. Kinzie Jr. 7. Robert Allan Kinzie 8. Gwinthlean Kinzie.

used his nullification order to point out that, while generals didn't have the authority to free people, he himself *did* (a major statement at the time). It also gave him an opportunity to urge the border states not to be "blind to the signs of the times" and abolish slavery on their own.[71]

But Hunter went ahead and organized 750 "contrabands" into the First South Carolina Volunteers, with Arthur as their colonel.[72] Though not officially recognized, this was the first known army unit made up of Black soldiers. When Kentucky congressman Charles Wicklife demanded an investigation, Hunter wrote that he *hadn't* recruited "fugitive slaves," but "a fine regiment of loyal persons whose late masters are fugitive rebels."[73] Some members of congress cheered and laughed, and, though Wickliffe criticized Hunter's lack of civility,[74] the questions of Emancipation and forming Black regiments were now pushed to the forefront of a government that had tried to ignore them. Lincoln echoed Hunter's language when he used the phrase "forever free" in the preliminary Emancipation Proclamation months later.

As colonel of the unauthorized regiment, Arthur Magill Kinzie praised the abilities and potential of Black soldiers. Though his reasoning that they were naturally "imitative" and "obedient" was hardly progressive,[75] he deserves credit for helping to form the regiment at a time when such actions were illegal, and made him a particular target for confederates.

John H. Kinzie Jr. and Arthur's sister, Nellie, married a southerner and moved to Savannah shortly before the war. Though she became devoted to the southern cause, and was friendly with Robert E. Lee, local residents threw excrement on her door when they found she was related to David Hunter and Arthur Kinzie, which soured her a bit on her neighbors and their cause.[76] She is buried in Savannah, as is her own daughter, Juliette Gordon Low, the founder of the Girl Scouts.

■ ■ ■

Just north of the Kinzie plot is the large obelisk at the center of the Sherman family plot; this is Station 2. Turn to page 53.

The Sherman obelisk

STATION TWO

THE SHERMAN PLOT

Station two is the Sherman plot, near the intersection of Main Ave and Fairview Ave, just north of *Eternal Silence*. Look for the large, faded brown obelisk, on which the name "Sherman" is very faintly visible, surrounded by nearly fifty individual markers.

The Sherman Family Obelisk

"Mother, war is a horrible trade."
—Francis Trowbridge Sherman, *Letter to Electa Sherman*

Though best remembered for building the Sherman Hotel, a Chicago landmark for decades, **Francis Cornwall Sherman (1805–1870)** also served multiple one-year terms as mayor of Chicago, the first in 1841 when it was a brand new town of a few thousand people, and the next in 1862, when the now-exponentially larger city was just coming to realize the horrors the coming Civil War would bring. In 1863, he won a third time, this time for a two-year term.

At a time when his Democratic party was widely viewed as antiwar, if not actively pro-confederate, his 1862 election was a viewed by some as a defeat for the more progressive Union supporters. However, the Republican-leaning (though aggressively middle-of-the-road) *Chicago Journal* wrote, "Since the Fates have decreed that we must have a Democratic mayor, we know of no man in that party whom we would more willingly see occupying that office than Francis C. Sherman."[1]

He had beaten out National Union (Republican) nominee and Graceland founder Thomas B. Bryan by only a couple hundred votes, and Bryan's friends urged him to contest the results. But Bryan didn't *want* to be mayor badly enough to press the issue and simply conceded.[2]

Perhaps to show that there were no hard feelings, Francis purchased the family plot—consisting of nine lots, with spaces for about a dozen burials each—just a few months after the election.[3]

Francis had a personal reason to support the Union: his son, **Francis Trowbridge Sherman (1825–1905)** was serving as a Colonel in the 88th Illinois Volunteer Regiment. Letters that "F.T." wrote from the front show that he was uneasy about his father's political career; there was a general sense among soldiers that even "war democrats" were too soft on the confederates, and he often pleaded with his father to "cast aside all considerations of party."[4] But he needn't have worried; in his third inaugural address, his father said that if anyone in the city wanted to recognize the Confederacy or withdraw troops from fighting them, "such men are strangers to me personally and politically. I have no relations with them of any kind. I am not their friend, nor are they my friends." F.T. was promoted to Brigadier General toward the end of the war.

■ ■ ■

From Station two, paths go North (Route 2-A) and East (Route 2-B).
For route 2-A, go to page 57.
For route 2-B, go to page 91.

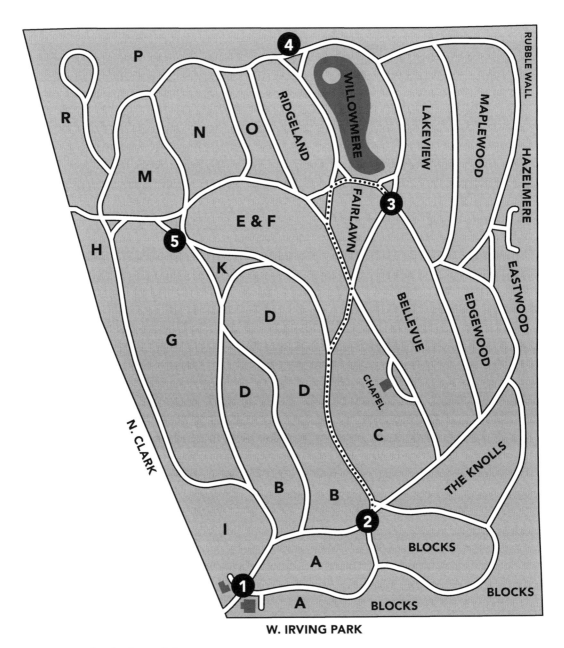

Map for Route 2-A

Proceed north up Center Avenue. On the left, beside the Zimmerman plot, is the unmarked grave of **Melville Reeves (c1888–1938)** who was known as "The Skyscraper Burglar." Over a 25-year career, he stole millions of dollars worth of valuables from office buildings in the loop, and, though police suspected him, they couldn't pin anything on him until he was caught stealing $53 in stamps from the London Guarantee Building in the early 1930s. He died in prison.[1]

North of Zimmerman will be three dark "table" style graves that resemble sarcophagi. **Daniel Elston (1790–1855)** was a London-born business man; a friend described him in a eulogy as "dignified in appearance and courteous in manner."[2] He served as an alderman in the 1840s, a time when the oath of office included a portion in which he was ordered to swear that he had never been involved in a duel, either as a duelist or a second.[3] He hadn't. Phew.

Daniel married **Blanche Marie Elston (1799–1895)** in London in 1832. Two years later, he chartered a ship and filled it with farm tools, furniture, and a massive art collection to emigrate to America, where they purchased 160 acres near Division Street, alongside the north branch of the Chicago River on the old trail that would one day be named Elston Avenue. Blanche was noted for her encyclopedic knowledge of English literature.

Proceeding past Elston, on the right, in the Curtis plot is a very, very old marker, set into the ground. No last name is given, but it's for a woman named **Adele** who died in August 1849 (presumably part of that year's cholera epidemic). There are also inscriptions for two children, **Charles Edgar** and **Charles Garr**, whose dates of death appear to be 1831 and 1833—well before even the old City Cemetery was established. These two may, like John Kinzie, be in their third or fourth graves.

A bit north of Curtis, behind the Wheelock plot, is the lonely, faded marker to **Jeremiah Price (c1793–1854)**, a land speculator remembered solely for being spectacularly boring. "If he had any imagination," wrote one contemporary, "it . . . never went beyond the alphabet, the multiplication tables, and

The Stevens Tumulous

the rule of three." When stricken by the cholera epidemic of 1854, he insisted he could cure himself with peppermint lozenges. It didn't work. The next morning, he was found dead, with $20,000 in cash, securities, and promissory notes strapped to his body as though he were trying to take it with him. Dying alone without a will,[4] it took decades for his estate to be settled; a judge let his lawyer, L. C. P. Freer (page 59) use some of it to move his body and monument here from City Cemetery in 1870.[5]

On the left you'll see a mausoleum built into the hill bearing the name G. M. Stevens. This tomb was originally built by dry goods merchant H. H. Magie and was pointed out as a highlight of the cemetery in many early articles.[6] [7] However, a few decades after his death, Magie's son-in-law, Judge Lambert Tree, sold the tomb to lawyer **George M. Stevens (c1847–1923)** and had the bodies removed and reburied in the Tree-Magie plot (page 137).[8]

Just north of the tomb is the Freer obelisk.

Luscious C. P. Freer and the Vigilance Committee

"(We) had worked for thirty years against the encroachment of slavery, but all the time the slave power grew stronger with the National Government, and all the time it was making inroads. War was the lesser of the two evils, and we believed that war was inevitable."

—L. C. P. Freer, "Slavery in Chicago"

In October 1846, three men on Lake Street were seized by a man claiming to represent a St. Louis enslaver who claimed the three as his property. The slave catcher was assisted by Deputy Sheriff Henry Rhines (page 252). "Rhines," wrote the *New York Tribune*, "is a degraded, drunken wretch, ready and accustomed to assist in the most nefarious schemes for money or office."[9]

Just how a New York paper would know about Rhines' drinking habits is impossible to know, but most of Chicago seemed to be on the *New York Tribune's* side—lawyer **L. C. P. Freer (1813–1892)** and his partner James H. Collins (page 61) had worked hard to create an antislavery atmosphere in the city, despite strong pushback from a vocal minority. A crowd estimated at 2000, more than 10 percent of the city's population at the time, gathered outside the office of Justice Kercheval, where the three alleged refugees were being held.[10]

Freer and Collins appeared as lawyers for the men, but in talking to the judge their real goal was creating a distraction that allowed the three to escape. It worked; they slipped out the door and down the stairs, where the crowd held Rhines back while the men were hustled to safety. Collins and Freer then convinced Justice Kercheval that he didn't have the authority to issue the writ he'd issued to arrest the men, and he agreed to quash it.[11]

Years later, when Lincoln was elected president and southern states began seceding, citing northern hostility to slave catchers as a major grievance, the new U.S. Marshal of the Northern District of Illinois, J. R. Jones, appeared to be trying to appease them by cracking down on adherence to the Fugitive Slave Law. This created an emergency situation for refugee enslaved people—or anyone who might be mistaken for one.[12] Freer put an ad in the paper saying "The new United States Marshal is inaugurating a reign of terror among our colored population. Do you wish to take any steps in the matter? If you do, you are invited to meet at my office this evening . . . None but live men are invited."[13]

In Freer's office that night, a "vigilance committee" was formed, with John Jones (page 68), Philo Carpenter (page 30), and Freer himself as officers. Funds were raised to put hundreds of endangered people on trains to Canada,

The Collins marker

and bodyguards were arranged to make sure they weren't apprehended on the way.[14]

Freer died in 1892, outliving most of the rest of Chicago's antislavery legal force. Among those interred with him is his wife, **Esther Freer (1815–1873)**, and seven of their children. Both L. C. P. and Esther were active in the Underground Railroad.[15]

• • •

Across the road from Freer, a bit up the hill, is the faded old cream-colored monument for James H. Collins, who was Freer's mentor.

James H. Collins: "A Most Violent and Extreme Abolitionist"

"The Fugitive Slave bill recently passed is a most daring violation of the law of nature and of revelation, an outrage upon the Constitution, an assault upon liberty, an insult to the people of the free States, and ought to be disobeyed and trampled in the dust."
—James H. Collins, "The Old Liberty Guard"

Chicago's first murder trial was held in 1834, when a man was accused of killing his wife. Years later, no one could remember or locate the man's name.[16] But all remembered that **James H. Collins (1799–1854)** was the lawyer for the defense and got the man acquitted on what amounted to a technicality.[17] This likely didn't make Collins popular in the city, but that sort of thing never bothered him. Indeed, from various anecdotes one gets the impression that he almost delighted in making people mad. He was burned in effigy when he bought the land where the old Fort Dearborn stood, evicting an early settler many believed was entitled to the property.[18]

But this attitude was perfect for antislavery and Underground Railroad work, where you couldn't be afraid of a fight, and it was his efforts in that field that made him famous. Isaac Newton Arnold (page 190) said that Collins was "as combative as an English bulldog . . . an early, and most violent and extreme abolitionist."[19] Frederick Douglass' newspaper praised him as a man who "Stood against the whole combined force of slavery."[20]

Collins came to Chicago in the 1830s, and at first lived with his family in an apartment so small that the cooking had to be done outdoors, where cows would sometimes steal his vegetables.[21] He first made a national name for himself in 1843 with his courtroom defense of Owen Lovejoy, who was accused of aiding enslaved people who were attempting to escape. Collins had already defended several other "fugitives" and people who assisted them in court, including Julius and Samuel Willard (page 209), but the Lovejoy case was national news, as Owen's brother, Elijah, had been murdered by an anti-abolitionist mob, despite the efforts of W. F. DeWolf (page 63). Lovejoy was acquitted after Collins addressed the jury for seven solid hours, and one paper noted that "the courthouse was crowded, and very many were present and heard a genuine abolition speech who never could have been induced to hear one on any other occasion."[22]

In 1846, following the arrest of three men believed to be escaping enslaved people and the ensuing uproar (see the story on page 59), Collins appeared at a public meeting, railing against the newspaper editors who'd tried to "stigmatize the [crowd who'd come to help] as an 'armed negro mob.'" He said that the crowd had been peaceful, but that if they *had* attacked the police, he would have been happy to help: "For my part, I would spit upon and trample them under (my) feet in scorn . . . all who act the part of slave hounds do it out of pure love for the devil, and if they continue their evil practices, I will see the question tried before the highest tribunal."[23]

In a letter the next day, he asserted his view that no judge or magistrate had any power to issue a warrant to arrest anyone as a "fugitive slave," that no officer had any obligation to aid in their capture, and that citizens could use force against such officers. "No officer, therefore . . . while engaged in the arrest, detention, or surrender of a fugitive slave, can claim any more protection from the law than any private person who may be mean and vile enough to engage in such an employment."[24]

His work extended to helping on the underground railroad; in an 1846 letter, he said that he and his colleagues had just helped thirteen people escape to Canada, "and hundreds more are on their way."[25]

In 1854, Collins argued a case in Ottawa, IL, with his usual vigor, but that evening he began to feel ill. It was cholera, and he died the next morning.[26] Initially buried at City Cemetery, he was moved to Graceland in 1866.[27] Later, his friends would muse that if he'd lived until the Civil War, he could have ended up in a position of high command as his abolitionist goals, which seemed impossible to many at the time, finally became mainstream.

■ ■ ■

Return to the route. Among the older graves alongside the road on the right is a tall white marker on which the name **Emily Shrigley (c1801–1884)** is faintly visible; the name of her husband **John Shrigley (c1794–1853)** is easier to read on the back side. John served as the second High Constable of the police department, and in 1840 catered Chicago's first known cricket match, which was played at Dutchman's Point (now Niles).[28]

On the left, behind the monument to teamster **Henry Borman (1834–1897)**, will be a family plot centered on a monument in the form of a draped sarcophagus. The inscription on the ruffled drape must have been difficult to read even when it was newly installed in the old City Cemetery. It's the largest monument in the plot of the De Wolf family.

The De Wolf Family Plot

"Such a hotel (as the Alton House in 1836) . . . would now, in 1882, be considered very inferior. But we had made up our minds to meet the deficiencies of the new West with the best grace we could, and soon came to enjoy the life about to be entered upon."
—William Frederick De Wolf, "History of Madison County"

In 1837 a meeting was held in Alton, Illinois, regarding what should be done about Reverend Elijah Lovejoy, a local abolitionist newspaper editor who was considered a dangerous radical in the small, conservative town. **William Frederick De Wolf (1811–1896)**[29] stood up for Lovejoy's right to freedom of the press, and the mob not only shouted him down, but murdered Lovejoy. Years later, Judge Joseph Gillespie lamented that "If the counsels of Mr. De Wolf had prevailed, we would have been spared the necessity of having to apologize for the greatest iniquity of the 19th century; the atrocious murder of one of the greatest and best men in the land, by a worthless mob."[30]

A cousin of abolitionist Calvin De Wolf, lawyer William Frederick and his wife, **Margaret Padelford Arnold De Wolf (c1810–1877)** moved their family to Chicago in 1847, and William eventually became city treasurer. While in New York in 1853, they took their eight children on a trip on the steamer *Bay State*. When a cylinder on the ship exploded, sending massive amounts of steam into the state rooms, four of the De Wolf daughters were badly injured. Three died within hours at a hospital; a fourth, teenage Ann, lingered for several days before succumbing.[31]

A mourner wrote after her funeral that "One of (Annie's) innocent amusements with her bright sister Charlotte and some other little friends was to describe the house and gardens where they should like to live. I can always call to mind these imaginary abodes. Princes might envy them their galleries of statues and pictures."[32]

William purchased his City Cemetery lot only days after the accident.[33] While there's strangely no record of the girls' bodies being moved to Graceland,[34] their monument was; the draped sarcophagus monument is a memorial to them.

Son **William De Wolf (1842–1862)** joined Taylor's Battery in March 1862; he saw action almost immediately in the battles of Belmont and Fort Donelson before being assigned to the Army of the Potomac. He was shot off his horse in a skirmish the day before the Battle of Williamsburg, and promptly hopped onto another horse, continuing to fight although he was badly wounded.[35] After the battle he was taken to the Washington, D.C. residence of congressman Isaac Newton Arnold (page 190), where he died of his wounds four weeks later. The *Tribune* wrote that "Truly has the dart of the 'insatiable archer' found a shining mark."[36]

William Frederick himself remained active politically all his life, even insisting on being carried to the polls in 1890 when he was unable to walk there on his own to vote.[37]

. . .

Proceed North. On the right will be the tall white marker for pioneering urologist **Louis Ernest Schmidt (1869–1957)**.[38] A few rows behind Schmidt are two small monuments listing the various Civil War battles in which their occupants participated.

Captain Lucius Larrabee: From the Zouaves to Gettysburg

> "Captain Larrabee of Company B was saying in his cheery voice, 'Major, these two left companies are under an enfilading fire.'. . . . I said to myself: 'Enfilading. Never heard that word pronounced before, though I have read it all my life. Now, first time I hear it, I am enfiladed.'"
> —Col. Charles Sprague, "Octogenarian"

At the second Battle of Bull Run in 1862, **Lucius Larrabee (1837–1863)** had one of his fingers shattered by a bullet. A former member of Ellsworth's Zouaves (page 17), he declined to take anything to numb the pain when it had to be amputated, and even remained awake to watch the operation performed. Afterward, he casually remarked that it had hurt more than he thought it would, and agreed that if he needed *another* finger amputated, he'd take the ether.[39]

Larrabee had followed Ellsworth to New York to form the Fire Zouaves when the war began. After Ellsworth's death, Larrabee ended up in the 44th New York Volunteer Infantry, who found themselves at The Battle of Gettysburg in 1863. On the second day of the battle, Larrabee told others that "Since our last battle I have known that I would be killed the next time I was under fire," and begged them to take his valuables for safekeeping. They laughed it off (such premonitions were common), but Larrabee was so spooked that he left his watch and the address of his brother with the quartermaster.[40]

As the line formed on Little Round Top, he was ordered to move his regiment down the slope of the hill. Captain Bourne wished him luck, and Larrabee, still haunted by his premonition, said, "Good bye, Billy, I shall never see you again" and led his troops forward.[41]

They advanced about 200 yards down the slope before meeting enemy fire, and Larrabee was shot and killed. Captain Nash wrote that "No braver soldier, no purer or truer spirit took its flight from that blood-drenched field."[42]

Right near Larrabee is a nearly matching grave for **Captain Peter Preston Wood (1834–1865)**, whose sister, **Mary Ann Wood Larrabee (c1827–1913)**, was married to Captain Larrabee's brother, **Charles Larrabee (c1825–1899)**.

Wood and Larrabee had marble pillars as gravestones at first, but they were replaced with the current matching granite mark-

Larrabee

ers in 1948.[43] Behind the plot is a tree with a small stone marker of its own, identifying it as a "Pickett's Charge Black Walnut." A company called Famous & Historic Trees was selling "Scion trees" in the late 20th century, along with optional granite markers, so this was likely a tree grown from a seed from the black walnut that still stood on the grounds in Gettysburg where Union forces decimated the famous Confederate attack.[44] A few are around Graceland; in front of the marker is a tree marked as "Gettysburg Spruce."

■ ■ ■

Return to the route. On the left side, set back from the road behind the plot of farmer **Zoroaster Culver (1794–1878)**, will be the large Dexter plot, most recognizable for a boulder grave that sits near several gray "cradle" style graves from the Dexter's Prairie Avenue neighbors, the Walkers. The boulder is for Katharine Dexter McCormick and her husband.

Katharine Dexter McCormick: Love and Science

"I was sharply commented upon [at MIT] about the shorter length of my dress. I responded, 'I don't want it to touch the unclean floors.'"
—Katharine Dexter McCormick[45]

A corporate lawyer who headed relief efforts after the Great Fire, **Wirt Dexter (1832–1890)** was always political; family stories said that his boyhood home in Michigan was an Underground Railroad depot run by his father. He raised his daughter, **Katharine Dexter McCormick (1875–1967)**, with his same sense of idealism. Though the family lived on the "Millionaire Row" on South Prairie Avenue and were a part of high society, it's said that young Katharine was more interested in searching Prairie Avenue for relics of the Battle of Fort Dearborn, which had been fought on the grounds in 1812, than in going to parties. However, she attended such famous functions as the Fields' Mikado ball (page 174) and dutifully became a debutante at 18.[46]

After the early deaths of her father and brother in the 1890s, Katharine decided to become a doctor and studied biology at M.I.T. There, she successfully challenged a dress code that required women to wear fashionable hats and long skirts. She was one of the first women to graduate from the school, and later provided funds and lobbying to get the school to build more womens' dormitories, overdue efforts that allowed the number of women enrolled as students to rise exponentially.[47]

But she gave up plans to go on to medical school in order to marry **Stanley McCormick (1874–1947)**, one of the sons of Cyrus McCormick, the "reaper king" (page 176). Cyrus had died when Stanley was just a boy, and he was raised largely by his mother, Nettie (page 177), who steered Stanley away from his desired career in the arts and toward the family business. Invariably portrayed as domineering in biographies, Nettie kept Stanley at home well into adulthood; even as a grown man he was not allowed to close the door to his bedroom, and he was subjected to breath checks to see if he'd been drinking, among other indignities.[48] She was whispering unkind words about Katharine into Stanley's ear on the day of the wedding.[49]

Stanley's friend Arthur Meeker Jr. (page 112) wrote that the McCormick family was known for "a certain not undistinguished goofiness."[50] In reality, many of the McCormicks suffered from severe mental health issues, and Stanley may have been the most affected of all.

By the time of his marriage to Katharine in 1904, Stanley's sister Mary Virginia (page 177) had already been institutionalized for mental illness, and within a few years of his wedding to Katharine, Stanley, too, had deteriorated mentally. The marriage was never consummated; he would lock himself in his room to avoid Katharine. When the couple moved to Massachusetts so Katharine could do graduate studies, Stanley's mental health collapsed completely. After a series of alarming episodes, he was confined to a full floor of a mansion in Santa Barbara, where he was attended full time by nurses for the rest of his life.[51]

Katharine exhibited her scientific knowledge in court regularly as she battled to be given a leading role in his care, while the McCormicks urged her to have the marriage annulled, offering her a generous settlement. But even as she fought to manage Stanley's treatments, and visited the Santa Barbara mansion often, she wasn't allowed to see him personally for two decades. His attendants believed that seeing *any* women was bad for Stanley's mental

Katharine Dexter McCormick, Library of Congress.

health; during the two decades he was barred from seeing Katharine, he didn't see a single other woman, either.[52]

Though she continued fighting, Katharine had no choice but to get on with her life. She became treasurer for the National American Woman's Suffrage Association and often acted as a spokesperson for the women's movement in the press. Stanley had introduced her to Jane Addams of Hull House, whom he counted as a good friend, around the time of their wedding.[53]

Katharine remained politically active after Stanley's death in 1947, almost single-handedly funding the research behind the first birth control pill.[54] When she died at the age of 92 she was buried beside Stanley in the Dexter family plot (it's notable that he was buried in *her* family's plot, not the McCormick's). Their lives and relationship were the subject of the 1998 novel *Riven Rock*, by T. C. Boyle, and she was the subject of a 2003 biography by Armond Fields.

The family plot beside the Dexters is that of railroad president **James M. Walker (1820–1881)**. The largest of the gray cradle-style graves is that of his daughter **Mary Walker Root (1858–1880)**, whom poet Harriet Monroe described as "Alert, brilliant, keenly intellectual, she won friends by her eager loyalty; and enemies, perhaps, by her sharp wit."[55] She died of tuberculosis at 21, only six weeks after her wedding to architect John Wellborn Root (page 114).

■ ■ ■

Proceed north along the road. On the right will be a marker for **Rush Johnson (1880–1952)** and **Edna Shaw Johnson (1881–1940)**. The unmarked spot behind it is the Atkinson-Johnson-Greenwood plot. **Isaac Atkinson (c1816–1884)** and his wife, **Emma Atkinson (c1820–1906)** (misnamed as Annie in Graceland records), were said to have worked on the Underground Railroad 1840s. Isaac was of Scottish and Cherokee descent, and his wife was half Black and half Cherokee; their large family became prominent in Black society in the late 19th century.[56] The family's papers and photographs, featuring several prominent Black citizens and celebrities of the era, were donated to the Chicago Public Library in the 1990s.

■ ■ ■

Just behind the Johnson plot, and a bit to the left, is a dark "base, dye and cap" style marker for John and Mary Jones.

John Jones and Mary Richardson Jones: Chicago Crusaders

"It is not the complexion or shades of men that we are discussing, it is the rights of all inhabitants of the State . . . the white, the black, and the colored. The interest of one, is the interest of all."
—John Jones

In the early 1840s, Black settlers were required to put up a bond of $2000 even to live in Illinois—an impossible sum for most. But one Black old timer in 1898 noted that "to the honor of Chicago the law was never enforced and the setting of every sun marked the arrival of a strange Negro."[57]

Arriving in town in 1845 with $3.50 to his name, **John Jones (1817–1879)**[58] established himself as a tailor and arranged for papers to be drawn up showing that he and his wife, **Mary Richardson Jones (1820–1910)**, were "free persons of color." Though both were born free, and Chicagoans tended to be hostile to people who tried to claim other Chicagoans as slaves, they couldn't be too careful.[59]

John's tailor shop was a huge success; by the end of his life he was thought to be the wealthiest Black man in town, and Mary was the head of the Black society circle. But their work and social obligations, to say nothing of their

John Jones

precarious status as free people, didn't stop them from being outspokenly political. Their Dearborn Street home soon became a known depot on the Underground Railroad; John even put ads offering aid to anyone who arrived in Chicago in *Frederick Douglass' Paper*, stating that he was adept at finding people jobs, and that "Families and those that need help will find it to their advantage to apply at my office for their supplies."[60] Shortly after setting up their house, the couple came to the aid of three women who'd escaped by hiding under the hay in the back of a wagon; John and Mary kept them in their home all winter until it was safe to put them on a boat to Canada.[61] These were perhaps the first of hundreds of refugee slaves the couple would shelter and assist.

In 1852, John Jones (page 68) and lawyer L. C. P. Freer (page 59) purchased a man, Albert Petit, from his Tennessee enslaver. He was freed in the same document that transferred ownership.[62] In some accounts "Albert" was Alfred Richardson, his wife's brother;[63] and it may or may not be the same time that he raised $800 from friends and neighbors to free a man described by a Wisconsin paper as "his sister's husband."[64] It may be that Jones and Freer employed this technique more than once. Abolitionists didn't consider this sort of transaction ideal, but it worked.

John was uneducated and illiterate when he arrived; L. C. P. Freer (page 59) wrote his first documents for him, but insisted he learn to do so himself.[65] Jones proved to be a highly effective writer. In 1864, he wrote a pamphlet arguing for the overturn of the "Black Laws" that kept his family second-class citizens in Illinois. The *Tribune* championed the pamphlet, writing that the Black laws were "in part useless, in part unconstitutional, and wholly barbarian and disgraceful."[66] They were repealed only months later.

Shortly after the war, John was one of the delegates who went with Frederick Douglass to Washington, D.C., and was present at an interview in which President Andrew Johnson made a complete buffoon of himself; he asked Douglass if he'd ever been on a plantation, then called himself "the black man's Moses" while declining to support suffrage (a line that earned particular ridicule from Emery A. Storrs, page 116).[67] In 1871, John was elected to the board of commissioners, making him the first Black man to be elected to public office in Chicago.[68]

> "We want more justice to women and more virtue among men."
> —Mary Richardson Jones, "Cultured Negro Ladies," *Chicago Tribune*

Mary continued fighting long after John died of Bright's disease in 1879.[69] Though she had many stories to tell by the 20th century, there was one she was called on to tell at one meeting after another: the story of the day radical abolitionist John Brown showed up at her door with several of the "fighters" he had recruited for his planned rebellion.[70]

Brown had first been brought to the Jones home by Frederick Douglass years before, when starting a rebellion was only an idea in his head. But by

1858 Brown had become famous and had a price on his head. Mary thought his "fighters" were "the roughest looking men I ever saw" and wasn't sure she wanted them in her home, but she reluctantly harbored them while her husband and Allan Pinkerton (page 76) went around the city raising funds to get them to Canada. She also sent a man who she figured was about Brown's size into town to be fitted for a new suit Brown could wear. Only months later came Brown's raid on Harper's Ferry and his subsequent execution; years later Mary wrote, "I guess John Brown was hung in those same clothes."[71]

In 1893, Mary became the first president of the Ida B. Wells Woman's club, at famed activist Wells own insistence. "I wanted Mrs. John Jones to head the

Mary Richardson Jones

movement," Wells later wrote, "because . . . it would lend prestige to have such a genteel, high-bred old lady of the race to lead them."[72] Though initially fairly conservative about womens' suffrage, Mary devoted herself to the cause in later years. Her own grave is marked in the plot by the white stone that simply says "Grandma Jonesie."

In the plot with them are their daughter, **Lavinia Jones Lee (1843–1933)**, who later recalled that her father had helped hundreds of enslaved people escape.[73] The most recent interment in the plot was Lavinia's daughter, **Theodora Lee Purnell (1871–1967)**, who passed on stories of the old family home as an Underground Railroad station.[74]

In his 1864 pamphlet, Jones wrote that "Today a colored man cannot buy a *burying lot* in the city of Chicago for his own use."[75] Lake View would not be absorbed by Chicago for several years, so he may not have been counting Graceland as Chicago. Black burials had certainly taken place in the cemetery by then.

Graceland records did not typically note the ethnicity of interments, which was fairly progressive for the 1860s. But it can present difficulties for modern research; without records, it's impossible to know when the first Black interment took place at Graceland, or how many people of color had been buried there by 1865. Occasionally, though, a clerk would write "(Colored)" next to a name in the interment book. The first that are so noted are Octavia, John, and Henrietta Johnson, three young children who had died from 1861 to 1862 and were buried in July, 1862. They were interred in a section of single graves noted only as "N. end of Div," the meaning of which is now obscure.[76]

. . .

Directly east of the Jones plot is a small marker on which the name "Bradford" can be made out. Jones owned this plot, as well.

Henry Bradford and Ailey M. Bradford

"Whereas The Fugitive Slave Bill has just been passed into a law . . . We are determined to defend ourselves at all hazards, even should it be to the shedding of human blood . . . We who have tasted of freedom are ready to exclaim in the language of the brave Patrick Henry, 'Give us liberty or give us death.'"
—Resolution drafted in part by Henry Bradford, 1850

Ailey M. Bradford (1810–1886) was Mary Richardson Jones' sister, according to a letter from Mary in the Graceland files (page 70).[77] She and her husband, **Henry Bradford (1809–1880)**, are sometimes listed as "lesser leaders" in the abolition movement.[78] They share the plot—which was owned by John Jones—with their son, **Frankie Bradford (1863–1869)**, as well as the Wheel-ers (page 73). It's to be assumed that they helped John and Mary Jones with their Underground Railroad activities.

Born in Virginia (likely enslaved),[79] Henry's name begins appearing among committees and as a signatory to political resolutions in Chicago around 1850.[80] He and John Jones both contributed to a letter of tribute to James Collins (page 61) upon Collins' death in 1854,[81] and Henry was part of a reception for Frederick Douglass at Jones' house in 1859.[82] From mentions in the press, Henry seems to have been most active during the war years; he assisted "contrabands" who were brought to Chicago in 1862,[83] and was made the chair of a committee to fight for public schools in Chicago to be integrated in October 1864.[84]

Ailey's name is sometimes given as "Elsie." She was treasurer of the Colored Ladies Freedmens Aid Society of Chicago, which gathered and shipped supplies to freedmen during the war.[85]

An 1870 census lists Henry as a saloon keeper; the census from the year of his death a decade later says he was a barber.[86]

■ ■ ■

Though he has no marker of his own, the ashes of John Jones' nephew by marriage, Lloyd Garrison Wheeler, and his wife Ramie are buried in the Bradford lot as well.

Lloyd Garrison Wheeler: The First Black Lawyer in Illinois

> "When the growing mind of thoughtful man finds expression in new truths and new orders of things, it is met with a skepticism based on no higher authority than individual belief. When Franklin demonstrated the impotency of church bells to dispel lightning . . . by simply gathering it around a metal key, the anathemas of the faithful knew no bounds . . . Lightning, the evil and tumultuous spirits of the air, was so easily tamed by the well-organized brain of Franklin as now to serve mankind as the winged messenger of peace and light and health."
>
> —Lloyd Garrison Wheeler, in a philosophy lecture

Born in Ohio around 1848, **Lloyd Garrison Wheeler (1848–1909)** came to Chicago at 11. As a teenager he studied law while working as a mail carrier, and in 1869 he became the first Black man admitted to the bar in Illinois.[87]

After practicing law in the south for a time in the 1870s, the terror of the Ku Klux Klan drove him back to Chicago, where he gave up law to manage the business interests of John Jones (page 68), eventually expanding to several other business interests of his own that made him a wealthy man. Once he was established, he became a prominent philanthropist and got involved in a number of reform committees.

In 1882, a Chicago grand jury made a sweeping move, indicting dozens of gamblers (guys with names like "Dirty Shirt" Brown and "Kid Leonard") who were operating out of hotel rooms. For good measure, the grand jury also indicted their landlords, including both Wheeler, who was running a hotel at the time, and Potter Palmer (page 148). Having been a lawyer himself, Wheeler knew how hard it was to prosecute such indictments, and simply laughed it off, telling a reporter "It's my impression, dear fellow, that the grand jury has woke up more snakes that it can kill."[88] He was right to laugh; the case was soon dismissed.[89]

In 1888, he cofounded the Prudence Crandall Club, a Black literary society known as a haven for "free thinkers," along with his friends Mary Jones (page 70) and Daniel Hale Williams (page 115). In the club, Wheeler was the head of the philosophy discussions.[90]

Besides the Bradfords, Lloyd shares the plot with his wife, **Ramie Sarah Wheeler (1843–1917)**, a niece of John Jones whom John and Mary had raised as an adopted daughter. Lloyd and Ramie's infant daughter, **Louisa Wheeler (1874)**, is in the adjacent Jones plot, with a small marker to the right of the tree. (The markers next to her, for "Eddie," "Nellie," and "Baby," are children in the adjacent lot of manufacturer **Eber C. Prieble**.) In an affidavit, Mary Jones wrote that, after Henry and Ailey Bradford (Mary's sister) died with no surviving children, John granted the remaining space in the plot to Wheeler "for no other consideration than personal regard and a desire to be buried near each other."[91]

. . .

A little bit south of the Bradford and Jones markers, and near the rusticated cylindrical stone Rickords marker, is an unmarked space for a fascinating author and adventurer.

Mary Hastings Bradley: Author and Adventurer

"People ask what my ambition is. What kind of book I want to do next, what new jungles I'm going to explore. I've never had a goal. I've always lacked ambition because I've enjoyed life too much doing what I happened to be doing at the time."

—Mary Hastings Bradley, "An Unclassified Author"

A movie about **Mary Hastings Bradley (1882–1976)**[92] would seem like an old-fashioned serial thriller. She was a novelist, archaeologist, and big game hunter while maintaining a schedule of society dances and operas. Her daughter described her as "a kind of explorer-heroine, highly literate, yet very feminine whatever that is. You help her through doors—and then find out she can hike 45 miles up a mountain carrying her rifle and yours. . . . And dazzling looks . . . I am still approached by doddering wrecks . . . who want to tell me about Mother as a young woman."[93]

Raised by firm Victorian parents, Mary began her career writing light fiction for magazines and then found fame as a travel writer. Her books on Africa, which encouraged women to travel there, were hits, but by the 1930s she was focusing more on historical fiction and mystery novels (including the hits *Palace of Darkened Windows* and *The Fortieth Door*), which paid better at the time. The U.S. Government sent her to Germany after World War II to document the remains of Nazi death camps.

She died at 92 in 1976, having lived in the same Hyde Park apartment for more than 60 years; her obituary said her last wish was that there be no services "Of any kind, nature, or description," which probably explains the fact that her grave is not visibly marked.[94] The daughter who traveled with her in Africa, Alice, became a successful science fiction writer under the name James Tiptree Jr.[95]

. . .

Return to the road and continue north. On the right, shortly past a fork in the road (stay right), you'll see an obelisk with a metal plaque marking the Pinkerton family plot.

Allan Pinkerton: "A Friend to Honesty and a Foe to Crime"

"Legitimate, honest detective business . . . approaches
the dignity of an art."
—Allan Pinkerton, *The Somnambulist and the
Detective*

Scottish-born **Allan Pinkerton (1819–1884)** first attracted notice for his work on the Underground Railroad—as early as 1851; when he came to Chicago to lend his support to the Moses Johnson case (page 14), one reporter called him "The indefatigable Allan Pinkerton of Dundee."[96] L. C. P. Freer said that "[Pinkerton] came to Chicago to help us manage the Underground Railway, and his instincts as a natural detective developed in that work. He knew when there was an escaped slave in town, where he was, and also where were those who were hunting for him to take him back into slavery. I have seen Pinkerton drop down on his hands and feet and go galloping along the unpaved and unlighted streets as rapidly and as noiselessly as would a dog when he was following a clew [*sic*] or watching some slave-owner or officer who was on the track of the escaped slave."[97] Philo Carpenter described him as "an anti-slavery warhorse."[98]

In 1852, seeing that the city police were too susceptible to political influence, Pinkerton used the skills he'd learned in abolition work to launch his namesake detective agency. The company immediately became associated with high-profile cases around town—including catching the city sexton (cemetery manager) helping Rush University students rob graves from the old City Cemetery in 1857.[99]

In 1861, when Abraham Lincoln was about to travel to Washington, D.C., to assume his office, Pinkerton uncovered an assassination plot, and was put in charge of Lincoln's safety. He and his detectives came up with an elaborate plan to help sneak the president-elect into the capitol under the would-be assassins' noses, and when the war broke out months later Lincoln put Pinkerton in charge of organizing a "secret service" division of the army.

After the war, Pinkerton and his organization became best known for breaking up organized labor groups, a move that has cost his modern reputation considerably. He always insisted that he supported workers' right to organize, and that his group stopped only violent uprisings, though his writings do indicate a certain amount of contempt for striking workers and trade unions.[100]

In 1869 he suffered a stroke that left him largely unable to do active detective work, so he put his energy into writing novels based on his adventures. In most cases, it appears that they were only very loosely based on true stories, but they do give us some idea of what sort of work his detectives did.

Pinkerton, left, with Abraham Lincoln

Allan's wife, **Joan Carfrae Pinkerton (1822–1887)**, met Allan while she was singing in a church choir in Glasgow; she later worked with Robert Fergus (page 17) on publishing *Old Country Ballads*, a now-lost collection of traditional Scottish songs. The Pinkertons had been taken in by Fergus when they first arrived, destitute, in Chicago after the ship they had sailed from Scotland was wrecked near Nova Scotia, costing the young couple most of their savings.[101]

Family members and friends in the plot include his son, **William Pinkerton (1846–1923)**, who was only a teenager when he was put to work in his father's Secret Service during the Civil War. Being younger and lighter than the others, he was chosen one day to try doing some reconnaissance work in a newly invented weather balloon, making him, by some accounts, the first person to engage in military aerial recon.[102] Behind the family is **George H. Bangs (1831–1883)**, the first detective Pinkerton hired.

5	6	9	10	15	16	12	21	23	30	33
PH DAVIS 12/25/1867 age 60	JAMES FORREST 1/4/1867 scarlet fever, no age given.	CHARLES F. FOX 5/31/1868 age 32	KATE PRESCOTT BRACKET 2/9/1869 age 29 (no stone)	Wm T BROWN 10/28/1872 age 27 (no stone)	JOSEPH WICHER 3/10/1874 age 27 (James Gang victim)	JULIUS HOUSDORFF ?/1874 Age 36 (date 12/1874, but internment 11/8/74)	JNO McEWEN 9/9/1880 (moved here in 82, same day as 23) age 50	BOTELLA OLSON 5/7/1882 age 27 from norway	JOHN C CAMERON 5/1/1893 age 37	NELSON WENLOFF 1/19/1907 age 65

29	13	17		28	XX	32	8	XX
WILLIE RANSOME 2/25/1889 age 6mos	NELLIE C ROBERTSON 2/4/1872 age 8 mos (moved to 85 blk in 1873)	WILLIE H CLARK 1/25/1874 age 9		THOROLD LUND 4/13/1888 age 38	TITLE STONE	BERNHARD SANFTLEBEN 1/1/1896 age 43	ANGIE WARREN AKA KATE WARN 1/28/1868 age 38	TIMOTHY WEBSTER (memorial only)

18	19	22
HENRY M ROBINSON 7/5/1874 age 1	MARGARET LINDEN 3/13/1875 age 6mos	GEORGE KIMBLE 4/23/1882 diptheria age 2

**PINKERTON EMPLOYEE LOT
GRACELAND CEMETERY**

The Pinkerton lot. Most of the stones are no longer legible, but good records have kept the identities of those buried here from being lost, even if most of their biographies remain largely mysterious.

∎ ∎ ∎

Despite the need for secrecy, Pinkerton was a shameless self-promoter. Perhaps his strangest—and most interesting—form of publicity was the burial plot for his detectives, which is just southwest of his family plot. Details of the elaborate floral tributes he put on the graves each New Year's Day were often announced in the press, thus keeping his agency and their past exploits in the news.[103]

Look for a plot of gray stones, including a large gray marker that says "In Memory of the Employees of Pinkerton's National Police Agency." The larger stones in the plot are mostly detectives; the smaller ones to the left are the children of detectives who died in infancy.

Few of the unpolished stones are legible, and in most cases very little is known about the life and adventures of the detectives they commemorate. But all of the names are known, and some of the stories are, as well.

The Pinkerton Detective Lot

Kate Warn

"Undoubtedly the best female detective in America, if
not the world."
—Kate Warn's obituary in the *Chicago Republican*

Very little is known of **Kate Warn (c1830–1868)**—even her proper name is
something of an enigma. According to the Graceland records, her real name
was Angie M. Warren. The sparse info in the interment book, indeed, furnishes
some of the best data we have about her: it gives her address at the time of
her death as 94 Washington (63 W. Washington in modern numbers; this was
the Pinkerton office, where most women employees had living quarters), and
her cause of death as "congestion of the lungs."[104]

As one of the first women to be a professional detective in the United
States (the very first in some accounts), she has become something of a cult
hero, the subject of TV segments, comic books, and novels—there's even currently talk of a movie. But all draw heavily on her appearances as a character
in Pinkwater's novels, in which she undergoes such tasks as impersonating
a fortune teller to gain the confidence of a rich man's wife. The novels don't
tend to hold up to fact-checking, but they do probably give us a reasonable
idea of the sort of work she did.[105]

Her 1868 obituary in the *Chicago Republican* says that she was born in
Chemung County, New York, around 1830, and called upon Pinkerton for a
job as a detective in 1855. "Up until that time," the obituary said, "he had
never dreamed of employing females, and even then (he) could not realize
how they could be employed consistent with a strict regard for the prejudices
of the community. After several interviews, however, Mrs. Warn succeeded
in convincing Mr. Pinkerton that the innovation could be realized, and she
entered his service."[106] Soon, Pinkerton had a whole women's department,
of which Warn became the head.

Among her known activities are helping to recover money stolen from the
Adams Express Company in Alabama and arranging for private sleeping cars
for Abraham Lincoln when Pinkerton was helping him sneak past would-be
assassins into Washington, D.C. Lincoln was disguised as an invalid, and Warn
played the role of his sister. During the war, when Pinkerton was in charge
of the secret service, she headed the female department of the Pinkerton
agency in Washington, D.C., working to keep tabs on the many "secession-
ists" among D.C. society ladies. She frequently visited the enslaved people
who were held in the D.C. jail, possibly assisting Pinkerton agent Seth Paine
(page 181) in his efforts to help them escape.[107]

She returned with Pinkerton to Chicago in 1863 and then worked in the New Orleans office beginning in 1865. She died in Chicago on January 28, 1868, leaving behind a biography full of more questions than answers. Despite the lack of solid data, she's been the subject of a few recent children's books, including Kate Hannigan's *The Detective's Assistant* and Greer Macallister's *Girl in Disguise*, and she and her headstone appear in Emil Ferris' 2017 graphic novel *My Favorite Thing Is Monsters*.

Timothy Webster

To the right of Warn's marker is a monument for Timothy Webster, whose epitaph calls him "The Harvey Birch of the Rebellion," a reference to *The Spy* by James Fennimore Cooper. Working undercover during the war, Webster was captured and hanged as a spy by the rebels. Though his body was recovered from Richmond in 1871, he was reinterred in Onarga, IL, not at Graceland. The monument to him is merely a cenotaph; it functions mostly as an advertisement for the Pinkerton company.[108]

. . .

Joseph Wicher

Buried at the left end of the row behind Warn, the Iowa-born **Joseph Wicher (c1847–1874)** had just gotten married in 1874, and he told his wife he was going off on just one last dangerous mission as a Pinkerton detective before settling down.[109]

Taking a train to Independence, Missouri, Wicher spoke with a few local officials before making his way to a farm owned by Zerelda Rubens, where he told her he was a farmhand looking for work. Perhaps the local officials had tipped her off, or perhaps she saw Wicher's smooth hands and could tell he wasn't really a farm worker. Either way, Rubens seems to have realized very quickly that he was really a detective in pursuit of her sons: the outlaws Frank and Jesse James. They had just returned home.[110]

The James-Younger gang was an attractive target to an old abolitionist like Pinkerton. Though mostly remembered as an ordinary wild west train robber today, in the 1870s Jesse James was widely understood to be a neo-Confederate terrorist. During the war the James Brothers joined Quantrille's raiders, a guerilla group that would ride into towns and kill anyone they judged to be insufficiently supportive of slavery and then ride out with their scalps trailing from their horses. They once ambushed a train full of Union soldiers going home on furlough, killed them, and mutilated their bodies. They never accepted that the war had ended; Jesse made it known in the press that he recognized no authority but that of the Confederate States of America, and the trains he targeted were generally associated with the Union.[111]

Shortly after the day Wicher arrived at the farm, a man who ran a ferry across the river described seeing the James boys with a prisoner tied to a horse; they told him they were lawmen who'd caught an outlaw. The next day, Wicher's body, bound and shot several times, was found nearby a set of crossroads near Liberty, Missouri.[112] In some later accounts there was a note pinned to his shirt saying "Let sneaking detectives beware of Jesse James."[113] He was briefly buried in Missouri, but within two weeks had been disinterred and conveyed to Graceland.[114]

Pinkerton continued to hunt Jesse, at one point killing his eight-year-old half-brother and badly wounding his mother with an incendiary device. A cousin of the James brothers later claimed that Jesse spent a few months in Chicago attempting to assassinate Pinkerton.[115]

Two Other Mysterious Women

In an unmarked grave to the left of Wicher is **Kate Prescott Brackett (c1840–1869)**, another detective from the women's department. Even less is known about her than is known about Kate Warn, though theories abound that she was really Hattie Lawton, a Pinkerton detective who posed as Timothy Webster's wife during the Civil War, and about whom no real details are known. Cemetery records add a couple of clues: the interment book notes that Brackett lived in St. Louis and died of cancer at 29 in February 1869. At least one researcher has connected her to Kitty Brackett, a St. Louis madame who may have doubled as a spy.[116]

A few spaces to the right of Wicher is a marked grave for **Botilla Olson (c1855–1882)**, once described in a report on floral tributes at the plot as a "Norwegian detective."[117] Such records and stories of Botilla that survive form a particularly interesting mystery. Botilla (whose name is variously given as Botella, Betalla, Bortella, Bertha, Bessie, or Betsy) was described as "small in stature, with light hair and sallow complexion."[118] She and her sister lived with the ailing Allan Pinkerton in 1880; they were listed in the census as "servants."[119] By May of 1882, Botilla was living in an apartment above the Pinkerton office (women who worked for the company generally lived in the living quarters); she died there that year at the age of 27 from the effects of an abortion.[120] After Botilla died, a midwife named **Augusta Hinz (c1834–1899)** was arrested as an abortionist, along with Lionel Bush, a former Pinkerton clerk who had apparently been Botilla's boyfriend ("the author of the girl's ruin,"[121] in the newspaper parlance of the day). Bush was only held as a witness, but Hinz was brought to trial.

Olson was disinterred for a second autopsy, which indicated that she had certainly undergone an abortion, but may not have been pregnant to begin with. This created a loophole that required Hinz to be released, as it wasn't illegal to perform abortions on people who weren't pregnant. The *Tribune* said that when the judge discharged her, "there was loud applause from the friends and acquaintances of Mrs. Hintz [*sic*], a number of whom were women."[122] (Hinz is buried in the Fairview section at Graceland, not far from the Pinkerton lot; her grave does not appear to be marked.)

Most papers referred to Olson as a servant who worked as a "domestic" or "servant girl."[123 124 125] But the fact that she was given such a prominent place in the employee burial lot—despite the fact that it could have caused controversy and bad publicity for Pinkerton—suggests that she may have been playing a more prominent role in the company.

Could she have been disguising herself as a domestic as part of her job as a detective? It's tempting to imagine, but remains strictly in the realm of speculation.

■ ■ ■

Return to the road. Just north of Pinkerton is a tall, light gray headstone reading "Platt," and also featuring the name of Richard T. Greener.

Richard T. Greener: The First Black Harvard Grad

> "The field is comparatively clear now that some old hacks have fallen by the way . . . Will the young men of color throughout the country resolve to begin now to take part in public affairs . . . and show that the young may be safe in counsel as well as good for war? . . . Young men to the front!"
> —Richard T. Greener, "Young Men to the Front"

Jacob F. Platt (1814–1882) didn't get as wealthy from his lumber yard at State and Taylor as some of the white lumber men in Chicago became, but when he died in 1888 he was estimated to be worth around $100,000—no small amount in those days.

Born in upstate New York, he and his wife, **Amelia Matthews Platt (1819*– 1902)**, came to Chicago around 1852. In his home state, Jacob had been an agent for *The North Star*, an antislavery newspaper published by Frederick

Douglass.[126] He helped welcome Douglass to Chicago in 1859,[127] served as secretary of the Suffrage League in the 1860s to fight for Black voting rights,[128] and rode alongside John Jones (page 68) in an 1870 parade celebrating the ratification of the 15th amendment, which finally guaranteed Black men the right to vote.[129] Amelia served on the board of the Colored Women's Freedman's Aid Society of Chicago with Ailey Bradford (page 72) during the Civil War.[130]

After a stroke in 1876, Jacob was an invalid for the last 12 years of his life. His *Inter-Ocean* obituary describes him as "a self-made man in the highest sense of that term" who had no formal education, but was "a great reader (who) seemed to forget nothing" and taught himself a great deal of mathematics, as well.[131] He certainly made sure his children got the education he'd been denied: one of Jacob and Amelia's daughters, Ida B. Platt, became the first Black woman admitted to the bar in Illinois (she is buried in the U.K.). Another daughter, **Amelia Platt (1851–1934)**, finished a law course in the 1890s and became a clerk and stenographer in a prominent loop law firm.[132]

In the early 20th century, the Platt household was joined by **Richard T. Greener (1844–1922)**, a distant relative. Born in Pennsylvania in 1844, Greener became the first Black graduate of Harvard University in 1870.

After graduating, he taught moral philosophy at the University of South Carolina while studying the classics and law there (the University later honored him with a statue). He was admitted to the bar in Washington, D.C., in 1877, and spent two years as the dean of Howard University School of Law.

Though initially fairly conservative about postwar reform movements, Greener was galvanized by the 1883 supreme court decisions that struck down civil rights advances and initiated the Jim Crow era. "I myself would much rather be deprived of my political rights than my social ones," he wrote. "I can live without suffrage, I can exist without office, but I want the privilege of traveling from New York to California without fear of being put off a car or denied food and shelter solely because I have a trace of negro blood in my veins."[133]

In the 1880s, Greener served as secretary for the Ulysses S. Grant Monument Association, and in 1898 was appointed U.S. Commercial Agent in Vladivostok, Russia, by President McKinley. After leaving public service in 1905, he moved in with the Platts in the Kenwood neighborhood of Chicago (very near President Obama's future house). He was the subject of a 2017 biography, *Uncompromising Activist*, by Katherine Reynolds Chaddock.

■ ■ ■

Across the paved road from the Platt-Greener marker is the massive family monument marked "Hoyt," topped by three roughly life-sized statues.

The Hoyt-Fox Monument and the Iroquois Theatre Fire

"Horrors sometimes occur the character of which may not be adequately described. The quality of the English, or any other language, does not suffer for all the dreadful shadings. Such an awful event was that of yesterday afternoon, when the new and beautiful Iroquois Theatre was destroyed."
—*Chicago Daily Inter-Ocean*, Dec 31, 1903

It's impossible to miss the magnificent monument to **William Hoyt (1837–1925)**, a grocer who came to Chicago in the 1850s. The granite base is topped by a life-sized statue of a woman pointing upward toward heaven; a seated figure to her right holds an anchor, and one to her left is cradling a child. It was built long before anyone was buried in the plot and pointed out as a highlight of the cemetery as early as 1885.[134] Though not unique—the same monument can be seen in other cemeteries—it serves as a magnificent example of Victorian funerary monumental art. The three figures are representations of "Faith, Hope and Charity," a reference to the verse in 1st Corinthians that is usually translated today as "faith, hope and love."

Easier to miss, though, is the row of graves at the back, including William's daughter, **Emily Hoyt Fox (1867–1903)**, three of her children, and her husband. Emily and her children all have the same date of death: December 30, 1903, the day of the Iroquois Theatre fire, which killed around six hundred people—roughly twice the estimate of the people who were killed in the Great Chicago Fire a generation before.

On December 30, barely a month after the Iroquois Theatre opened, a calcium light set the drapes on fire during a matinee performance of a panto called *Mr. Blue Beard*. The flames caught on the freshly oiled ropes and canvas scenery in the rafters. The builders had cut every possible corner to get the theater open in time for the holidays; there was no sprinkler system, and the fireproof curtain, required in every theater by law, had been made from a less-than-fireproof blend of asbestos, cotton, and wood pulp.[135]

But the real danger wasn't so much from the fire as the rush to escape. The main doors opened inward, toward the lobby (which had already been illegal for years, though few seemed to pay attention to the rule), and, additionally, were locked. They could be unlocked if one took a moment to experiment, but, as the *Tribune* raged in the aftermath, "it is known by all except theater managers that in a panic people lose their heads."[136]

Emily Hoyt-Fox and three of her children had come down from their home in Winnetka to see the show. Their bodies were found scattered among the nearby stores and rooms that were pressed into service as makeshift morgues.[137]

The estimate of six hundred victims only includes those who died in the fire and its immediate aftermath; such estimates don't take into account the people whose health never recovered, those who died years later as a result of the injuries they sustained, or the dreadful effects of the tragedy that spread even to those who weren't there. When looking at the graves of the four victims in the Hoyt plot, it's hard not to notice that **Frederick Morton Fox (1865–1904)**, Emily's husband, didn't live long after the fire; the shock was a terrible blow to his health, and he died barely two months later.[138]

William Hoyt was one of the primary contributors to a hospital raised as a memorial to the victims,[139] and built Christ Episcopal church in Winnetka as a tribute to his daughter and grandchildren. He had come to Chicago in 1855 and started his first fruit business a few years later on an $89 investment. He lost his building in the fire in 1871, but signed a lease on a new location the very next day. The new landlord suggested that they wait until the fire was truly extinguished, but Hoyt said, "No harm in executing the lease now; as in case the store goes the lease goes with it." He signed the papers and then promptly boarded a train to New York to convince his suppliers that Chicago would be rebuilt and that they should extend him the necessary credit to stock a new shop. They did.[140]

Hoyt died in 1925, decades after his own monument was built.[141]

■ ■ ■

Just beyond Hoyt will be a fork in the road. Standing in the middle, the Bellevue section will be on your right. Near the monuments to Meyer and Haberkampf in Bellevue is a section of single graves, among which is a shared marker for **Richard Brown (1927–2019)**, the academic vice president of the Newberry Library, and **William Lloyd Barber (1943–2018)**, a teacher. They were partners for thirty-eight years and married for seven.[142]

On the left edge of the fork is the obelisk for lumber merchant **Eli Bates (1807–1886)**. Veer left at the fork and continue north. A few plots beyond Bates on the left will be a large marker for another lumber man, **Willis H. Estey (1813–1917)**, whose plot also contains a small marker for his son-in-law, architect **Lawrence (or Lars) Gustav Hallberg (1844–1915)**. His best-known work today is perhaps the old Chase and Sanborn Coffee Warehouse on the Chicago River at 325 N. Wells.[143]

To the right of Hallberg is the Chalmers monument, which consists of four white columns designed by architects Graham, Anderson, Probst and White. The head of a prominent manufacturing concern, **William J. Chalmers (1852–1938)** was the husband of **Joan Pinkerton Chalmers (1855–1940)**, the daughter of detective Allan Pinkerton (page 76). Joan grew up in Gilded Age society and lived long enough to be perhaps the city's most prominent source of nostalgia for the "Elegant Eighties." "There was a such a thrill living back then," she said in 1932, as she recalled taking a coach and four to Derby Day, one of the highlights of the social season. "We gave so much more time and thought to good grooming in those days and clothes were truly beautiful. There was an air of elegance in the colorful parasols and dresses."[144]

■ ■ ■

A little to the right of Chalmers is the MacVeagh plot, including **Franklin MacVeagh (1837–1924)**, who served as secretary of the treasury under President Taft. Among the section of single graves behind Franklin is a marker for **Lillian Julia Davenport Partac (1980–2013)**, a Chicago activist and graphic designer whose headstone includes the epitaph "Lilly, my one and only," the first line of the song "Lily" by The Smashing Pumpkins. In her final tweet before her untimely death from cancer, she said, "Everything I've ever learned about typography, I learned from watching *The Price Is Right*."[145]

Continue north on the road. On the right just before the next fork in the road will be the curved marker for Melville Fuller.

Melville Fuller: The "Separate but Equal" Judge

> "If slavery is the cause of the war, is not abolitionism? Supposing slavery to be as explosive and destructive as gunpowder, where does the guilt lie in the catastrophe following the ignition—on the inert material, or on him who applies the lighted brand thereto?"
> —Melville Fuller

Melville W. Fuller (1833–1910) was only in his 20s when he managed Stephen A. Douglas' 1860 presidential campaign against Abraham Lincoln, and he continued to scorn Lincoln throughout his presidency. He particularly disliked the Emancipation Proclamation. By some accounts he abhorred slavery and even wrote a college paper on the "tyrannical cruelties" and "wickedness" of the institution,[146] but he was the sort of antislavery man who abhorred abolitionists even more.

His hostility to the war effort played well in southern-sympathizing Springfield, where he served as a member of the state house of representatives during the war. When he voted against extra funds for wounded soldiers, the *Chicago Tribune* railed that "We tell these Copperheads—little Mr. Fuller

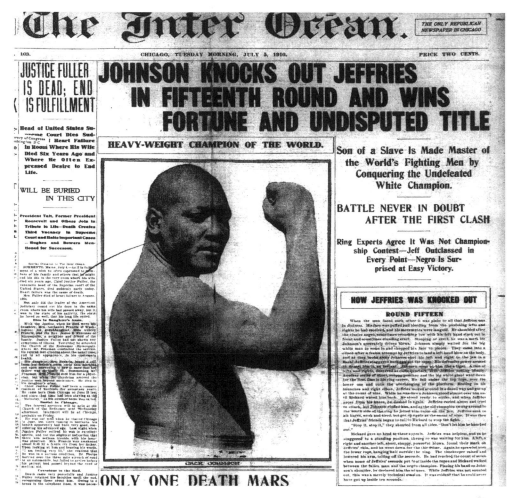

The *Inter-Ocean* announcing Fuller's death (and Johnson's victory).

included—that there is a deep damnation awaiting them. . . . There will be heaped up wrath against the day of wrath for such heartless villains."[147]

But the political damnation the papers predicted for Fuller did not come to pass in his lifetime; twenty-five years later, President Cleveland named him Chief Justice of the Supreme Court, a position he held from 1888 until his death in 1910. Under his leadership, the "Fuller Court" was often preoccupied by issues of race, immigration, and labor—issues on which he remained conservative. Perhaps his court's most notorious decision was in *Lone Wolf v Hitchcock*, in which they unanimously agreed that Congress could break treaties with Native American tribes without the tribe's consent,[148] though it's infamy is rivaled by his establishing the "separate but equal" rule in *Plessy vs. Ferguson*, which was cited when statues of him were removed in his home state of Maine.

When Fuller died, the news was secondary in most papers to banner headlines about Jack Johnson (page 102), who defeated Jim Jeffries to become the heavyweight boxing champion the same day.[149]

In the plot with him is his wife, **Mary Coolbaugh Fuller (1845–1904)**, whose father was Chicago banker William Coolbaugh (page 235). Their daughter, **Mary Coolbaugh Fuller White (1867–1910)**, was largely raised in Berlin and grew up to be a concert pianist.

■ ■ ■

Veer right on the fork just past Fuller. On your left will be a triangle occupied by the magnificent Kranz vault, a sort of outdoor mausoleum.

The Kranz Mausoleum

"People will eat candy. The tariff discussion, so far as I
  see, has had no effect on my business."
—John Kranz, "Hope for Good Times"

After moving to Chicago from Germany, **John Kranz (1841–1919)** opened his first candy store in 1868. In 1881 the store was moved to a prominent location across the street from Marshall Field's department store (Block 37 stands on the spot today) and became something of a landmark. The shop was colorful wonderland, with art nouveaux fixtures and life-size swan statues that could move.[150] The chocolate mice were a longtime favorite.

John's daughter, **Florence Kranz (1870–1952)**, took over as head of the company after her father's death in 1919. Depending on whom you ask, the style of chocolate cookie known as Florentines are named either for her or her mother, **Florentine Kranz (1849–1915)**, who is interred here as well.[151]

By the 1930s, the shop was an institution in the loop, though by then the whole store was coming to be seen as a relic of a bygone time, as were all survivors of the 1800s in those days. "Afternoon coffee with cinnamon rolls is an afternoon feature at Kranz's (today)," the *Tribune* wrote in 1938, "[just] as it was in the days when ladies in leg-o'-mutton sleeves and wide rustling skirts were driving up the door in victorias. Nor has the style of the shop with its marble floors, ceiling adorned in the style of the last century, and counter lamps with yellow silk flower petal shades, been changed since it was open."[152] The store closed after Florence retired in 1946.[153]

■ ■ ■

Turning to the right to follow the road along the southern edge of Lake Willowmere, in front of the Hoffman marker on the right is a small monument to architect **George Veronda (1941–1984)**. Beside him is a cenotaph to his partner, artist and Chicago LGBT Hall of Fame member Roger Brown (1941–1997), who is buried in Alabama. Near them is a marker for **Alan F Saake (1948–1993)**, a lawyer who appears to have died in the AIDS epidemic (the family asked for donations to AIDS research in lieu of flowers)[154] and his partner **James Hamman (1957–1995)**.

Behind the Hoffman monument is a flat, square grayscale stone for **Arthur Siegel (1913–1978)**, an innovative photographer who studied under Laszlo Moholy-Nagy (page 94) and went on to be the subject of multiple solo exhibitions at the Art Institute of Chicago. The design of his monument evokes a snapshot.

Further along the road on the right is a large monument featuring a partially draped sarcophagus for **Columbus R. Cummings (1834–1897)**, who began as a clerk in Potter Palmer's store (page 148) and became president of the New York, Chicago, and St. Louis railroad, commonly known as The Nickel Plate Road.[155]

■ ■ ■

Just beyond Cummings on the right is the large column for George Pullman, in front of which is Station Three, between Pullman, the Schoenhofen pyramid, and the Ryerson tomb. Turn to page 119.

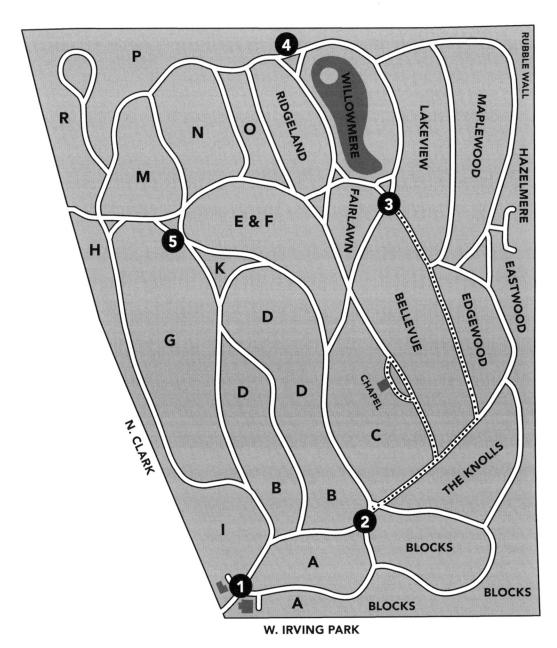

Map for Route 2-B

From Station two, take a right, heading up "Mausoleum Row."

On the left will be the vault of **Tobias Allmendinger (1832–1889)**, a sand and gravel dealer who was an early member of Chicago's volunteer fire departments. His son, **George Allmendinger (1852–1901)**, died of apoplexy in the middle of a waltz in 1901.[1]

Next will be the vault of business executive **William Kubel (1874–1956)**, the son of **Seraphin Kubel (1830–1913)**, a butcher. Beyond the Kubel vault is that of **Dr. Robert D. MacArthur (1843–1922)**, a physician.[2] Also on the row is **John A. Linn (1849–1910)**, a clerk of the circuit and superior courts.[3]

■ ■ ■

At the fork in the road, there will be a large monument to patent medicine baron **Peter Fahrney (1840–1905)**, including a boulder for his son, **Emery Fahrney (1876–1935)**. Fahrney's medicine, a cough syrup, was popular long after his death in 1905, selling particularly well in the 1920s, probably due in no small part to its being 14 percent alcohol.[4] [5] His granddaughter, Merry Fahrney, gained the nickname of "Madcap Merry" for the marvelous time she had blowing through her fortune as heir to the last great American cough syrup dynasty. Cheerfully telling reporters she didn't even know what medicine she was heiress to, she married and divorced eight times, crashed airplanes, and somehow managed not to get in much trouble when she killed her new brother-in-law by driving drunk on her wedding night, or when she volunteered to spy for the Germans during World War II. One husband, the dressmaker Oleg Cassini, married her in 1938 and described her decades later as "one of only a few purely evil people I've met in my life."[6] Though there is a space that would have been hers near the boulder for her father, when she died in 1974 her ashes were scattered in the Atlantic Ocean.

On the path, walk alongside the Fahrney plot toward the chapel building. On the left will be two more mausoleums: **George N. Neise (1853–1933)**, a banker, and **John K. Stewart (1870–1916)**, who made millions inventing and manufacturing automobile accessories, most notably speedometers. His wife, **Julia Stewart (1875–1917)**, died shortly after he did; it was widely reported that among her effects was found a suitcase containing nearly a million dollars in cash and checks.[7]

On the left, you'll soon see the honeycombed red stone columbarium, which sits adjacent to the chapel. Among the many notables whose small memorials can be found here is perhaps the most prominent woman among Graceland's many architects.

Marion Mahony Griffin: Architect and Artist

"What the gods have given us we are under obligation to share with humanity."
—Marion Mahony-Griffin, *The Magic of America*

Architecture is generally a collaborative effort, and **Marion Mahony Griffin (1871–1961)**[8] was instrumental in developing and publicizing Frank Lloyd Wright's signature "prairie style."

One of the first women to graduate from M.I.T. (a few years ahead of Katharine Dexter McCormick, page 66), Marion became the first woman to be licensed as an architect in Illinois and worked in the same office as Wright at Dwight Perkins' firm (page 29). After joining Wright's own studio, she worked with him for over a decade, designing several buildings on her own, while also producing gorgeous Japanese landscape–inspired lithographs of Wright's designs. A published portfolio of paintings of Wright's buildings made him famous—and more than half of the paintings were by Marion.

Though she wrote that "Chicago architects welcome women into the profession with open arms,"[9] she also wrote that her treatment by Wright was not entirely pleasant. She rarely mentioned him by name, but she was probably referring to him when she spoke of one architect as "a canker sore . . . who originated very little but spent most of his time claiming everything and swiping everything. . . . whose vanity and malice killed the so-called Chicago movement in architecture."[10]

When Wright left his family to live in Europe in 1909, Marion worked with Hermann Von Holst, who took over the studio and is said to have continued Wright's practice of taking credit for much of Griffin's work.[11] Between a lack of recognition and her own apparent preference not to promote herself as more than a supporter (she received little public attention in her lifetime), she is now considered a pioneer in her field.[12] Her 1400-page autobiography, *The Magic of America*, was finally made available online in 2008 after decades as

Starrett

an object of cult status among architects.[13] Her husband, the architect Walter Burley Griffin, is buried in India.

■ ■ ■

Walk behind the columbarium. Behind the back-left wall is a Sherlock Holmes–themed gravestone shaped like an open book on a black pedestal.

Vincent Starrett: The Last Bookman

> "There can be no grave for Sherlock Holmes or Watson . . . Shall they not always live in Baker Street? Are they not there this instant, as one writes? Outside, the hansoms rattle through the rain, and Moriarty plans his latest devilry. Within, the sea-coal flames upon the hearth, and Holmes and Watson take their well-won ease. They still live for all that love them well: in a romantic chamber of the heart: in a nostalgic country of the mind: where it is always 1895."
>
> —Vincent Starrett, *The Private Life of Sherlock Holmes*

A newspaperman by trade and longtime book critic for the *Tribune*, **Vincent Starrett (1886–1974)** had a side career writing mystery novels and short stories for publications like *Weird Tales*. He even wrote several books *about* books, once saying that "When we are collecting books, we are collecting happiness."[14] Carl Sandburg, who worked with him at the *Daily News*, called him, "One of those few men whom I have little difficulty in placing in most any previous era of civilized mankind."[15]

He remains best remembered, though, for his writings about Sherlock Holmes. Particularly beloved is his 1942 sonnet, "221B," which famously ends with the lines

"Here, though the world explode, these two survive
and it is always 1895."

He also used that line in a section, quoted earlier, of his book *The Private Life of Sherlock Holmes.*[16]

When his supporters raised money for the gravestone in 1986, they had the famous line carved in the stone, next to an image of Starrett's Holmes-themed bookplates. His expertise on Holmes is even noted in the Graceland lot card.[17]

· · ·

In the section of single graves just behind the Starrett plot is a simple gray marker for one of the 20th century's most innovative artists. The first director of the New Bauhaus School of design, Hungarian-born **Laszlo Moholy-Nagy (1895–1946)** had taught at the original Bauhaus School in Berlin before being forced to flee Germany in 1933 (he was a noncitizen and born to Jewish parents, both of which made him a target as soon as the Nazis took power). In the United States he became a pioneer in the use of modern technology in art. Though perhaps best known for his constructivist paintings, he also worked in photography, film, sculpture, and light.[18]

His work began to be rediscovered in the 21st century; he has been the subject of several recent books, as well as a 2019 documentary, *The New Bauhaus*, in which Art Institute curator Elizabeth Siegal describes him as "probably the most versatile artist of the 20th century."[19]

The Chapel

The original chapel at the cemetery was near the front entrance. The current one was designed by Holabird and Roche and built of Waupaca granite[20] in 1885, near a now-defunct Buena Avenue entrance. A crematorium—the only one in Chicago at the time—was added in 1893.[21]

The first cremation was a man named Gustav Schroeder who had died a year before; his family had been keeping his remains in a vault while they waited for a crematory to be available.[22] A cremation service at the time cost $25, including a service and an urn. It was still a highly controversial practice in those days, with some clergy even refusing to officiate at cremation services, and management had to be a little sneaky in opening the crematory at all. O. C. Simonds, the superintendent at the time, said, "Undoubtedly there would have been opposition, more or less violent, from a majority of lot-owners had our proposition been presented to them . . . so we determined to make the crematory an accomplished fact first, and ask afterward."[23]

As late as 1898, the *Tribune* noted that there were only enough crematoriums in the country to accommodate 600 cremations per month.[24] As such, bodies for cremation came to Graceland not just from Chicago, but from all over the Midwest. Among the bodies cremated here, but not interred here, were executed labor leader Joe Hill, photographer Jun Fujita, Hull House cofounder Mary Rozet Smith, and one of the children of Mamah Borthwick Cheney, the mistress of Frank Lloyd Wright, who was murdered along with her children in 1914.

. . .

Back on the road, to the right of the chapel is a large edifice for the Swan and Coburn families.

Annie Swan Coburn: Eccentric Collector

"Because they're such good company."
—Annie Swan Coburn on why she bought paintings,
  "Chats with Well Known Chicagoan and
  Connoisseur"

Like Bertha Palmer (page 148), **Annie Swan Coburn (1856–1932)** was one of the primary donors of impressionist paintings to the Art Institute. However, while Bertha lived in a palatial mansion, Annie lived in The Blackstone Hotel. To those who could get an invitation, her suite was among the most incredible art galleries in the world. "It is a great adventure to see it," wrote the *Tribune*. "And they are all canvasses that one can more or less live with—and still find life beautiful; indeed, more beautiful."[25]

The daughter of anti-slavery advocate **Albert Swan (1826–1860)**, Annie married patent attorney and Gettysburg veteran **Lewis Larned Coburn (1834–1910)**.[26] Upon Lewis' death in 1911, she moved into the Blackstone hotel and crowded every inch of her suite with priceless works of art. A reporter who visited in 1931 found Picassos, Monets, and Renoirs shoved into every nook and cranny. A Degas functioned as a fireplace screen, and a Van Gogh was stashed under the bed.[27] Even the bathroom was lined with French paintings. Though the suite was not open to the public, Coburn was happy to receive visitors and show off her makeshift gallery.[28] Most of the collection was donated to the Art Institute upon her death.

She came into the news again in 2017 when word spread that Donald Trump showed visitors his copy of Renoir's "Two Sisters (on the Terrace)" and claimed it was the original; the Art Institute noted that the original painting in question had been donated to them by Mrs. Coburn in 1933 and had been in their museum ever since.[29]

• • •

Across the road and a bit further up from Coburn, behind the monument to candy maker **James C. Simm (1832–1904)**, is a flat black marker to the Hunter and Elmslie families, including **George Grant Elmslie (1871–1952)**, a Prairie School architect who worked with Frank Lloyd Wright and Louis Sullivan, for whom he served as chief draftsman and ornamental designer.

Double back down Greenwood Avenue, going back past the chapel. In front of it, note a memorial boulder to Lucile Pepoon, a Chicago nurse who became sick and died during World War I while working in France. She was buried in a military cemetery there with full honors; the boulder was added to Graceland in 1966.[30]

Turn left at the Fahrney plot, returning to "mausoleum row."

Architecturally, one of the most interesting crypts in this section is the one at which Greenwood Avenue terminates: that of **Lewis H. Boldenweck (c1835–1896)**, a businessman who died falling down an elevator shaft at his own factory.[31] It is often mistaken for a Louis Sullivan design.

To the left of the first Boldenweck vault is an oblong red granite mausoleum (which is also sometimes mistaken for a Sullivan design)[32] for contractor **Gustav Wilke (1853–1915)**, one of the first builders to make use of William Le Baron Jenney's steel frame concept (page 40). Red granite was also used for his Chicago mansion and his most famous building, the Texas State Capitol, on which he may have done much of the architectural work after the principal architect was fired.[33] Legend has it that the mausoleum, built nearly twenty years before his death, was made from leftover granite from the Texas capitol.[34]

The next mausoleum on the right will be that of **Amariah G. Cox (1849–1941)**, which was originally built as a vault for William Wrigley Jr., the chewing gum kingpin who owned the Chicago Cubs. When Wrigley moved to California, he sold the unused tomb to Cox, one of his vice presidents. A blueprint for the mausoleum bearing the name "Wrigley" survives in the Graceland office.[35]

Beyond Cox will be the tomb of **Augustus B. Raffington (1865–1932)** and his family, including his son, Miami hotel owner **Thomas Raffington (1901–1973)**.[36] Just past the Raffington vault, take a sharp right turn into the grass, past the mausoleum and into the section behind the mausoleums. Among the stones on the ground is a small red marker for Robert Fitzsimmons.

Robert Fitzsimmons:
Boxer and Movie Star

> "Some cold mornings you will get up, possibly after a hard night, feeling languid and unrefreshed. Instead of taking your cold bath, rub-down and exercises, you may be tempted to say 'Oh! I'll just skip it this once, and jump into my clothes.' Such weakness is fatal. Persevere!"
>
> —Bob Fitzsimmons, *Physical Culture and Self Defense*

In the early 1890s, nearly every reporter who saw a demonstration of moving pictures had the same thought: "We could use it to preserve prize fights!" The reaction was so common that when Edison was explaining the "kinetograph" he hoped to display at the 1893 World's Fair, he said "I can reproduce a prize fight without much difficulty" before the reporter could ask.[37] Boxing held a place in the public imagination hard to imagine today—far before most people could watch a major fight, newspapers the world over covered title bouts in exhaustive detail.

It almost must have seemed natural that the first "feature length" movie shown in Chicago (or pretty much anywhere) was footage of the 1897 bout between "Gentleman Jim" Corbett and **Robert Fitzsimmons (1863–1917)**, but the film was really far, far ahead of its time. Projected movies were still brand new in 1897, and most were still under a minute long. The film captured every round, more than 70 minutes in all.

The Chicago premiere of the fight film came at the Grand Opera House in June 1897 (with the actual referee on hand),[38] and by all accounts the crowd was just as rowdy as the crowd at the real match had been, even though most patrons already knew that Fitzsimmons was going to knock Corbett out with his famous "solar plexus punch" in round 14. Even those who didn't care for boxing got to see the possibilities of the new medium first-hand.[39]

Fitzsimmons was born in England in 1863, and grew up mainly in New Zealand, where he built his powerful arms working as a blacksmith. As a boxer, he had little patience for training or "the sweet science" of pugilism, instead preferring simply to punch his opponents really hard. And he punched hard

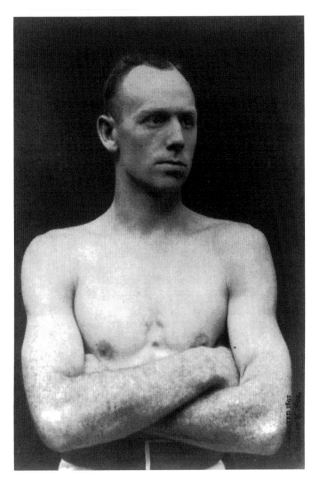

Fitzsimmons, Library of Congress.

enough to become champion in multiple divisions (though a late career match with Jack Johnson, page 102, ended quickly with Johnson victorious).

After his career, Fitzsimmons began appearing on the vaudeville stage, sometimes performing a skit written for him by Jack London; he died of pneumonia while appearing in Chicago.[40]

. . .

Return to the road and proceed north. On the right will be the tomb of leather dealer, **T. C. Hammond**, and that of **William Boldenweck (1851–1922)**, who was the last mayor of Lake View before it was absorbed by Chicago, and a brother of the nearby Lewis Boldenweck (page 96).[41]

Next is that of **Arthur C. Geist (1885–1949)**, a chemical engineer who often made the news for his habit of giving lots of money to random strangers—the *Tribune* called him "the genial gentleman with the bulging wallet." At 63, he explained that his friendly nature was covering up a broken heart he'd nursed since a woman rejected him 45 years earlier.[42]

On the ground to the left of the Geist vault will be several small markers for the family.

The De Priest Plot

> "I saw in a paper the other day that Tom Heflin, the senator from Alabama, said that if I showed up in the senate rest rooms he would throw me out. Well, just for that, I'm going over there and see if he's big enough."
> —Rep. Oscar De Priest, "Heflin-De Priest Battle Looms as Negro Takes Dare"

The parents of a United States Congressman, **Neander De Priest (1837–1925)** and **Martha De Priest (1845–1928)** were born enslaved in Alabama; a mid-20th-century article says that Neander repeatedly defied his enslavers, but was of such slight stature that they were afraid to punish him physically, lest he be killed or incapacitated. After emancipation, he married Martha, worked as a teamster, and became involved in local politics in Florence, Alabama.[43]

But Florence, Alabama, during the postwar Reconstruction era was a dangerous place for Black families, as the Ku Klux Klan and other terrorist organizations used violence to maintain the old order. As late as 1903 a speaker at the dedication of the town's confederate monument said, "In this our Southern land flows the purest Anglo-Saxon blood. . . . In the Northern states . . . they look upon a negro as a white man with a colored skin, and believe education to be the one thing needful. We of the south know better."[44] A local paper called the unveiling "The greatest day in the history of Florence,"[45] and the monument is still in place as of 2022.

His political activities made Neander a target, and when a lynching took place in front of their house in 1878, he and Martha, with their son **Oscar De Priest (1871–1951)**, moved to Kansas. After finishing school, young Oscar ran away to Chicago, where he began his own political career. In the 1920s he became Chicago's first Black alderman and then ran a successful campaign to become the nation's first Black congressman of the 20th century.

Perhaps the most memorable event of his first term occurred in 1929, when First Lady Lou Henry Hoover organized a tea party for the wives of congressmen at the White House. Such parties were a White House tradition, and, as a matter of course, Oscar's wife, **Jessie Williams De Priest (1873–1961)**, was invited.

Mrs. De Priest said that it was a charming affair, and that Mrs. Hoover was a gracious hostess. "The other ladies at the party discussed such problems as you and I might discuss at a Sunday afternoon in this church," she told a gathering the next month. "There was no excitement when I entered the White House. All the storm of criticism has been stirred up since."[46]

But to say there'd been a "storm of criticism" was putting it very mildly. Several southern state governments even issued formal condemnations of the

Oscar De Priest, Library of Congress.

fact that a Black woman was invited to tea with the First Lady. Senator Morris Shepard of Texas—best known as the author of the 18th amendment, which banned the sale of alcohol—ranted, "I deplore the incident beyond measure. It is recognition of social equality between the white and black races and is fraught with infinite danger to our white civilization."[47]

Though Mrs. De Priest was very gracious in simply dismissing the controversy, Oscar was having none of it. "They're a lot of cowards," he said of the southern politicians, whom he proceeded to thank for being "So barbaric they drove my parents to the north. If it hadn't been for that, I wouldn't be in congress today." He threatened not to vote for a single penny to enforce the 18th amendment if the government didn't agree to spending similar sums to enforce the 13th, 14th, and 15th, which dealt with slavery and civil rights.[48]

New headstones for Oscar and Jessie were placed in the plot very recently; Jessie's refers to her as "a gracious yet forceful civil rights advocate for Black women during the 'White House Tea Incident'—1929."[49]

. . .

Jessie De Priest, Smithsonian.

Just north of the De Priests is a small stone marked "Our Daughter" for **Ruth Johnson Wanderer (1898–1920)**, whose murder by her husband, Carl Wanderer—along with a "ragged stranger" Carl had hired to pose as a mugger—was one of the biggest true crime stories of 1920. Carl was hanged the next year.

Returning to the road, double back slightly and turn onto Main Avenue at the fork marked by the large monument to lumber baron **S. K. Martin (1837–1896)**.

Walk up the road, and on the left will be a large white marker bearing the name Johnson.

Jack Johnson:
Heavyweight Champion

"I have no quarrel with fate, nor do I cling to the absurd belief that fate has set any special mark upon me. Yet fate must have intended me for adventures and experiences that do not fall to the lot of the average man."

—Jack Johnson, *In the Ring—and Out*

When **Jack Johnson (1878–1946)** was about 11, he was sitting in church when a clearly drunken preacher asked the congregants to consider a conversation between Paul and the apostles; the slurring preacher asked, "Dear brothers and sisters . . . what does Paul say?"

From his seat in the back, Johnson cracked, "He says, sir, that he won't give you any more gin until you pay for last night's bottle." The pastor came running for young Jack, and Jack ran from the church and straight onto a ship that was sailing out of Galveston. "It seemed utterly tragic to me at the time," he later wrote, "but now I realize that it was a joke."[50]

Young Johnson, in his telling of the story, ended up all the way in Boston, and stayed there for four years, all because of a wisecrack in church. When he got back home, at the age of 15, he took up boxing. In his first professional fight in 1898, he knocked Charley Brooks out in the second round to become the Texas State Middleweight Champ. In 1900, he defeated Klondike Haynes, a Chicago boxer who was billed as the "Black Heavyweight Champ," in a bout that made national news.[51]

By 1907, Jack Johnson should have been the heavyweight champion of the world, but the title wasn't open to Black boxers at the time. Instead of a true title bout, he had to settle for boxing the former champ, Robert Fitzsimmons (page 97), who by then was 44 and past his prime. After a first round in which the two mainly circled one another, Johnson knocked Fitz out with a few punches in round two.[52]

He was finally given a shot at the world title in a bout against Tommy Burns in late 1908. After 18 rounds, the referee gave the match—and the crown—to Johnson.

For the next ten years, Johnson may have been the most famous Black man on the planet, fighting a series of matches with white boxers who were each billed as the "Great White Hope," most of whom ended up being utterly humiliated. Films of his matches were major hits—at the end of a 1909 film of his match with Stanley Ketchel, Johnson can be seen brushing Ketchel's teeth out of his glove.

Jack Johnson

His marriage to **Etta Terry Duryea (1881–1912)**, a white Brooklyn social-ite, ended with her death in 1912; she was the first to be interred at the plot Johnson purchased in Graceland.

When Johnson married Lucille Cameron, another white woman, he was arrested on the grounds that the marriage constituted a violation of laws prohibiting transporting women across state lines for "immoral purposes." To avoid going to prison as a "white slaver," he left for Europe on the advice of his mother, **Elizabeth T.M. "Tiny" Johnson (c1857–1918)**, for whom he'd bought a mansion on South Wabash.

Born enslaved in Galveston, Tiny (pronounced "Teeny") may well have been among the people who heard they were free on the famous "Juneteenth." In 1912, she said, "The world can say what it pleases about (Jack), but when it does my answer is 'his old mammy lives in a $12,000 house, has everything she wants to eat and wear and don't have to work no more.'"[53]

Jack was still in exile in Europe when Tiny died of pneumonia in March 1918 (his father, Henry, is buried in Galveston).[54] He returned to the United States and served a prison term in 1920 and then returned to the ring. He had lost his title in a match in Cuba in 1915 but continued to box professionally until he was 60 years old. Since his death from a 1946 car accident, he has been the subject of numerous films and plays, as well as a Ken Burns documentary and a Miles Davis album.

· · ·

Proceeding up the path beyond Johnson, notice the monument to **Frederick W. Wolf (1837–1912)**, an architect who primarily designed breweries. The monument features a shaft topped by a statue of a woman descending a staircase. Cemetery statues of figures in motion usually appear to be ascending to heaven; for a statue to be heading *down* is highly unusual!

Across the path are two stone sarcophagi for **Benjamin Honore (1826–1913)**, a brother of Henry H. Honore (page 151), and his wife **Laura Honore (1833–1922)**. Among the single graves in the section behind them and to the right is an unmarked spot for **John Levinsky (c1874–1892)**, an 18-year-old newsboy who drowned in Lake Michigan. Fellow newboys who were members of the Waifs Mission raised money for a funeral, and he was buried in a plot donated by Bryan Lathrop, then president of Graceland.

In the distance to the left, toward the wall, you'll see a large pink columnated monument for **Peirce Anderson (1870–1924)**, an architect whose firm, Graham, Anderson, Probst & White, grew from the old Daniel Burnham company after Burnham's death. The firm designed his monument, not to mention such iconic Chicago buildings as the Merchandise Mart, The Wrigley Building, the Civic Opera House, and many other icons of the 1920s and '30s.

Continuing up the path, just beyond the Honore monument on the right will be a large statue of a knight, known as "The Crusader" by Lorado Taft.

Victor Lawson and the Crusader

"I've made it a general rule of life that if I can't punch,
I'll hold."
—Victor Lawson, *Chicago Tribune*

When he died, **Victor Lawson (1850–1925)** had been the publisher of the *Chicago Daily News* for nearly fifty years. He was known as something of a workaholic, even avoiding a private golf course built on his Green Lake estate. A colleague at the time said, "I used to feel sorry for him, but I finally ceased when I found that work was his life and his joy. It was his recreation. He had no other. Golf he tried to please Mrs. Lawson **(Jessie Larson 1851–1914)**, but he dropped it, saying 'I can't get interested enough in it to get mad at it.'"[55]

By most accounts, Lawson was a practical, businesslike man whose favorite book was a dictionary; he avoided the high-society scene and was "no back slapper nor ever wishful to be slapped on the back," though after his death

The Crusader

his friends pointed out that he had a sense of humor: his employees enjoyed playing pranks on him, and he accepted them with a hearty laugh.[56]

Curiously, when he died, it was announced that there would be no elaborate memorial at his gravesite, reflecting his "plain taste." The *Tribune* said "There will be a marker, carved with the dates of birth and death at the head of the grave. Naught else."[57]

It was somewhat odd to describe a man whose Lake Shore Drive mansion was called a "castle" as a man of plain taste, and the plan for a plain marker was abandoned when the heirs—perhaps feeling that *something* had to be done with an estate valued at millions—commissioned Lorado Taft, known for his memorial to Henry Graves (page 41), to erect a statue of a crusading knight. Perhaps in keeping with the plan for simplicity, though, no names are visible on the statue; one simply has to *know* that it's a monument to Victor Lawson.

■ ■ ■

Across the road from Lawson, there will be a miniature Parthenon-style monument for General Strong.

General William Emerson Strong of the Freedman's Bureau

"Most assuredly no white man in Texas had anything to do with gathering the crops, except perhaps to look on and give orders. Who did the work? The freedmen, I am well convinced, had something to do with it; and yet there is a fierce murmur of complaint against them everywhere that they are lazy and insolent, and that there is no hope for a better condition of affairs unless they can be permitted to resort to the overseer, whip, and hounds. Two thirds of the freedmen in the section of the country which I traveled over have never received one cent of wages since they were declared free."
—General W. E. Strong, *The Congressional Globe*

After being made a brigadier general for his services in Sherman's Atlanta campaign and March to the Sea during the Civil War, among the more than twenty battles he fought during the war,[58] **William Emerson Strong (1840–1891)** served as inspector general of the Freedman's Bureau, the government office set up to promote the welfare of the recently freed people, when the war ended. Pushing against the then-common stereotype that freedmen were lazy, dangerous, and getting rich on free government money, Emerson testified that the freedmen were frequently beaten and murdered, and that, while they were doing *most* of the work that was being done in Texas, more than half had never received a cent in wages. Indeed, following his trip south several months after the war ended, he wrote, "I saw freedmen east of the Trinity River who did not know that they were free until I told them."[59] This would have been months after the famous "Juneteenth."

He pushed for a far stronger federal presence in Texas to enforce civil rights, believing that conditions were worse there because most of the white residents had never seen a Union army unit in their town, but President Andrew Johnson was uninterested. Strong returned to civilian life, though he also collected dozens

General Strong

of photos of Confederate officers into an album, now at Duke University, that he titled "Notorious Characters of the So-Called Confederate States."[60]

Though he was always referred to as "General Strong" in the press, his time as Inspector General of the bureau seems to have been quickly forgotten; he was spoken of locally more for his time in the lumber business after his death in 1891, though fellow soldiers remembered him as "a capital story teller, and inimitable in the rendition of army songs—the life, soul and center of every gathering of his old comrades."[61] As a singer, he once performed in an amateur opera at William Ogden's house under the name Signor Guglielmo Emersonio Strongini.[62]

Strong's wife, **Mary Ogden Strong (1843–1901)**, was the daughter of Mahlon Ogden (page 228).

■ ■ ■

To the right of the Strong monument, you'll see a broken-looking monument to the **Kroeschell** family, who made their fortune in steam tunnels and pipe fitting. It's widely said that the monument is purposely "unfinished" to signify a life broken off too soon, but what a person had in mind when commissioning a monument is seldom actually written down, and no record seems to confirm this story.

If you walk off the path, walking between Kroeschell and Strong and into the Bellevue section, there will be a low stone wall surrounding a plateau. In front is a plaque marking a plot once owned by Graceland landscape architect O. C. Simonds, though he's buried elsewhere. On the left, near the steps onto the plateau, is the Holabird plot.

The Holabird Plot: An Architectural Dynasty

"[William Holabird was] gruff, with a deep voice. He could scare the daylights out of any draftsman. He did pretty well with his small grandson, too."
—John A. Holabird Jr., quoted in Bruegmann, *The Architects and the City: Holabird and Roche of Chicago, 1880–1918*

After working in the office of architect William Le Baron Jenney (page 40), **William Holabird (1854–1923)** founded Holabird and Roche, the firm that helped pioneer the "Chicago School" of architecture with works such as the Marquette Building—in addition to designing many of the buildings in Graceland Cemetery itself, such as the chapel and the main office. A coworker, Edward Renwick, said, "In the office, Holabird never made any drawings; he was not a designer. He never did much in engineering, either. He was an excellent critic; he knew the styles, and he had good taste . . . one time, Roche had a design made and Holabird, looking at it, said 'It looks just like a Saratoga trunk.' From that time on that was all you could see in it."[63]

One son, **William Holabird Jr. (1884–1902)**, was a well-known golfer when he died of typhoid fever in 1902.[64] Another, **John Auger Holabird (1886–1945)**, became an architect himself and teamed up with John Root Jr. (page 115) to form Holabird and Root, which designed many of the city's Jazz Age gems, such as the Palmolive Building, The Daily News Building, 333 N. Michigan, and the spectacular Board of Trade at La Salle and Jackson, which upon completion in 1930 became the tallest building in the city, narrowly beating out his father's Chicago Temple. It held the title for more than twenty years.

His own son, **John Auger Holabird Jr. (1920–2009)**, won a silver star for his service attacking a German-held bridge in World War II, the battle that inspired the 1977 film *A Bridge Too Far*. After the war, he worked as a TV set designer in the 1950s before joining his father's architectural firm. He became a partner in 1987, at an age when most would be retiring.

・ ・ ・

Coyotes are common in urban cemeteries. Shy around people, Graceland's resident coyotes are a vital part of the cemetery's ecosystem.

Near the Holabird plot is the small staircase up the plateau. Walk onto it; on the left will be a small marker for **Wilhelm Rapp (1827–1907)**, a German-born Jew[65] who, like Dr. Schmidt (page 253), had to flee Germany after the failed radical uprising of 1848. Relocating to Baltimore, he ran an anti-slavery newspaper until a pro-slavery mob forced him to flee Maryland. Disguised as a minister, he walked to Washington, D.C., where Abraham Lincoln offered him the job of postmaster general. He turned it down and chose instead to move to Chicago and to publish the *Zeitung*, a German-language newspaper.[66]

Just north of Rapp, find the Kirkland-Hill plot on the left.

Caroline Kirkland: Madame X

> "It made quite a talk when my stuff, reeking with indiscretion, first appeared. One friend, now deceased, said, 'You'll never be invited to dinner, my dear, if you go on writing for the Sunday Tribune.' 'Then I'll have to eat at home,' I replied."
> —Caroline Kirkland, "News of Chicago Society"

Among the Kirkland-Hill markers is **Caroline Kirkland (1865–1930)**, who wrote a society column for the *Tribune* under the name of "Madame X." She began her career as a travel writer. Though her book on travels in Uganda in 1906 was intended to encourage other women to go to Africa, it also served as an inspiration and guide for Theodore Roosevelt on his famous 1909 safari.

In 1909, Kirkland started her gossip column, which she cheerfully described as "reeking with indiscretion," after Medill McCormick offered her a sum she assumed was for a month but turned out to be for a week. Confident she'd never truly earn such an amount, she signed on for just one issue, but stayed on for more than twenty years. [67]

While reporting on the moving of society in the city, she spearheaded the movement to save the old water tower when it was slated for destruction in 1917 and used her columns to push for better treatment of World War I vets.[68]

Elsewhere in the plot is her niece's husband, **Boyd Hill (1897–1964)**, the architect who designed the Aragon Ballroom and the nearby Lawrence Hotel.[69]

■ ■ ■

Further along on the plateau, you'll find the Meeker-Murray plot on the right.

Madame X (Caroline Kirkland) in 1917, *Chicago Daily News* Collection, Chicago History Museum (DN-0068212).

Arthur Meeker Jr.: Chicago with Love

"Compared to New York, Chicago is like good roast beef medium after a diet of assorted pastries. . . . Even its faults are dear to me. I glory in the cruel Northeasters sweeping in from the lake; the foghorn's keening note, the smoke that descends on the loop on windless days in winter like a dismal beach blanket; the rush and bustle and wild confusion in the streets that are, after all, only surface things—for, as we've already decided, Chicago is a town where you can live."

—Arthur Meeker Jr., *Chicago with Love*

Only five years old at the time of the Great Chicago Fire, **Arthur Meeker Sr. (1866–1846)** later said that the main thing he remembered about it was that he was wearing his first pair of long pants that night.[70] As an adult, he became vice president of Armour and Co., the sort of position in which one was expected to be a leader in Chicago society in addition to his duties as a business man. Well into the 20th century, his wife, **Grace Murray Meeker (1869–1948)**, would occasionally reminisce in the press about Gilded Age society events she'd attended as a child, like the Mikado Ball the Fields threw in 1886[71] (page 174).

Their son **Arthur Meeker Jr. (1902–1971)** became an author and journalist. Experiencing the last gasps of the Gilded Age with a young man's cynicism, he had an interesting take on the Prairie Avenue culture of his parents' generation; as an adult he wrote, "In the 1880s and 1890s, taste in America, we must admit, was as bad as it has ever been."[72]

Though he viewed it with a certain aloofness, Meeker Jr. was a part of Chicago's high society world himself and praised it as unique among high societies. He noted that while it took centuries for an aristocracy to develop in Europe, Chicago developed its own very quickly. "I wonder," he wrote, "if in any (other) city the horsy set is also the artistic set? Do other communities blend a talent for square dancing with a passion for politics? Are their civic figureheads successively absorbed all in one season by social reform and symphony concerts; herb gardening and 'Great Books' courses, deep sea fishing and the dog show? In the Windy City you see the same old faces everywhere, year in, year out . . . Yes, we get tired of them, too; but if we stayed away, who would come?"[73]

Arthur Jr. never married, but he lived for thirty years with a partner named Robert Molnar, who was his heir when he died in 1972.[74]

It you take a left (west) from off the ridge, among the Bellevue section graves is a small cenotaph for Colonel John Weir, who perished aboard the *Titanic* in 1912. Before embarking, he had told the manager of the Waldorf hotel, "I'll be hanged if I go tomorrow. I know it sounds absurd, but I've got a funny feeling about going."[75] His body was not recovered. The marker is in the plot of Dr. James F. Graham (1847–1923), a veteran of the Battle of the Crater (page 8) whose connection to Weir is a mystery. Another *Titanic* victim marker is in section N (page 193).

. . .

Return to the road. Just north of the Kroeschull marker is Alfeo Faggi's elegant monument to businessman **Charles Hutchinson (1828–1893).** (This is not the same Charles Hutchinson who founded the Art Institute; he is in section E&F.)

To the right of Hutchinson is **Robert Wilson Patterson Jr. (1850–1910),** who married a daughter of Joseph Medill (page 138) and became editor of the *Tribune* himself; he was the father of Cissy Patterson (page 139).

At the fork in the road, in the triangle a little way off the path on the right will be a very large marker for M. A. Owens. The "M.A." is **Mary Ann Owens (1854–1931)**. Other than the fact that she died after a long illness in an Indiana hospital in 1931,[76] little can be confirmed about Mary. The lack of information makes her one of the cemetery's most puzzling enigmas. The momument is large enough that one assumes she must have been well off financially, but few clues have been found to tell the story of her life.

Behind the Owens stone is the stately white mausoleum for the family of **Ernest J. Lehmann (1849–1900)**, founder of The Fair, a now-defunct State Street department store. Behind that are two small mausoleums for the family of **Francis J. Dewes (1845–1922)**, a brewer whose phantasmagoric beaux arts mansion still stands at 503 W. Wrightwood.

Back on the road, north of the Hutchinson marker on the left will be the Celtic cross marker for John Wellborn Root.

The Root Cross

"What could be more stupid and uninteresting than Tennyson's 'Brook' if we had not heard the low thrilling murmur of some mountain rill?"
—John Wellborn Root, quoted in Monroe, *John Wellborn Root*

Mary Root used to say that her son, **John Wellborn Root (1850–1891)**, could sing before he could talk and never "made a discord" on the toy violin he was given at the age of two.[77] Root was a fun-loving prankster with a deep love for the arts and a never-ending urge to spend money. His instinct for beauty led him to a career in architecture, and the work he did as one of the heads of the firm of Burnham and Root helped put Chicago on the map as an architectural city. Though he loved the newfound freedom architects were finding in what they could create, as new technology allowed architects of the late 19th century to experiment with design, height, and forms, he felt that Queen Anne–style Victorian houses, with their turrets and spindled porches, tended to "suddenly jump up and howl" as people looked at them.[78]

He died of pneumonia in 1891, just as the firm was at the height of its popularity and preparing buildings for the upcoming Columbian Exposition. The Celtic cross marker, designed by Burnham and Co., includes a design Root had just drawn for the entrance of the Phoenix Building in the loop, which was demolished in 1958. His first wife, Mary, who died only weeks after their wedding, is buried with her parents in the Walker plot (page 68); his second wife, **Dora Monroe Root (1857–1913)**, is here. Her sister, poet Harriet Monroe, wrote a biography of John.

In the plot with John and Dora is their son, **John Wellborn Root Jr. (1887–1963)**, who partnered with John Auger Holabird (page 108) to form Holabird and Root, the architectural firm best known for its jazz-age art deco skyscrapers such as the Board of Trade, 333 N Michigan, and the *Daily News* building.

• • •

Just past Root on the left will be a large stone marker for cigar dealer **W. H. Heegaard (1845–1899)**. To the right of it is a delightful red single marker for Joseph Jude McCaskey (b 1961) with a smiley face, a peace sign, and the epitaph "He was Tidy—Love Yourself." Joseph is still alive as of this writing; he is the son of Virginia McCaskey, owner of the Chicago Bears.

Behind Heegaard is a small marker, flush to the ground, for one of the most prominent surgeons of his era.

Dr. Daniel Hale Williams: Pioneering Surgeon

"A people who do not make provision for the sick and suffering are not worthy to be called a race."
—Daniel H. Williams, "Stab Wound of the Heart and Pericardium"

In 1893, the *Inter-Ocean* opened an article by saying, "One of the most surprising yet encouraging signs of progress and adaptability on the part of the colored people of this city is found in their efficient and successful management of Provident Hospital." Like most articles on the hospital, it was complimentary in spirit, but terribly patronizing at the same time. The hospital was run mainly by Black staff, and catered largely, though not exclusively, to Black patients.[79]

That day, though, the paper was covering a recent event at the hospital that would go down in medical history: **Dr. Daniel Hale Williams (1856–1931)** had successfully performed open heart surgery on James Cornish, who had stumbled into the hospital after being stabbed in the chest with what papers called "a sailor's knife."[80]

An initial probe showed only a superficial wound, not the giant gash described by papers. But Cornish's condition worsened overnight, and a further examination the next morning showed that the knife had penetrated all the way to the heart.[81] Almost any physician would have assumed that the wound was fatal—so far as anyone present knew, no open-heart surgery had ever

Dr. Williams, National Institute of Medicine.

been performed successfully. But Williams believed it was worth a try. Accompanied by a team of doctors, he cut into Cornish's chest and exposed the heart, which revealed the wound. Timing his stitches to the beat of the heart, Williams successfully sewed up the wound, and Cornish survived. Williams saw him working, perfectly recovered, at the Union Stock Yards two years later.[82]

The operation—the first of its kind by some measures—made Dr. Williams famous, though it was hardly his only major achievement. Around 1892, he successfully removed a 110-pound tumor from a woman who survived, as well. "It was the work of Dr. Dan and the Lord," the woman said.[83]

Born in Pennsylvania, Williams had graduated from the Chicago Medical School (now Northwestern) in 1883. Besides a stint running a hospital in Washington, D.C., he spent most of his adulthood in Chicago, dying there in 1931. Several buildings, schools, and parks in the Chicagoland area are named for him.

. . .

In the triangle southern tip of the Lakeside section, northeast of Heegaard, is the art nouveau urn monument to the family of lumberman **Herman Hettler (1863–1929)**. South of it is the large plot for lumberman **Augustus Carpenter (1825–1911)**. Behind Carpenter is a grave that remains unmarked but for a tiny section marker bearing the name "Emery A. Storrs."

Emery A. Storrs: The Great Advocate

"Slavery has a hundred arms, and may assume almost innumerable forms . . . The negro is not yet free. For, if today we adopt the policy of Andrew Johnson, tomorrow every state has it within its power to annul all its previous action, and by such hampering legislation as their ingenuity would readily devise, reduce the negro to a condition of slavery in fact, whatever it might be in name."

—E. A. Storrs, Speech in Ottawa, IL, 1866

It seems as though there was hardly a rally from 1858 to 1885 where lawyer **Emery A. Storrs (1833–1885)**, didn't steal the show with his blistering wit and forceful oratory. He was as central to Chicago politics as anyone of his era who held no office. Robert Todd Lincoln urged then president-elect James Garfield to make him attorney general. After the Civil War, Storrs fought to remind people that if people weren't vigilant, the south would continue to make laws restricting freedom and civil rights.

Arriving in Chicago in the late 1850s, Storrs was a lawyer in many cases of note, but truly made a name for himself in politics, first by making speeches supporting Abraham Lincoln, and then for his fierce advocacy of civil rights—and his raging criticism of Andrew Johnson. One phrase he used frequently—applied to people who tried to stop abolitionism, or the impeachment of Johnson, or the election of Garfield—was, "They had better have been in a boat of stone, with sails of lead and oars of iron, the wrath of God for a gale, and Hell the nearest port." At one point he suggested that on his next speaking tour, Johnson should go to an island plagued by earthquakes and volcanoes. "I would like to see all the copperheads colonized there. Ashamed of their company, volcanic mountains would become quiet. A desert would cover the land, and Andrew Johnson would be master of the territory he is just fitted to rule." In one speech, he summed up his attitude: "I am not blood-thirsty, but I mean business."[84]

In the aftermath of his early death, biographies and books of his speeches appeared. But he wasn't the "first" anything, never achieved high office, didn't end up with his name on a foundation or a building, has no large memorial, and was damaged by rumors of his wilder side. He was nearly forgotten soon after his death. But his speeches, many of them still thrilling to read, and even still relevant, are now easy to find online; a biography by Isaac Adams contains many of them in full. Adams was assisted in writing it by Emery's wife, **Caroline Storrs (c1836–1888)**.[85]

At the time of Emery's death, Caroline claimed to be destitute, and sought charity for the near-anonymous burial, but on her death three years later it was a minor scandal when it was found that she was in fact very well off. It was suggested that she had been hiding her money from their son, **George Storrs (1860–1896),** who was in and out of trouble and was given to tempestuous marriages, one of which led him to be put in, and later escape from, an asylum.[86]

■ ■ ■

Proceed back up the road to the Station three, in front of the instantly recognizable Schoenhofen pyramid.

The Schoenhofen Pyramid

THE PYRAMID, THE COLUMN, AND THE MASTABA

At Station Three, you'll find yourself surrounded by three wildly different, but equally remarkable monuments—and the pyramid of Peter Schoenhofen, the forty-foot Corinthian column for George Pullman, and the dark Egyptian crypt of Martin Ryerson.

Peter Schoenhofen's Pyramid

Graceland is a nonsectarian cemetery; people of all faiths can be and are buried here. Though religious iconography isn't exactly in short supply, one sees less overt religious symbolism than one might see at the nearby Catholic or Jewish cemeteries.

In the case of brewer **Peter Schoenhofen (1827–1893)**, it's an old joke among cemetery tour guides that when he commissioned his mausoleum, he was really hedging his bets. He was not religious himself—the press made a great deal of his son being given an entirely secular funeral[1]—but his vault contains symbols from a number of different religions.

The Egyptian pyramid features the staff of a Greek god above the door, which is flanked by a Christian angel and an Egyptian sphynx (whose face is variously described as resembling Spiro T. Agnew or Mikhail Gorbachev). The fantastic door handle features a single snake wrapped around a staff, a three-dimensional version of a symbol that appears in both Greek and Jewish traditions. The joke that Schoenhofen was making sure he was in the good graces of whomever he met on the other side is actually backed up by his will, in which he left large sums to Catholic, Protestant, and Jewish charities, as well as such nondenominational groups as the Home for the Deaf, the Newsboys and Bootblacks Association, and the Chicago Orphan Asylum.[2]

The pyramid was designed by architect Richard Schmidt, who also designed the monument for his parents (page 253), as well as some of the Schoenhofen brewery buildings and the mansion of Peter's son-in-law, the brewer **Joseph Theurer (1852–1912)** (now known as the Wrigley mansion).[3] Though usually said to have been built when Peter died in 1893, lot records indicate that it was built in 1888, when Peter's son, **Peter G. Schoenhofen (1869–1888)**, died from injuries sustained in a diving accident.[4][5] More than twenty more interments were added over the next century.[6]

The Impenetrable Plot of George Pullman

"I suppose you will be shocked when I tell you I am at the office instead of in church, but you can see a man is apt to become demoralized especially with regard to a proper observance of the Sabbath in the absence of a wife to remind him of his duties!"
—Letter of George Pullman to Hattie Pullman, May 1879

Legend has it that **George M. Pullman (1831–1897)** was buried in a manner designed to protect his remains from disgruntled employees, who, it was feared, might wish to dig them up and damage them. It's probably not *entirely* true, but the fact that the story even exists speaks volumes about his reputation.

When Pullman's luxury train cars made him fabulously wealthy, he built an entire town—now the neighborhood of Pullman—for his employees. The town was looked on as a grand, progressive experiment at the time, and was certainly far nicer than most factory towns of the era. But what seemed like benevolence at first soon began to seem overly paternal, especially Pullman's strict regulations for conduct that his employees and their families were expected to follow. One common line around the town went, "We are born in a Pullman house, cradled in a Pullman crib, fed from a Pullman store, taught in a Pullman school, exploited in a Pullman shop, and when we die we'll go to a Pullman hell."[7]

In 1894, when Pullman cut the workers' pay but didn't lower the rents on the apartments they were required to rent from him, there were strikes that erupted into violence, and President Cleveland had to send in federal troops.[8]

By the time Pullman died in 1897, the practice of stealing bodies for medical students to use as cadavers was far less common than it had been a generation before, as laws had changed to allow schools to acquire more bodies legally. However, in 1876, there had been a highly publicized attempt to steal Abraham Lincoln's body from his Springfield tomb and hold it for ransom.

Solon Bemen's Pullman Monument

Not long after, the body of A. T. Stewart, the merchant prince of New York, was stolen from his own crypt and held for ransom in what became one of the most scandalous stories of 1878.[9]

It was Lincoln and Stewart, not fear of vengeful employees, that newspapers noted when they talked about precautions taken with Pullman's interment.[10] According to *Tribune* reports, an 8-foot grave was dug, 13 feet long and 9 feet wide. An 18-inch concrete base was poured in and strengthened with bands of metal. The lead-lined mahogany coffin was placed on top of these and then wrapped in tar paper and coated in an inch of asphalt. More concrete was added until the entire casket was buried. On top of the concrete were eight steel T-rails, more tar paper, and then more concrete.[11]

The *Daily News* was even more explicit, saying that a few curious gawkers were still lingering after the graveside service when "roughly garbled men with grimed faces stepped out from behind the shrubbery . . . carrying paviors' rammers, shovels, and long iron rails. Others rolled barrels of concrete out into the open."[12]

Today, no one is entirely sure if the story was true, or just a myth the family circulated to discourage anyone from getting ideas. After all, it does beg the question of how his wife, **Hattie Sanger Pullman (1842–1921)**, could have been added to the plot right beside him when she died in 1921, not to mention their daughter, **Harriet Pullman Schermerhorn (1869–1956)**, who was buried there in 1956. The *Daily News* spoke of the shadows of nearby obelisks falling on the grave, but no obelisks are nearby. The plot is also too close to Lake Willowere for an extra deep grave to be practical. The *Chicago Chronicle*, which was always up for a good sensational story, covered the burial service in detail, and didn't mention anything out of the ordinary at the time.[13] The next day, though, they noted that the coffin was "incased in stone work, cement, and asphalt."[14]

Above the ground, splendid benches and a promenade are topped by a 40-foot Corinthian column. Designed by Solon S. Beman, architect of the Pullman town (as well as the mansions of Marshall Field Jr., page 174, and W. W. Kimball, page 143), the monument consists of some 25 tons of Hallowell granite.[15]

Their other daughter, **Florence Sanger Pullman Lowden (1868–1937)**, is in the Lowden plot, directly to the left of the Pullman marker, along with her husband, former Illinois governor **Frank O. Lowden (1861–1943)**, and their daughter, **Florence Lowden Miller (1898–1988)**. Lowden was governor during the 1918 pandemic and the race riots of 1919, which were chronicled in Gary Krist's book *City of Scoundrels* in 2012.

The Ryerson Tomb

"[On our automobile trek in France] I found a small shop in which gasoline could be had. The woman in charge brought out a six-ounce bottle of the precious fluid. I asked to see all she had in store, and, after an interval, a two-gallon can was produced as the whole village stock. My offer to purchase it all was the source of so much surprise that the poor woman could not decide how much to charge for it."

—Martin A. Ryerson, "Off the Tourist Route"

The black mausoleum across the triangle from Pullman is an Egyptian-style vault designed by Louis Sullivan (page 145), though it's very atypical of his architectural style. It combines two forms of Egyptian mausoleums: the top is a pyramid, and the bottom portion is a mastaba, a style of tomb which predated the pyramids.

Louis Sullivan's Ryerson tomb

Martin L. Ryerson (1818–1887) left his New Jersey home to seek his fortune and adventure in the frontier when he was just a teenager. At 16, he was in Michigan, trading furs with Native American tribes. At one point he was married to an Ottawa woman whose name is not known; she is thought to have died shortly after the birth of their daughter, **Mary Ryerson Butts (1843–1888)**, and was presumably buried at Old Indian Cemetery in Muskegon, Michigan (though some dispute this and say she died in Chicago).[16] Martin eventually commissioned a statue, *The Alarm*, that would portray peaceful Ottawa in contrast to the then-common statues depicting them in battle; it still stands on Lake Shore Drive.[17]

Martin eventually made millions through lumber and real estate in Chicago. In the vault with him is his third wife, **Mary A. Campau Ryerson (1832–1907);**

Martin A. and Carrie Ryerson, from a passport photo.

· · ·

their son, **Martin A. Ryerson (1856–1932)**, who took over the lumber business after his death; and daughter-in-law **Carrie Hutchinson Ryerson (1859–1937)**. Martin A. and Carrie traveled frequently with the Hutchinsons, including a 1900 trip to Russia, where they met with such people as Leo Tolstoy and the Czar.[18]

The interior of the mausoleum features a bust of Martin L Ryerson over his crypt, likely sculpted by J. J. Boyle, who also created "The Alarm." He made at least one bust of Ryerson in 1883.[19]

■ ■ ■

For Route 3-A, turn to page 127.
For 3-B, turn to page 143.

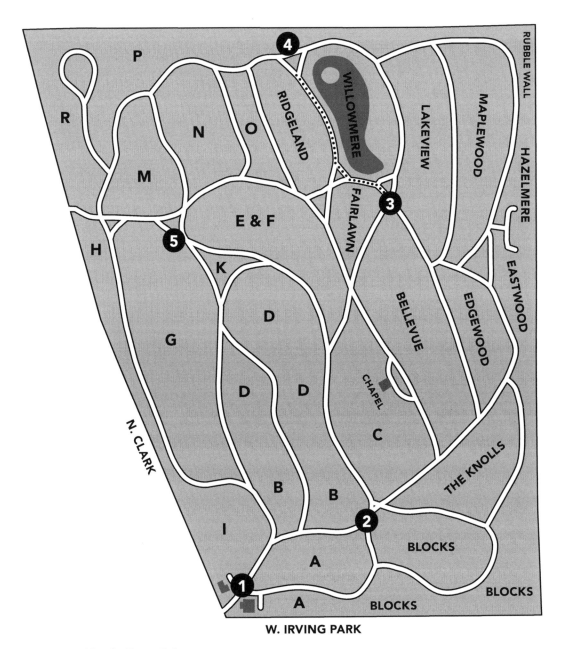

P

R

N

O

RIDGELAND

WILLOWMERE

LAKEVIEW

MAPLEWOOD

RUBBLE WALL

HAZELMERE

M

4

3

H

E & F

FAIRLAWN

BELLEVUE

EDGEWOOD

EASTWOOD

5

K

D

CHAPEL

G

D

D

C

THE KNOLLS

N. CLARK

B

B

2

BLOCKS

I

A

BLOCKS

1

A

BLOCKS

W. IRVING PARK

Map for Route 3-A

ROUTE 3-A

At the foot of the pond is the marker for **John Nash Ott (1909–2000)**, a photographer who developed the technique known as "time lapse photography."[1]

To the left of Ott is the flowerbed Insull plot, including actress-turned-socialite **Margaret Bird Insull (1873–1953)**, but not her more famous husband, utilities kingpin Samuel Insull, who is buried in the U.K.

Proceed left, along the edge of the pond. In the triangle on your left at the southwest edge will be a triangle of small single graves. Among them is jazz legend Bud Freeman.

Lawrence "Bud" Freeman: Jazz Pioneer

> "When I got home with all my money my father said, 'Now son, where did you get all that?' I said 'Playing in the band and playing a slot machine.' It took him a while to believe my story, but afterward he felt better about my future . . ."
>
> —Bud Freeman, *Crazeology*

In the early 1920s, when jazz was still new, dangerous, and scary, the *Tribune* called the saxophone "(the) symbol of lost souls who drift to the port of missing men."[2]

Such critics never dreamed that jazz also may *inspire* education. In this uptight world, five boys from Austin High School began ditching school to study and practice music in the back room of The Spoon and Straw, an ice cream parlor at 5613 West Lake. Over time, they became a bit of a clique; when one lanky boy wanted to hang out with them, they chased him off because he was wearing uncool knickerbockers. That lanky boy was Benny Goodman.[3]

Bud Freeman. Gottlieb Collection, Library of Congress.

The clique formed a band known as the Austin High Gang. With their jazz dreams constantly overshadowing their school obligations, each member was expelled from school at least twice, but saxophonist **Lawrence "Bud" Freeman (1906–1991)** led that pack with five expulsions.[4]

Their truancy paid off; the Austin High Gang helped shape the high-octane variation on New Orleans jazz that came to be called "The Chicago Style." They were even awarded honorary degrees from Austin High when they reunited to play the senior prom in 1942. Studs Turkel called Bud "a pioneer . . . a precursor to Lester Young in a way, with that cool, economic style."[5]

Freeman remembered the Chicago of his youth as "Bustling and crass. . . . Still raw, still a young giant with belching steel mills and sprawling stockyards. That was the town I grew up in, at a time when almost everyone played ragtime on their parlor pianos."[6] He also believed that "Chicago, not New Orleans, was the town that really cradled jazz. New Orleans, I think, spawned a kind of ragtime that developed into jazz in Chicago through the genius of King Oliver and Louis Armstrong (when they came here) . . . the men who developed the beat that will be with us forever."[7]

Freeman went on to play and record professionally for more than sixty years, performing with the likes of Tommy Dorsey, Mezz Mezzrow, Pee Wee Russell, and Benny Goodman (who had eventually convinced the Austin High Gang that he was cool after all). Ill health forced him to retire after a final show at the Field Museum in 1989; he died of cancer two years later.

■ ■ ■

Just beyond the triangle is a section whose most visible monument is to **Alfred Featherstone (1855–1924)**, a manufacturer of "velocipedes, tricycles, and bicycles."[8] He was among the first to introduce affordable bicycles to the market.

Nearby are several plots for the Mok family. **Mok Ming Chuen (1906–1998)** was in the restaurant business in his native China and believed that "food feeds the soul and a well-prepared meal warms the heart." In the United States, Mok retired from work to focus on his family. The stone features the names of the family's ancestors and their hopes for future generations, but, being written in an ancient form of Chinese, even the family has only a rough translation.[9]

Among the single graves surrounding these family plots are monuments to several architects; of particular note are Bruce Graham and Fazlur Kahn, whose similar-but-not-identical memorials are side by side, which is fitting, since they frequently worked together on buildings in which Graham was the architect and Khan the structural engineer.

Fazlur Khan:
Savior of the Skyscraper

> "The technical man must not be lost in his own technol-
> ogy. He must be able to appreciate life, and life is art,
> drama, music, and most importantly, people."
> —Fazlur Khan, Engineering Architecture

The inscription on this marker is a verse by Bengali poet Rabindranath Tagore, whom **Fazlur Khan (1929–1982)** adored; it translates to

> *"For you it is the beginning*
> *for me this is the end*
> *you and me together*
> *thus flows the current."*

Khan was a Bangladeshi-American engineer and architect, known as "The Einstein of Structural Engineering." Born in 1929 and raised in a village near Dhaka when it was a part of British-ruled India, Khan won a Fullbright Scholarship and traveled to the United States. Here, he studied at the University of Illinois in Champaign and began working in Chicago in 1955.

After the first great rush of skyscrapers that topped 1000 feet in the 1930s, "supertall" structures had fallen out of favor with the next generation of builders; they were simply too costly to build and maintain. The "bundled tube" system developed by Khan made them cost-effective again, and his ideas ushered in the next great era of skyscrapers. Working with Bruce Graham, whose monument is next to his own (though he is not buried here), he designed such iconic Chicago buildings as the Hancock Building and the Sears Tower. He was the subject of a 2004 biography by his daughter, Yasmin Sabina Khan.

Other architects interred in the section behind Khan include architectural photographer **Richard Nickel (1928–1972)**. Nearby are cenotaphs for Daley center architect **Jacques Brownson (1923–2012)**, and, beside him, brutalist **Stanislaw Gladych (1921–1982)**, who designed the F.B.I. Building in Washington, D.C., and Chicago's Chase Tower. Brutalist **Walter Netsch (1920–2008)**, designer of the Air Force Academy and University of Illinois at Chicago's University Hall, is in front of Featherstone.

Cross back over the road to the shore of Lake Willowmere, heading north up the road. The monument to "Mr. Cub," topped with a baseball glove, will be instantly visible on the right.

Ernie Banks: Mr. Cub

"It's a beautiful day for a ball game . . . let's play two!"
—Ernie Banks

Everyone in Chicago knows the legend of the Cubs Curse—how Sam Sianis, owner of the Billy Goat Tavern, cursed Wrigley Field when they wouldn't admit his pet goat during the 1945 World Series, leading the Cubs into a pennant drought that would last for seven decades. The story was popularized by columnist Mike Royko, who later said in his final column before his death that the *real* curse came because the Cubs took so long to start hiring Black players after Jackie Robinson broke the color barrier in 1947.[10] Other teams waited longer, but by holding off as long as they did, they missed out on the chance to hire players like Willie Mays and Satchel Paige.

The Cubs brought **Ernie Banks (1931–2015)** onboard in 1953. They had actually called Gene Baker up from the minors as their first Black player but realized that they'd need someone to be Baker's roommate when the team traveled, so they hired Banks from the Negro League's Kansas City Monarchs. But due to Baker nursing a pulled muscle when the two arrived, Banks played first. There was little controversy about the issue by then; a *Tribune* article about the two new players only mentioned that they'd be the first Black Cubs in passing.[11]

Banks remained with the team until 1971 and was named National League MVP in 1958 and 1959—which is particularly remarkable given that the Cubs lost more games than they won in those years. One can only imagine how much worse the records—and ticket sales—might have been without Banks, whose prowess on the field was complemented by a personality that made him a fan favorite.

Monuments to Page, Delfau, and Banks

He was elected to the Baseball Hall of Fame in 1977 and was awarded the Presidential Medal of Freedom in 2013. A statue of him was built at Wrigley Field, and on a clear day you can hear the crowds there at Graceland. A temporary headstone was in place in 2016 when the Cubs finally won the World Series, a feat they not only failed to accomplish while Banks was on the team, but during Banks' entire 84-year lifetime. The current version of the marker was unveiled in 2017.

• • •

Immediately to the left of Banks is the elegant marker for Ruth Page.

Ruth Page:
A Dangerous Dancer

"(Anna Pavlova's) manager took me backstage to meet
her, and I was thrilled to death . . . When she opened
the door, there she was, stark naked (and) picking her
teeth."
—Ruth Page, Interview No. 1

As a teenager **Ruth Page (1899–1991)** began touring with the legendary
Anna Pavlova, and she was soon dancing at functions such as the coronation
of Emperor Hirohito of Japan and the premiere of Stravinsky's *Apollo*. In addition to stage work, Page eventually appeared in films and such television
programs as *The Ed Sullivan Show* in a career that took her through most of
the 20th century.

Page was perhaps even better known as a choreographer; her works in that
field include a version of *The Nutcracker* that was performed in Chicago for
years. But the wholesome holiday piece is almost an anomaly in a career that
was frequently marked by controversy; her own 1938 production of *Frankie
and Johnny* was considered a landmark at the time, but it was banned in
some cities for its sexual content, which included a lesbian couple in a saloon
scene. Recalling the minor scandal in 1985, Page said, "If you just did what
people thought you should do, you'd be awfully limited, you know."[12]

Even when she was in her 70s, she wore leotards under her clothes every
day, and had not lost her eagerness to push boundaries: in an interview, she
enthused to a reporter about a ballet she wanted to stage based on the play
The Triumph of Death. "The director comes onstage naked," she said. "Stanley (the chairman of the Chicago Ballet) wouldn't like this—but (the director
is) sprayed with orange paint almost immediately. In Chicago I'd have him
wear tights. Chicago is so proper!"[13]

Right in front of her grave is that of **Andre Delfau (1914–2000)**, the artist who designed sets and costumes for many of her productions. Ruth and
Andre worked together for years before marrying in 1983, when they were 83
and 70 years old, respectively. At a dinner party the night after the wedding,
Ruth told dancer Rudolf Nureyev, "You really ought to try getting married.
It's fun!" Nureyev said, "You have only been married one day. I will talk to
you on Sunday!"[14]

· · ·

Just to the left of Delfau is the crystal-topped monument to Bruce Goff.

Bruce Goff

"Any time we experience a work of art for the first time, the only reason we notice it at all is because it completes a circuit within us and engages our attention . . . In order for a work of art to survive the moment of surprise, the work must contain mystery."

—Bruce Goff, quoted in Morris, "The Hidden Sides of Architect Bruce Goff"

Though perhaps less widely known than many of his colleagues in nearby plots, **Bruce Goff (1904–1982)** was one of the most delightfully eccentric architects of the mid–20th century. In an era when others were focused on boxes, he was building domes. When others seemed to be building almost exclusively in black, he was covering his buildings in lavender, pink, and blue. Modern commentators who look at his buildings—most of which were single-family homes—sometimes compare them to Pee-Wee's Playhouse. He was a critic of the "international style" of architecture that defined his own era and emphasized simple, non-showy buildings that showed the structure of a building prominently. "Some architects make a fetish out of structure," he said, "and I know it can be beautiful. A human skeleton can be beautiful, but who wants to shake hands with it?"[15]

Born in Kansas in 1904, and based primarily in Oklahoma throughout his life, Goff was advised to stay out of architecture school by Frank Lloyd Wright when he was only a teenager; Wright cautioned that academia would cause him to lose his already-unique style. The first home he designed was built when he was only 15. He designed the Boston Avenue Methodist Church, a structure in Tulsa that blended gothic and art deco styles, at 20. In the 1950s, he designed wildly eccentric houses that featured strange shapes, open floor plans, and bright colors. Many were decorated with found objects.

Focusing on smaller buildings for low-profile clients in far-flung localities probably contributed to his relative lack of fame, though some have also pointed to his being gay in a time when that was a career killer—he lost a teaching position at the University of Oklahoma in 1955 because of his sexuality. In recent years, there's been a revival of interest in his work; a 2018 *New York Times* headline called his work "gloriously disobedient,"[16] and the University of Oklahoma, the same school that fired him, hosted an exhibition dedicated to him in 2019.[17]

The blue crystal on the headstone is a piece of cullet—runoff from glass-making kilns, a material that was a Goff trademark. This particular bit was salvaged from Shin'enKan, a bachelor pad he designed for a patron in 1958, after it was destroyed by fire in the 1990s.[18]

Just north of Goff is an elegant black marker for **Jon Cockrell (1952–1988)**, a furniture designer who was lost to AIDS. Behind his monument and to the left, you will notice a stone with Greek characters.

J. Roderick MacArthur: One Foot in Fairyland

> "I have no fear of going to Hell. Nor of going to Heaven."
> —J. Roderick MacArthur, *Chicago Tribune*

A flamboyant social justice warrior and captain of the collectible plate industry, **Roderick MacArthur (1920–1984)** was a son of billionaire philanthropist John D. MacArthur. After working with French Resistance groups in World War II, he worked his way through several jobs, including a gig as a disc jockey, a stint as the editor of a theater magazine, and a period as a public relations man. By the early 70s, he was drawing a modest salary working for his father, who told him that a raise would only mean he had to pay more taxes. But Roderick saw an opportunity in the growing world of collectors' plates, and founded his own company, The Bradford Exchange, to produce and sell them. He initially ran afoul of authorities when his ads guaranteed that the plates they sold would double in value, but the company was a huge success.[19]

When his father tried to claim ownership of the company, Rod launched what he later called "The Great Crockery Raid." In broad daylight on a May afternoon in 1975, he brought a crew to a suburban warehouse, showed the police invoices to establish that the plates inside were his, and drove off with seven truckloads of them. Chicago history is full of stories of gangsters hijacking booze or other valuables, but this may have been the only major instance of piracy centered on commemorative dishware.[20]

Rod's father, impressed, worked out a deal to let Rod have ownership after all, and the company was grossing $75 million per year within three years, eventually focusing more on brokering sales of plates than manufacturing them. In the world of plate collecting, Roderick liked to say, they were the New York Stock Exchange.[21]

With his new fortune, he formed a foundation to support civil rights and social justice, which had been passions for him since the 1930s, when Florida police had arrested him and his friends simply for being in a Black neighborhood. The MacArthur Justice Center is still active, fighting for prisoners' rights and against racist laws, police misconduct, the mistreatment of immigrants, and similar causes. The Greek characters on his monument spell out "One Foot in Fairyland" in English.

Just in front of Roderick is a marker for his sister, **Virginia Cordova MacArthur (1922–2002)**. Never one for the spotlight, she spent much of her life living modestly in Mexico, where she taught English[22] and worked part-time jobs to supplement the modest monthly allowance she received from her father's estate. The marker features an excerpt from Robert Browning's poem "Pippa Passes."

. . .

Just north of Goff and MacArthur is the primary architect associated with the "less is more" modernist style, **Ludwig Mies van der Rohe (1886–1969)**, whose sleek, elegant designs are perfectly echoed by his black rectangle marker. In his native Germany, his work earned the scorn of the Nazis, who preferred more traditional German styles. Before his ideas could get him into real danger, he was lured to Chicago to teach at the Illinois Institute of Technology. Here, he designed buildings such as the IBM Building (now the AMA plaza) and the new I.I.T. campus. Though critics complained that his modernist buildings were just plain black boxes, many look just as modern and elegant today as they did more than half a century ago. His life story is told in numerous biographies, such as Franz Schulze's *Mies van der Rohe: A Critical Biography*.

Continuing north, on the right will be monuments to **Laverne Noyes (1849–1919)**, a manufacturer of farm equipment, to the family of surgeon **Ralph Isham (1831–1904)**, and to **John and Frances Glessner (1843–1936, 1850–1930)**, a farm equipment baron (among other pursuits) whose Henry Hobson Richardson–designed Prairie Avenue home was called a "queer looking mansion" by the *Chicago Daily News* in 1887.[23] The house is now a museum.

On the left side of the road will be a vast expanse marked mainly by greenery and a boulder; this is the eastern portion of the "McCormick Wilderness," three adjoining plots for the family of Cyrus McCormick. It stretches to the next road and is covered in route 4-A (page 176).

North of the Glessners on the right is a gorgeous high-relief statue of a hooded woman honoring paper manufacturer and real estate investor **Lucius Fisher (1843–1916)** (namesake of Burnham's stunning Fisher Building on Dearborn Ave). For some time, Fisher resided in the Nickerson Mansion, now the Driehaus Museum in River North. Designed by Peter J. Weber, an architect in Daniel Burnham's firm, with a sculpture by Richard W. Bock, the Fisher monument is actually a miniature columbarium; his ashes are behind the figure, which Bock referred to as a "door."[24] The keyhole is below one of the sleeves.

Nearby is the seashell-marked gravestone of investment banker **Howard Buhse (1906–1994)**, and a lakeside plot for the family of restaurateur **William M. Collins (1905–1909)**. Across the road from them is the large Armour plot.

Princess Aleka,
and the Armour Family

> "(Phillip Armour) can estimate the number of grains on
> an ear of corn, can guess the weight of a steer, or size
> up a human being better than any man in Chicago."
> —Mayor "Long John" Wentworth, "House of Armour"

As you pass the Armour plot, feel free to start singing the Armour Hot Dogs jingle. It wasn't written until decades after **Phillip Armour (1832–1901)** died, but it certainly kept his name alive.

Armour opened his first Chicago meatpacking plant in 1867, and eventually ran the largest plant in the city. A firm man of business, he would amuse friends by "sizing up" people on the street, noting whether he'd hire them based on a glance with such quips as "Late hours—booze—too smart—will be old at forty," "Thinks more of clothes than books—gets fifteen a week and is worth ten," or "He's needlessly sensitive and foolishly good—he'll have to be coddled, or he'll get a sour spot in his soul and imagine you have it in for him."[25]

Princess Alexandra "Aleka" Pavlovna Galitzine Armour (1905–2006), who is also in the plot, was born into Russian royalty. "I'm sure I had the happiest childhood any little girl ever had," she once said. "It never occurred to me . . . that the days of the empire were numbered. I remember so well the day five soldiers appeared at our house."[26]

After being imprisoned with her family for a time during the Russian Revolution as a teenager,[27] Aleka fled to London, where she met Prince Alexandrovich Romanoff, a nephew of the czar (and brother of one of Rasputin's killers). Making her way to Chicago, Aleka was quickly adopted into society, but, being broke, she took an ordinary job at Marshall Field. Prince Romanoff followed her to town and took a job in another department store—when they married in 1928, papers couldn't resist commenting on the wedding between a "royal shopgirl" and a "royal clerk."[28] They divorced in 1949, and a few years later Aleka married **Lester Armour (1895–1970)**, a grandson of Phillip who won the Legion of Merit award for his service in the Navy during World War II. In an interesting coincidence, besides marrying into the Armour family, one of her cousins on her mother's side was thought to be the namesake of beef stroganoff.[29] Meat seemed to be a recurring theme in her life.

During her first marriage, Aleka opened a clothing store of her own, and in her 70s she volunteered in the stock room of the gift shop at St. Luke's Medical Center. She seldom spoke of her background; when asked about her father, she'd simply say that "He worked for the government." Upon her death in 2006, age 101, her granddaughter said, "The only things she wanted in life were the ability to read a hardback book and to have fresh orange juice every morning. And she did that every day up to the day she died."[30]

■ ■ ■

Immediately past the Armour plot is the black stone marked "Tree-Magie" for **Judge Lambert Tree (1832–1910)** and his father-in-

Lambert Tree, Library of Congress.

law, dry goods merchant **H. H. Magie (1806–1879)**. Mr. Magie, who leased Potter Palmer space for his first store, was originally interred in the hillside tomb further south that Judge Tree sold to G. M. Stevens (page 58).

Tree wrote that during the Great Chicago Fire he saw several people hauling goods into the yard of Magie's River North house, which appeared to have enough empty space around it that it wouldn't be burned. The Trees and several other families were taking refuge there, but soon it too caught fire.[31]

The Tree and Magie families both survived, and Judge Tree served as U.S. Minister to Russia from 1888–1889. He and his wife, **Anna Tree (1830–1903)**, built the artists' colony Tree Studios on the old Magie property at State and Erie in 1894; the building still stands.

Just beyond to the right of them is the Medill plot.

The Medill-McCormick-Patterson Family

"(Lincoln) came forward with a giraffe-like swing . . . I do not pretend to remember (the words of Lincoln's famous, now-lost radical anti-slavery speech in Bloomington, 1856), (but) when the speech was finished I found myself standing at the top of the reporters' table shouting and yelling like one possessed."

—Joseph Medill, "Recollections of Lincoln as Furnished by Joseph Medill"

The Medill family is one of Chicago's most tangled dynasties—which is saying something. Though best known for their newspaper editors, the family history contains soldiers, socialites, politicians, royals, heroes, and villains. Many of the family members were more than one of those. The family is the subject of a multi-generational biography, Megan McKinney's 2011 epic, *The Magnificent Medills*. The children and grandchildren of the family married into the McCormicks (**the William McCormick branch,** page 244), the Higinbothams (page 158), and others. Later generations would marry into the Albrights and Guggenheims.

Tribune publisher **Joseph Medill (1823–1899)** is sometimes credited with getting Abraham Lincoln elected president. This is probably a bit of an exaggeration, but Medill certainly helped Lincoln get the Republican party's nomination in 1860, perhaps more than any single other person. As the country geared up for the election that year, several Southern states and counties adopted resolutions promising to secede from the union if anyone even remotely anti-slavery were ever elected president.[32] [33] [34] Against this backdrop, Medill published his endorsement of Lincoln, who was best known for his antislavery speeches, in February 1860, and kept ads on his front page promoting Lincoln for president throughout the Republican Convention that took place in Chicago that summer, where the groundswell of home-state support helped him become the surprise nominee. Medill's remarkably early endorsement of a man few spoke of as a serious candidate at the time was likely a key factor.

Joseph left the *Tribune* to devote himself to politics in 1864 and served two years as mayor of Chicago before returning to the newspaper world. He died in 1899; several sources said that just before he passed away, he turned to his doctor and said, "My last words shall be, 'What is the news?'"[35]

William Medill (1835–1863), Joseph's brother, was a member of the 8th Illinois under General Farnsworth, a company that was known as "Farnsworth's Big Abolition Regiment." The regiment was put in charge of guarding Alexandria, Virginia, which was then under the rule of a military governor who didn't approve of secession but hated abolitionists and felt that the war was all their fault. Out of pure spite, he had the regiment moved to a swampy, disease-ridden camp far south of the city.[36]

William's letters home showed a deep dissatisfaction with officers who seemed unwilling to truly fight against the south and its institutions. He was greatly encouraged when the Emancipation Proclamation went into effect, writing to his sister only days later that after taking over a Virginia plantation, he'd helped himself to some food from the owner's kitchen and then "for dessert I started 75 of his slaves on their way rejoicing."[37]

William was mortally wounded while attacking a band of confederates who were retreating from Gettysburg in July, 1863. He lingered long enough for his brother to be

Joseph Medill, Library of Congress.

summoned from Chicago to his deathbed, where William lamented, "I am going to die without knowing that my country is saved and the slave holders' accursed rebellion crushed."[38]

Joseph's granddaughter, **Eleanor "Cissy" Medill Patterson (1881–1948)**, found fame as "The Battling Countess of Newspaper Row."[39]

> "Why do you want to go back to Chicago to live, anyhow? The climate is simply awful. It's always too hot or too cold. The wind is forever blowing. I remember the newspapers forever blowing down the streets."
>
> —Eleanor "Cissy" Medill Patterson to Al Capone

Cissy grew up splitting her time between the Stanford White–designed McCormick-Patterson mansion, which still stands on Burton Ave, and Patterson House, a Washington D.C. mansion, also designed by White, so large that it was later used by presidents when the White House was under repairs. The finishing schools she attended prepared her mainly for life as a socialite, and she married a Polish nobleman, Count Gizycki, in 1904.

Cissy Patterson, Library of Congress.

In 1908, though, the count kidnapped their daughter, leading to an international scandal; divorce was very difficult to obtain in Europe, and it took an intervention from President Taft to get Cissy's daughter back. Reverting to her maiden name, Cissy went on to try her hand at acting and then published two novels in the 1920s (both of which were said to be thinly veiled attacks on her former friend, Alice Roosevelt). While working on the books she lived in Paris, where biographers portray her talking about guns with Ernest Hemingway and drinking with F. Scott Fitzgerald.

In 1930, when she was nearly 50, Cissy persuaded William Randolph Hearst to make her editor of the *Washington Herald*. Soon, the paper had merged with the *Washington Times*, and she was publishing 10 editions a day of the *Times-Herald*, a heavily illustrated tabloid that was unafraid of sensationalism. In addition to editing (and eventually owning) the paper, Cissy personally wrote stories on people such as Al Capone, with whom she landed an interview simply by driving past his Miami estate and catching him outside. "Women have a special kind of sympathy for gangsters," she wrote. "If you don't understand, consult Dr. Freud."[40]

In 1931, while attempting to seek out and interview Albert Einstein, Cissy found him sunbathing "relatively nude" and decided to leave him alone. A few nights later, at the premiere of Charlie Chaplin's *City Lights*, she saw the professor, seated next to Chaplin and weeping like a child at the famous ending. She decided that this image was better than any interview could have been. "Why ask him if the universe, space, and time are finite or infinite?" she wrote. "It's all the same to you and me . . . Isn't it more interesting to know that Einstein, who understands better than anyone else the sublime arrangement of the universe, can also understand and weep to see the heartbreak of a little clown?"[41]

It was, frankly, an uncharacteristically human thing for Patterson to write. Her paper became the best-selling in D.C., and in 1946 *Collier's* magazine called Cissy "Probably the most powerful woman in America. And perhaps the most hated."[42] By then, the "most hated" part was becoming more prominent; she'd used the paper as a weapon in feuds with her many, many enemies, both social and political. Her daughter had even publicly "divorced" her in 1943. And like her cousin Colonel McCormick, who edited the *Tribune* at the time, her isolationist views and rants that people concerned about the rise of the Nazi party were being too alarmist badly tarnished her reputation.

She died of a heart attack at age 63 in 1948. Over the years she's been the subject of many biographies, perhaps the most thorough of which is Amanda Smith's exhaustive 2011 tome, *Newspaper Titan: The Infamous Life and Monumental Times of Cissy Patterson*.

■ ■ ■

Just past the Medill plot is the triangle featuring the Getty Mausoleum. This is Station Four: Turn to page 165.

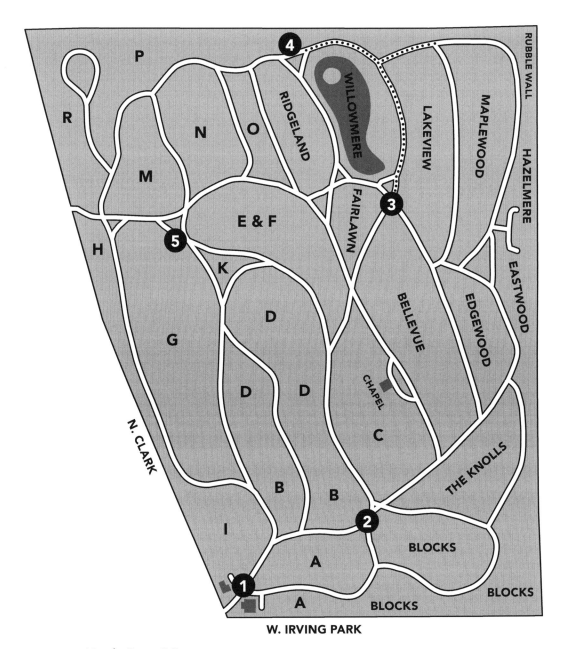

Map for Route 3-B

Walk north beyond the Ryerson mausoleum, veering to the right onto the path will lead up along the east side of Lake Willowmere. To the right, there is an arresting white monument featuring a colonnade of columns fronted by an angel statue kneeling at the back of a pair of slabs.

William and Evaline Kimball's Angel

> "At last I have found (a Rembrandt), and at a reasonable figure . . . There you see it—it has just been unpacked. It almost completes my collection."
> —Evaline Kimball, "New Rembrandt Owned in City"

If you look at the two marble slabs on the surface of the McKim, Mead and White-designed Kimball monument,[1] it can ever-so-subtly suggest the look of piano keys. It may have been intentional; after all, **William W. Kimball (1828–1904)** was the founder of the Kimball piano company. A traveling salesman in his youth, in 1857 when Kimball came to Chicago, he traded some Iowa land to a bankrupt dealer for four pianos. He knew nothing about musical instruments at the time, but sold them for a good profit and opened his first store months later. His wholesaling and use of installment plans brought music into countless households.[2]

Though they seldom made the news personally, the Kimballs spent great energy amassing an art collection, with a particular fondness for old masters—**Evaline Kimball (1840–1921)** believed she would have a "complete" collection, Arthur Meeker Jr. recalled, when she had one painting by each "master."[3] The highlight of their purchases was Rembrandt's *Old Man with a Gold Chain* (now in the Art Institute), which Evaline acquired for $110,000 in 1913.[4]

In 1920, it was said in the press that Evaline, now a widow, was suffering from dementia and was not even aware that she was living among a collection

The Kimball Monument by McKim, Mead, and White.

thought to be the second finest art collection in private hands, behind that of Martin A. Ryerson, who is interred very close to her (page 124).[5] Evaline died the next year.

. . .

Just behind the Kimballs and to the left is a marker for architect **Louis Sullivan (1856–1924)**, though perhaps a better memorial for him would be the tomb he designed for the Getty Family (page 165), which is the quintessential example of his architectural style.

Sullivan's grave was initially unmarked (when he died in 1924, he was out of fashion and in dire financial circumstances), but admirers added the stone five years later. It was initially announced that the boulder marking his grave would be seven feet high, but a more modest granite stone was eventually used.[6]

A few of his Chicago buildings survive, including the ornate department store he designed for Schlesinger and Mayer (better known as the Carson Pirie Scott Building on State Street, and now a Target), the Chicago Auditorium, and the old Kraus Music Store on Lincoln Avenue. His life and work have been the subject of dozens of books, not the least of which is his own third-person autobiography, *The Autobiography of an Idea*. He died at the Hotel Warner, on the site of the old Camp Douglas and a stone's throw from the old Henry Graves house (page 42), in 1924.

If you continue walking straight east past the Sullivan marker, you'll pass the excellent Westerly granite monument with four bronze friezes and sundials representing the four seasons, one of which features a skull topped by a raven. It's a monument to **Frederick Seymour Winston (1856–1909)**, a corporate lawyer.

Crossing the next road and proceeding past the small green "Isaacson" marker, there's a small stone for a man who could reasonably be called the first Hollywood director sitting beside a tree.

Francis Winter Boggs:
Hollywood's First Director

"The company is trying to get better talent and so raise the tone of the films. The work is new and some actors are reluctant to take it up. We paid one prominent actor in Chicago $1000 for four days work!"

—Francis Boggs on filmmaking, "How They Make Moving Pictures"

It's seldom remembered today that for much of the silent-film era, Chicago was the movie-making capitol of the United States—Hollywood before Hollywood. Thomas Edison had patented most of the movie-making equipment, and studios further east who weren't paying him off were frequently raided and broken up. Chicago was far enough west that filmmakers could stay under his radar. By 1910, there were two major studios in the city; Essanay operated on Argyle Street and Selig Polyscope had a studio at Byron and Claremont. The Selig studio space included a fake mountain range, an artificial lake, and a whole menagerie of lions, leopards, and apes.[7]

Of the two studios, Essanay created more surviving classics (due largely to Charlie Chaplin's stint there), but Selig Polyscope was broadly the more innovative, always eager to try new things in an industry and art form that they were making up as they went along. Selig was doing color, feature-length films as early as 1911, and pioneered cliffhanger serials, newsreels, and other advancements. In 1907, *The Fairylogue and Radio Plays*, a series of color shorts with which *Wizard of Oz* author L. Frank Baum interacted live on stage, were directed by **Francis Winter Boggs (1870–1911)**, who was one of Selig's top filmmakers.[8]

Boggs was also the first to shoot in Hollywood, by some metrics. In 1908, Boggs was at the helm when Selig produced a film version of *The Count of Monte Cristo*. Winter filming in Chicago simply wouldn't do for the "thrown into the sea" scene, so the whole production was put on trains to California, where the shot became the first narrative film scene to be shot in Los Angeles. Selig was so delighted with the results that he made plans to build a new studio there, beginning the shift of the industry from Chicago to Hollywood.[9]

Records of who worked on the films from Boggs' era are spotty and sometimes unreliable, but he's credited with directing nearly 100 films from 1907 until his career was cut short in 1911, when he was shot to death by a studio janitor.[10] Only a fraction of his films survive, but more prints are being discovered all the time. One, *The Sergeant*, was screened in the chapel at Graceland in 2019.

. . .

Return to the path in front of the Kimball marker and proceed North toward the pond. On the left, one can walk right onto the top of the Goodman Family tomb, which was designed by Howard Van Doren Shaw (page 239). If you can (carefully!) make your way through the bushes to the front, which is right on the edge of the water, there is an apparently original inscription above the door: "Lulled in that sweet and quiet sleep that hath no vexing dreams a deep and silent slumber."

With the doors facing the water, it is meant to look as though caskets would have to be sailed up to the door on boats, though whether this has ever been done is not known. About half of the interments have been urns.

Kenneth Sawyer Goodman, Playwright

"Office until noon, then went . . . to The Strand to see Cousin Jim and make some changes and additions. Saw the suffragettes parade in the rain. Got home about five o'clock."
—Kenneth Sawyer Goodman's Diary, June 7, 1916

The Goodmans were a lumber family and made a fortune to rival that of any other major lumber family in the city. **Kenneth Goodman (1883–1918)**, their son, has a diary preserved in the Newberry Library which paints a picture of a very busy 1910s high-society life, filled with club meetings, formal dinners, yacht trips, and being prescribed cocaine for headaches.[11]

But between his job and his social schedule, Kenneth was, first and foremost, a playwright—and a well-regarded one. One of his plays, *A Game of Chess*, was produced all over the world. The Newberry Library has most of his manuscripts, many of them handwritten, including the screenplay for *Cousin Jim and the Lost Fraternity Pin*, a now-lost film he and his fellow Casino

Kenneth Sawyer Goodman, Newberry Library.

Club members produced for charity in 1916. It is, in many ways, the first "indie" film to be made in Chicago.[12]

Kenneth joined the army when the United States entered World War I and then contracted influenza and died during the 1918 pandemic. His parents founded the Goodman Theatre in his name, and his plays are still occasionally produced; the Newberry Library hosted a production of *Back of the Yards* in 2019.

■ ■ ■

Just north of the Goodman family plot are two monuments facing each other across the road: on the left, the Parthenon-like monument is that of the Palmer Family, and across the path on the right is the smaller gothic crypt of the Honore family (Bertha Palmer's parents). Both were designed by the New York architecture film of McKim, Mead and White, who are best known for their works and exploits in New York.

Potter and Bertha Palmer's Parthenon

> "Even more important than the discovery of Columbus, which we are gathered to celebrate, is the fact that the general government has just discovered woman. It has sent out a flash-light from its heights, so inaccessible to us, which we shall answer by a return signal, when the Exposition is open. What will be its next message to us?"
>
> —Bertha Palmer, "Four Hundred Years Ago," at the Columbian Exposition dedication ceremony, Oct 21, 1892

When the Civil War ended, the prices of cotton goods plummeted. While this was good for consumers, a number of businesses, who'd bought their goods at wartime prices, were ruined. But **Potter Palmer (1826–1902)** had sold off his cotton interests and left retail merchandising only months before. It was not the first time he'd predicted how history unfolding before him would affect the retail trade.

A decade before, when he'd been starting out on his own as a merchant, he'd successfully banked on the way the early stirrings of modern feminism could be good for business. While many middle-class women in the 1850s were skeptical of suffrage and equality, they were attracted to the new idea that they should be allowed to shop on their own, and early icon Elizabeth Cady Stanton made "go out and buy" one of her mottos. When Palmer, a young Quaker from Lockport, NY, opened his first small Chicago store in 1852, he catered to women particularly. The store, P. Palmer and Co., was a

The Potter and Bertha Palmer Monument by McKim, Mead, and White.

hit; in 1858 he moved into a grand new building that was erected to replace several smaller ones that had burned in the 1857 fire (page 10).[13]

As a merchant, Palmer pioneered the use of window displays, free delivery, return policies, and special sales. Though uninterested in politics, he had the foresight to buy up cotton in the months before the Civil War began, just before prices skyrocketed, and to sell the business to Marshall Field (page 174) just before the war ended and prices plummeted. He began investing the fortune he'd accrued in real estate and new ventures, most notably his famous hotel, The Palmer House.[14]

While the hotel was being built in 1870, Potter married **Bertha Honore Palmer (1849–1918)**, who was less than half his age—they had met 8 years before through Bertha's parents, when she was just 13, and a persistent legend says that Potter had decided immediately that he'd marry her when she was old enough.[15]

Anders Zorn's portrait of Bertha. Art Institute of Chicago.

Bertha became the queen of Chicago's high society. Among her many achievements, she is often credited with inventing the brownie, an early version of which was made in the Palmer House kitchen under her direction as a "portable dessert" to serve in boxed lunches at the 1893 World's Fair, at which she was President of the Board of Lady Managers.[16]

Legend has it that Potter left a clause in his will donating a large sum to anyone who married Bertha after his death, remarking that "He's going to need it." This is a myth; Bertha was given control of the estate, and, though the Tribune wrote that "it is popularly supposed that Mrs. Palmer takes a proposal of marriage with her morning tea the way ordinary folk take their bread,"[17] she never remarried. She certainly didn't need to, financially—she was very astute with her fortune. While her will makes several bequests that may paint her as the very stereotype of a wealthy socialite (there are sums left to her footman, her cook, and her butler), she greatly increased the value of the estate with her own investments. She bought and promoted land in warmer climates, effectively creating Sarasota as a resort town.

As good as her real estate investments were, though, her art investments were even more sound: at the time of her death she had one of the largest collections of impressionist paintings in the world, many of which now make up the core of the Art Institute's collection. Some were bought for just a few hundred dollars but would likely sell for tens of millions today. Beyond simply being a collector, she was well acquainted with many of the major artists of the day, and even posed for the sculptor Auguste Rodin and the painter Anders Zorn.

Though Potter and Bertha are by far the most visible interments in the plot with their raised sarcophagi, there are actually many other family members buried inside of the monument, including **Arthur Macdougall Wood (1913–2006)**, the CEO of Sears and Roebuck who oversaw construction of the Sears Tower. Arthur was married to **Pauline Palmer-Wood (1917–1984)**, a granddaughter of Potter and Bertha who grew up in the now-lost "liver-colored" Lake Shore Drive mansion known as the Palmer "Castle."

■ ■ ■

Across from the Palmers are Bertha's parents, the Honores, in another McKim, Mead, and White monument. **Henry Hamilton Honore (1824–1916)** was an early city planner and businessman.

On the left as you proceed north will be the Deering and McCormick monuments. **William Deering (1826–1913)** was a grain harvester manufacturer, not unlike Cyrus McCormick (page 176). The two were rivals in the 19th century, but their two companies—and families—merged in the early 20th century, and the companies became International Harvester. In the plot with William are his sons, **Charles Deering (1852–1927)** and **James Deering (1859–1925)**. Charles was chairman of the board of International Harvester but seemed more interested in art than business; he studied painting under Anders Zorn and posed for John Singer Sargeant. Graceland landscape artist O. S. Simonds laid out the grounds of his Florida estate.

James posed for Sargeant as well; his own Florida estate, Vizcaya, has appeared in everything from Bettie Page pinups to Ace Ventura movies. Rumors continue to swirl about the bacchanalian parties held there by James, a lifelong bachelor, but actress Lillian Gish remembered that a night there consisted of a brief tour of the beautiful gardens, followed by being ushered into the house to watch a movie about germs.[18]

Adjacent is a plot for **Chauncey McCormick (1884–1954)**, a grandson of William McCormick (page 244), who married **Marion Deering McCormick (1886–1965)**, Charles' daughter, twelve years after the two families' companies merged. The couple were noted art collectors, and Chauncey was decorated for his services as a captain in the American Expeditionary Forces in World War I.

■ ■ ■

Across from Deering will be a Celtic cross marked "McClurg," designed by Charles G. Blake in 1903.[19]

Alexander C. McClurg and the Saints and Sinners

"What shocking cruelties and barbarities have been committed in the name of cheapness on the innocent works of Scot and Dickens, of Thackery and Macauly! [People] are beginning to seek and treasure the really fine old editions, not because they are rare . . . but because they are more beautiful, more readable, and perhaps more correct. The taste for good books is growing."
—Gen A. C. McClurg, "Cheap Bookmaking"

The namesake of McClurg Court, **General Alexander C. McClurg (1832–1901)** seldom spoke about his Civil War service. He cheerfully told stories about *other* soldiers with whom he'd served, but never about himself. Indeed, when the *Junction City Union* tried to write a profile of him, the reporter ended up writing that "Not one of the facts concerning his military services were we able to extract from him."[20]

From records and his own writings, we know that McClurg served as chief of staff to union Major General J. C. Davis and was with Sherman for the whole of the famous March to the Sea.

Davis urged him to stay in the army after the war, but McClurg preferred to return to his family and his real love: books. Before and after the war he worked in publishing, eventually running his own firm, A. C. McClurg and Co., which is perhaps best remembered for publishing the first Tarzan books.

The firm also maintained a retail space, McClurg's Bookstore on South Wabash, which became known worldwide for its section of rare and unique books known as the "Saints and Sinners Corner." Humorist Eugene Field (who was originally buried at Graceland, but moved to Kenilworth) regularly wrote about the eccentric collectors who hung around there in his *Chicago Daily News* column, transcribing the conversations and arguments of "book fiends" who pined after first editions, autographs, and curiosa.[21] McClurg was a collector himself, and his love of good, well-made books sometimes served literature more than it served his finances; indeed, a biography of Field called the general "a book fancier of rare good taste and eke (little) business judgement."[22]

His war memoir was unpublished, though a large portion was included in the book *Reminisces of Chicago during the Civil War* published by R. R. Donnelly in 1914. Among other things, he reminisced about his decision, as an officer, not to swear at his soldiers, of testing water in a well captured in Kentucky to see if it had been poisoned, and how he often fantasized about a girl who gave him a handkerchief during a soldier's parade down Michigan Avenue. He never saw her again.[23]

The plot is also the resting place of General McClurg's granddaughter, **Barbara McClurg Potter (1925–2012)**, who may have inherited a bit of Alexander's military modesty: she worked for the C.I.A. during the Korean War, but never told her family any details, no matter how often they asked. In an obituary, her son, Charlie, said, "To her dying day, none of us could pry it out of her."[24]

■ ■ ■

Just left of the McClurg plot is the mausoleum of **Henry S. Everhart (1851–1889)**, a realtor and businessman who made some news when he purchased the bell from the original courthouse from Thomas Barbour Bryan, who had bought it after the Great Chicago Fire destroyed the bell tower in 1871. Everhart, barely twenty years old at the time, melted it down and had it made into miniature "charm bells," which still turn up on the collector's market now and then.[25]

Past Everhart on the right will be the memorial to **Charles H. Wacker (1856–1929)** and his family. Wacker, a brewer by trade, was head of the committee that commissioned Burnham to draft his famous Plan of Chicago; part of the plan was a bi-level road circling the business district. It was named Wacker Drive in Charles' honor. His parents are interred in Section N (page 197).

Beyond him is the large, elegant monolith for **Henry Porter (1835–1910)**, a railroad and lumber executive. In 1860 Porter traveled to Havana, and later wrote that two southerners there who first heard the news of Lincoln's nomination from him immediately challenged him to a fight. Both, he claimed, went on to be killed in the war.[26] His Charles Platt–designed monument received a glowing write-up in *The Monumental News* in 1916.[27]

Turn right at the fork in the road, passing the mausoleum of brewer **Michael Brand (1828–1897)**. On the right-hand side will be a section of single graves, in the front row of which is a marker for David L. Hull featuring the quote "Alas poor world, what treasure thou has lost" from Shakespeare's "Venus and Adonis."

■ ■ ■

David Lee Hull, Philosopher

"On [the 2100 block of North] Clark Street, there were two bars, one called the Volleyball, the other called Scarlet Ribbons. Guess which was lesbian and which was gay? And there was a swinging door between the two. In the boys' part, it was packed with guys dancing their heads off, and the other part was seven women getting in a fight."
—David Lee Hull reminisces with Andrew Seiert in Pride 2008.

When **David Lee Hull (1935–2010)** and his partner, Richard Wellman, came to Chicago in the early 1960s, the gay community was very small and tight knit; in 2008 he recalled that police raids on the few gay bars in town were frequent.[28]

Hull became a famous philosopher; he practically invented the field of Philosophy of Biology. He wrote ten books, most famously *Philosophy of Biological Science* in 1974, *Science as a Process* in 1988, and *The Metaphysics of Evolution* in 1989. He served for a time as president of The Society of Systematic Zoology, as well as teaching at Northwestern.

Though many of his papers remain relevant after thirty years, upon retiring to write his memoirs, he dismissed his old works as "bo-ring"[29] and focused on writing about his experiences in the gay community in the mid–20th century. Richard had died of AIDS in 1985, and Dr. Hull was shocked at how badly he was treated in those early days of the epidemic. "I just cannot believe that the medical profession could be so cruel and evil as it was to gay people in the early stages," he recalled in 2008.[30]

After Richard's death, Dr. Hull opened his own home to AIDS patients, giving them such comfort and care as he could. During the height of the epidemic, the house was very crowded. One colleague said he was "The Mother Theresa of the gay community . . . all of 5'4", David Hull was the biggest man I ever knew."[31] The house became quieter as the disease became more treatable, but friends say that David was worn out and never quite recovered his stamina. He retired in 2000 and died a decade later of pancreatic cancer.

■ ■ ■

Proceeding past Hull, the mausoleums on the right-hand side include those of banker **Rudolph Schloesser (1825–1898)**, sand dealer **John C. Allmendinger (1853–1916)** (the son of Tobias Allmendinger, page 91), and real estate investor **Edwin F. Getchell (1850–1915)**, who was once part owner of Abraham Lincoln's log cabin (which was displayed at the World's Fair and then lost).[32]

The Altgeld memorial

In the section of graves behind them, look a few yards south and you'll see a small swooping obelisk with large metallic plaques on each side. This is a monument to former governor John Altgeld.

John Altgeld's Fight for Justice

"Every deception, every cruelty, every grasp of greed, every wrong, reaches back sooner or later and curses its author."
—John Peter Altgeld, *The Cost of Something for Nothing*

In 1886, workers held a rally for the eight-hour workday in Haymarket Square, located at Randolph and Des Plaines, in reaction to an attack on striking workers that had taken place at the McCormick plant and then run by Cyrus McCormick Jr. (page 179).

Mayor Carter Harrison (page 219) arrived on horseback, decided that the gathering was peaceful, and ordered the police to stand down. But the second the permit for the rally expired, officers armed with rifles marched toward the crowd. A bomb was thrown from a nearby vestibule, and in the ensuing chaos several police officers and an unknown number of protestors were killed. No one ever determined who threw the bomb, but many of the speakers associated with the rally were arrested, and five were sentenced to be executed. Four of them eventually were; a fifth bit into a dynamite cap in his prison cell the night before the hanging.[33]

The Haymarket Incident became one of the most important political events in American history, a flashpoint in the labor movement whose effects were felt for years.

John Altgeld (1847–1902) entered the world of politics around the time of the incident. A Union army vet who had made a fortune in real estate, he ran for congress in the 1880s pushing penal reform (he believed that prison only made criminals worse), losing the election but making enough of a name for himself to be nominated for governor. He was a progressive Democrat in an era when such a thing was still a novelty; Republicans and Democrats alike were puzzled when he expressed concern that the rich were getting richer and the poor were getting poorer. But the message struck home with voters: he was narrowly elected to the state's highest office in 1892.[34]

Though he served an eventful term, attempting to stop President Cleveland from sending in federal troops to stop the 1894 Pullman Strike (page 120), Altgeld is mainly remembered now for pardoning three surviving men who'd been convicted after the Haymarket affair. His explanation for the pardon is on one of the plaques on his gravestone: "If the defendants had a fair trial, there ought to be no interference; for no punishment under the laws could then be too severe. But they did not have a fair trial. The evidence utterly fails to connect the unknown who threw the bomb with the defendants; and I am convinced that it is my duty to act."[35]

Altgeld knew that issuing the pardon was probably political suicide, and, indeed, the press branded him an "anarchist," "arch-devil," and "murderer." He failed to win a second term as governor, and two years later he received only 15 percent of the vote when he ran for mayor of Chicago.

Following his defeat he went to work as a lawyer in Clarence Darrow's office, though he continued to make political speeches and write books, such as *The Cost of Something for Nothing*, in which he railed that "the very rich of our country are supported by dollars that are tainted by injustice, and they are slowly but surely destroying the people who have them."[36] He died of a cerebral hemorrhage at the age of 54.

■ ■ ■

If you want to take a side trip, walk clear across the Maplewood section toward the Eastern wall, which is sometimes known as the "rubble wall."

Among the single graves, in the third row from the wall, aligned with the part of the road where it begins to curve northwest, is a dark marker, flush to the ground, for a man who liked to be thought of as Chicago's last pioneer.

> The rubble wall is rumored to be built partly from gravestones from the old City Cemetery in Lincoln Park; another rumor has those old gravestones being used to line Lake Willowmere. Some of the stones in the lake, the wall, and the plateau in the Bellevue section (page 109) are certainly disused headstones and coping, but those on which dates can be discerned are far too recent to be from City Cemetery.

Captain George Wellington Streeter: The Pirate King of Chicago

> "I've been a sailor man 25 years. Mr. Fairbank, he said he'd burn me down and I said I'd shoot Mr. Fairbank's whiskers off if he tried it . . . I'm goin' to claim all this made land as a squatter. I'm goin' to carry it up to the Circuit court an' to the App'late Court an' to the Supreme Court . . . and' if Uncle Sam tries to fight 'em off this ain't no land of freedom."
> —G. W. Streeter, 1890, "He Stands by the Ship"

George Wellington "Cap" Streeter (1837–1921) ran his ship, the *Reutan*, aground on the shore of Lake Michigan at the foot of Superior Street during a terrible storm in July 1886. Days later, he began charging people money to dump their garbage around the ship, eventually creating the 186-acre landfill that forms most of the area north of the River and east of Michigan Avenue, which is still known as "Streeterville" today. Citing a map that said the old shoreline was the edge of the city, he claimed the land as his own independent country known as the District of Lake Michigan and then battled with "corrupt capitalists" for his rights as a landowner for more than thirty years.

Or, anyway, that's the way *he* told the story. But there was no storm on the night Streeter claimed to have crashed ashore, and all evidence suggests that he landed the ship where he did (in a spot where land was already being filled in by the city) intending to extort money from homeowners along the shore.

When the money wasn't forthcoming, he forged a few deeds and spent the next several years squatting on the land, selling lots to gullible buyers and defending the turf through trickery, fraud, and occasionally even violence. In 1891 he shot a father and son with duck shot when they tried to build a fence around his boat, and at other times took shots at police officers during land disputes.[37]

Streeter was more of a pirate and rascal than the All-American pioneer he claimed to be, but somehow the city kept a soft spot for the irascible villain. When he died in 1921, his body was laid in state at Grace Methodist church.[38] Today, a life-sized statue stands at Grand Avenue and McClurg Court, in the heart of his old "District," and he was the subject of a 2011 biography, *King of the Gold Coast*, by Wayne Klatt.

■ ■ ■

Double back toward the lake. Among the mausoleums on the right as you head west will be those of manufacturer **Hans Fuchs (1864–1904)**, postmaster **Ernest Kruetgen (1868–1848)**, and **Benjamin Allen (1848–1924)**, a jeweler and banker.

On the shore of the lake stand the Higinbotham plot and the Crane mausoleum. **Harlow Higinbotham (1838–1919)** was the credit manager for, and later a partner in, Marshall Field's company, and was president of the World's Columbian Exposition in 1893. A book collector, Higinbotham was often seen in McClurg's famous "Saints and Sinners Corner" (page 152) and hosted a lecture by Sir Arthur Conan Doyle in his home in 1894.[39] In 1917 he claimed to be the only living person who had been present with Abraham Lincoln when he finally met Ulysses S. Grant in person in March 1864.[40]

A daughter in the plot, **Florence Higinbotham Crane (1871–1949)**, married plumbing supply baron **Richard T Crane, Jr. (1873–1931)** and is interred with him in the Crane mausoleum in the plot adjacent to the Higinbothams. Another daughter, **Alice Patterson (1878–1966)**, married a grandson of Joseph Medill (page 138).

■ ■ ■

Follow the road as it bends along the north shore of the pond. Beyond the Crane mausoleum will be a spacious lakeside plot with a simple rectangular marker for a person once estimated to be the richest woman in the world.

Edith Rockefeller McCormick:
Opera Is a Necessity

"It is time we began to grow within us so that we will be so rich with good, so overflowing that the overflow will pick up our fallen brothers without any detriment to ourselves. This is the turn of the era—1931, 1932, 1933. This is the beginning of the new era."
—Edith Rockefeller McCormick, *Chicago Tribune*

It's difficult not to notice that nearly all of the large memorials in American cemeteries highlight the patriarch of the family; women are often relegated to "wife of" or "daughter of" status. The plot of **Edith Rockefeller McCormick (1872–1932)** is a fairly rare exception; her name is the only one on the front of the stone, and the only others in the plot with her are two young children.

Edith was the daughter of John D. Rockefeller, the founder of Standard Oil and by many metrics the wealthiest person in American history. In 1895, Edith married Harold Fowler McCormick (page 177), merging two of the country's greatest fortunes. The two focused a great deal of efforts, financially and otherwise, to supporting the opera in Chicago; Edith believed that opera was not a luxury, but a "biological necessity,"[41] and often gave large blocks of tickets to settlement houses and other charities.[42] She spent most of the 1910s in Europe, writing poetry and Italian dramas, among other pursuits. She underwent analysis by Carl Jung, then became an analyst herself, with several patients of her own.

But her relationship with Harold was always rocky, and they divorced in 1921 around the time she returned to Chicago.[43] Afterward, in somewhat reduced financial circumstances, she lived the life of a socialite and philanthropist—and turned several heads when she claimed to be the reincarnation of Egyptian royalty. "I married King Tutankha-

Edith Rockefeller McCormick, from a passport photo.

men when I was only 16 years old," she told party guests in 1923. "I was his first wife. Only the other day, while glancing through an illustrated paper, I saw a picture of a chair removed from the king's chamber. Like a flash I recognized the chair. I had sat in it many times."[44]

These stories could be awkward for her guests; Edith Ogden Harrison (page 221) wrote, "Can you imagine the consternation that followed her announcement? But she adhered to her statement and went on to tell of many incidents in her life when she was Queen of Egypt. Now this sounds like an impossible statement to be made by a normal woman, but Mrs. Rockefeller McCormick was so brilliant, so learned, so well-informed that we could only class her as normal."[45]

In the 1920s she was keeping a number of high-priced astrologists and fortune tellers off the streets and out of trouble, but none came close to accurately predicting her death; most told her she'd live to a much older age than she did. By the end of her life she was reported to be nearly broke (the financial crash of the late 1920s cost her greatly), and she was described in one paper as "the loneliest woman in local history."[46] Forced out of her heavily mortgaged mansion, she died of breast cancer in her suite at the Drake Hotel in 1932, just shy of her 60th birthday.[47]

Though initially reported to be buried in the McCormick Wilderness (page 176), her ex-husband Harold had purchased this plot for her upon her death. However, no instructions came to bury her there, and she was interred in a vault beneath the Graceland chapel until 1953, when her surviving son had her buried in the plot.

· · ·

Just north of McCormick is the art deco–styled mausoleum of real estate brokers **John S. Holmes (1863–1931)** and his wife, **Maud G. Holmes (1876–1955)**.

Beside their mausoleum is the elegant round columnated monument to the Lyon and Gary families. **Thomas R. Lyon (1854–1909)** was a lumber merchant and banker. A half-brother of John Lyon (page 237), he was the uncle and legal guardian of Clara Ward, who married a Belgian prince in 1890 when she was only 16. As Princess de Caraman-Chimay, Clara would keep gossip columnists busy for years. She posed for Toulous-Lautrec and G. P. A. Healy and inspired characters in works by Marcel Proust and Cole Porter. For all of this, though, Thomas frequently had to help her financially, especially after she left the prince to marry an itinerant violinist, and once had to go to court to refute a claim that the princess was Cap Streeter's stepdaughter (page 157).[48] She died in Italy in 1916; her own burial place is unknown.

The Lyon-Gary monument

Beside the Lyon monument is a bridge leading to an island which contains a single family plot.

Burnham's Island: Make No Little Plans

"Our city of the future will be without smoke, dust or gases from manufacturing plants, and the air will therefore be pure. The streets will be as clean as our drawing rooms today . . . Railways will be operated electrically, all building operations will be effectually shut in to prevent the escape of dust, and horses will disappear from the streets. Out of all these things will come not only commercial economy but bodily health and spiritual joy."

—Daniel Burnham, *Chicago Record-Herald*

In 1910, architect and city planner **Daniel Burnham (1846–1912)** stood before a crowd at a Town Planning conference in London and gave a speech on "The

Burnham and Root's Rookery Building, Library of Congress.

Cities of the Future." During his stirring oration, he said, "Make no little plans; they have no magic to stir men's blood and probably themselves will not be realized. Make big plans; aim high in hope and work." [49] In 1921 the "maxim" was printed in a biography, and the next year it began appearing everywhere. It's now painted on the walls of several Chicago tourist attractions.

Burnham, sometimes in partnership with John Root (page 114), was the architect responsible for the Rookery, The Fisher Building (page 135), and other Chicago landmarks, not to mention such structures as the Flat Iron Building in New York and much of the design of the 1893 World's Fair and Columbian Exposition, but for much of the 20th century, he was remembered even more as a city planner. His 1909 Plan for Chicago isn't something the city followed to the letter, but many of its suggestions were taken to heart, and it was considered a landmark in the field of city planning.

Among the innovations he pushed for were having a bi-level road around the business district (which was realized by Upper and Lower Wacker Drives) and leaving the lake shore free of development. In his 1910 speech, he said, "Where a town lies near water, keep all the shore for the people. Neighborhood parks are magnificent both from the standpoint of hygiene and the standpoint of moral purity. Those who grow up before the eyes of the community escape those poisonous practices that lurk in secret places."[50]

The island on which he's buried was almost certainly not intended to be used for burials; early photos show it with a gazebo. But a few months after

Burnham died, the cemetery sold the plot to his widow.[51] In total nine people (all cremated) have been interred there, most recently **Catherine Wheeler Burnham (1883–1977)**, a daughter-in-law of Daniel.[52]

Among the other interments are his sons, **Daniel Burnham Jr. (1886–1961)** and **Hubert Burnham (1882–1968)**, who formed the architectural firm of Burnham Brothers, perhaps best remembered for the Carbide and Carbon building, the green and gold art deco skyscraper that adds a glorious splash of color to the Michigan Avenue skyline.

■ ■ ■

Proceeding back across the bridge and continuing west on the road, on the right will be a tumulus vault with stairs leading downward.

Flush toilets were still a novelty in the late 19th century, when **Ludwig Wolff (1836–1911)** became the city's biggest dealer of toilets and plumbing supplies. Many of his old factories and warehouses are still standing around the city, his name still carved in the stone above the door of buildings that are now condos and micro distilleries. Two of his daughters and two of his grandsons were killed in the Iroquois Theatre fire on December 30, 1903. The older daughter and her children are in another cemetery; the younger of the daughters, **Harriet Wolff (1894–1903)**, was initially buried in the Lakeside section of Graceland, but moved to the new vault when it was built in 1905.[53]

To the left is the triangle occupied by the Getty tomb—this is Station Four.

Louis Sullivan's Getty Mausoleum

STATION FOUR

THE GETTY FAMILY TOMB

> "No, I'm not looking forward to nursing or doing hospital
> work (in Europe), but there are a thousand other things
> to do, and my place is there, doing what I can. Art?
> Music? Oh, there is so much suffering to think of now,
> I can't think of anything but people."
> —Alice Getty, "Cook or Move; 'I Moved'"

Around the same time he designed the tomb for lumber baron Martin Ryerson, Louis Sullivan (page 145) was also hired to design a tomb for Ryerson's business partner, **Henry H. Getty (1836–1919)**. The tomb (which records suggest was commissioned in 1889, the year before Henry's wife, **Carrie Eliza Getty (1843–1890)**, died) is the quintessential example of Sullivan's style, with all of the arches, intricate ornamentation, and mixture of floral and geometric details we associate with him. Echoes of the style can be seen throughout the Chicago Auditorium, which Sullivan was working on around the same time.

But the architecture of the tomb, which became a Chicago landmark in 1971, has attracted so much attention that the stories of its occupants have usually been overlooked.

Henry and Carrie owned a house in the fashionable district on South Prairie Avenue, but raised their daughter, **Alice Getty (1868–1946)**, mainly in Muskegon, Michigan. When Carrie died, Henry retired from business to travel the world with Alice. In 1893, Alice wrote to a friend from Egypt, noting that she could see the pyramids from her window.[1] The two Gettys eventually settled in France, where Alice focused on composing music, publishing several songs that brought her a measure of fame, most notably a musical adaption of Paul Verlaine's poem "Pluie."[2] When they returned to Chicago briefly in 1915, the *Tribune* wrote that "Miss Getty is one of the most erudite and accomplished women seen in Chicago in years, and the word 'high bred' in no way compasses the scope of her intellectual activity."[3]

Alice Getty, from a passport photo.

In the first decade of the 20th century, Alice had turned her focus from music to the study of Eastern art and religion, a fascination she shared with her father. Press reports circulated that she'd formally become a Buddhist in 1909,[4] and in 1914 her first book, *The Gods of Northern Buddhism: Their History, Iconography and Progressive Evolution Through the Northern Buddhist Countries* was published by Oxford Press. The press treated her interest in Buddhism as a society girl's whims, but the scholarly book remains a landmark work.

Like her father, Alice was also a collector, both of art and curiosa. Besides her world-class collection of Asian art, much of which is now in major museums, she and her father had a collection of musical instruments (including a lyre made from a human skull, which she presumably realized was made to sell to tourists and not a genuine sacred object),[5] and she amassed a collection of 180 snuff bottles that were auctioned after her death.[6] Though Henry came home to his house in Chicago far more than Alice did, she made occasional stateside trips; in 1915 both were booked to travel on the *RMS Lusitania* for the very passage on which the ship was sunk by a German torpedo. The two canceled at the last minute to join friends on a different ship.[7]

During World War I, Alice worked with blinded soldiers, eventually founding a braille publishing house, La Roue. In 1921 she was awarded Le Prix de Vertu from the French government for her work.[8] She took a fairly hawkish view on American involvement in the war, writing to a friend that Jane Addams' pacifist efforts in Chicago were doing "incalculable damage to the cause of the allies" and would only prolong the war.[9]

After Henry's death in 1920, Alice lived for a time in a temple on Japan's Mount Koya-san, where she studied the esoteric Shingon sect of Buddhism, eventually writing a manuscript for a book on her time there (the only copy of which is thought to have been destroyed when the Nazis raided her villa in Toulon, France).[10] She fled France for New York in 1941, where she spent her last years studying Inanna, the Syrian goddess of love. When she died there in 1946, a death record gave her occupation as "mender."[11]

For all her scholarly erudition, though, her friend and research partner, Florence Waterbury, wrote that Alice would be remembered for combining academic study with "gaiety, society, entertaining and a genius for friendship . . . I saw something of her precise and delicate methods of research, her intense enjoyment in her work, and her enraptured amusement over the vagaries of 'the pure Inanna.' . . . We remember her with admiration and deep regretful love, for we know we shall not look upon her like again."[12]

The tomb was built with room for only the three interments, stacked along the back wall. The interior is not as ornate as the exterior, but a death mask of Henry is mounted above the door to look down on the crypts.

■ ■ ■

From Station four:
For Route 4-A, turn to page 169.
For Route 4-B, turn to page 197.

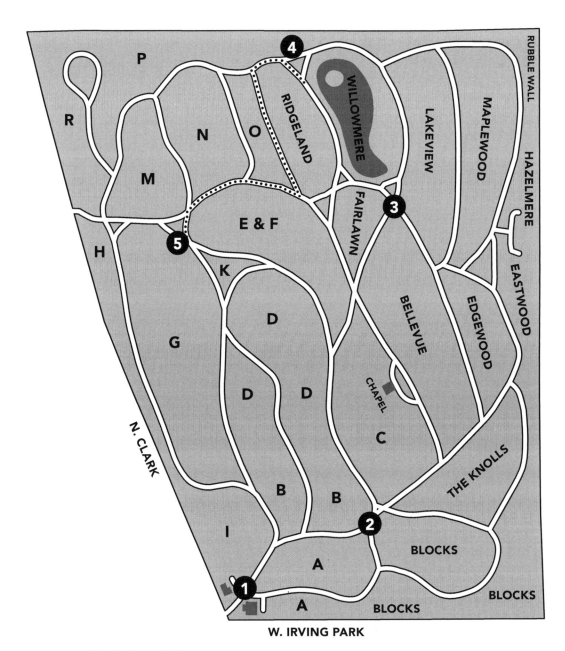

Map for Route 4-A

Proceed west from the Getty tomb and take the first left down Ridgeland Avenue. On the left will be the plot of **Sextus Wilcox (1825–1881)**, a lumber man whose plot includes his wife, opera singer **Sarah Adams Whittemore (1837–1907)**, a great-great-granddaughter of President John Adams. Sextus drowned in a fishing accident.[1] Sarah's D.C. mansion is still standing.

Across the road from Wilcox on the right will be the Potter vault designed by Henry Hobson Richardson in his signature "Richardsonian Romanesque" style.

Margaret Potter: A Dangerous Author

> "There are few large evening affairs in Chicago where some women, at least, do not defy every law of taste and propriety and appear in high-necked gowns with hats."
>
> —Margarter Potter, *The Fire of Spring*

Among the stranger claims of Cap Streeter (page 157), Chicago's squatter king, was that his wife was a niece of steel baron **Orrin W. Potter (1836–1907)**. Potter suggested that Streeter was confused by "some other Potter" in Mrs. Streeter's family tree, which was far more polite than simply saying that Streeter was after his money. The image-conscious Potter was not the kind of man who wanted to be dragged into a fight with a pirate.[2]

Large though the mausoleum is, it contains only the remains of Potter himself, his wife, **Ellen Potter (1842–1904)**, and their daughter **Margaret Horton Potter Black (1881–1911)**, an author who was only a teenager when she set the city on fire with her first novel, *A Social Lion*, in 1899.

A Social Lion told the tale of a drunken clergyman who was secretly the father of a dancer's daughter. The subject matter was shocking enough by 1899 standards, but the flames of controversy were fanned by the fact that the book was a thinly veiled satire of Chicago's high society and bohemian circles,

Henry Hobson Richardson's Potter vault

with a free-spirited character named Joan who was known to be based on Margaret's classmate, Joan Chalmers (whose grandfather was Allan Pinkerton [page 76]). When Mr. Chalmers (page 85) bumped his yacht into Mr. Potter's in Lake Geneva shortly after the book was published, the city whispered that it had been no accident.[3]

Margaret's image-conscious father tried to buy up and destroy every single copy. Naturally, this only made the book *more* desirable, and booksellers on both coasts were soon advertising that they could acquire illicit copies.

Margaret's literary career continued at a rate of more than a novel per year—mostly historical fiction—and a handful of plays through the first decade of the 20th century. Her sister said that Margaret would wake up every day at four to work, write until noon and then study all afternoon.[4] Her arduous research was said to amaze the librarians at the Newberry Library.[5]

She continued to court controversy; in her introduction to a Chicago novel, *The Golden Ladder*, she wrote, "As yet, but a very small number of the real American people feel the deep, throbbing pain of the cancerous growth of national Commercialism. Certainly, few seem to comprehend its menace to the strength and mental power of the next generation . . . but the growth of such a disease is terribly swift."[6] Some libraries publicly announced that the book was immoral and would be banned from their shelves, which, as usual, helped sales.[7]

Margaret and her sister were also avid baseball fans, with a private box at the old West Side park. Legendary Cubs first baseman Frank Chance remembered that they seldom missed a game; team president Charles Murphy said they were "Two of the most loyal fans the team has. It hurts them worse to see the Cubs lose a game than it does me, and that is saying a lot."[8]

Her 1902 marriage to lawyer John D. Black ended in divorce in 1909. During the divorce proceedings she was committed to a sanitarium for a few months after a nervous breakdown, the result either of morphine use, alcohol, or overwork, depending on who you asked.[9] Shortly after her release, she died of an accidental chlorodyne overdose in the Chicago Beach Hotel at the age of 30. Her name faded from the spotlight and doesn't appear anywhere on the tomb, but her books are in the public domain and are now easily available online. Even the banned ones.

. . .

Return to the road and proceed south. Across the road from the large family plot of lawyer **James L. High (1844–1898)** are unassuming markers for businessman **Jedediah Lathrop (1806–1889)** and his wife, **Mariana Bryan Lathrop (1820–1893)**, who was a sister of Graceland founder Thomas Bryan. Also in the plot is Jedediah and Mariana's son, former Graceland president **Bryan Lathrop (1844–1918)**.

Behind the Lathrop markers is the monument to **Christopher D. Manuel (1964–2005)**, which is topped by a statue of a boy playing a flute and features a verse of the jazz standard "For All We Know." Manuel was an anesthesiologist at Rush Medical Center who built a reputation for taking on challenging cases.[10] His mother, **Linda Manuel (1930–2007)**, is buried beside him.

To the south of Manuel is an elegant marker for architect **Stanley Tigerman (1930–2019)**. He told the *Chicago Reader* in 2011 that he knew where his future lay: in Graceland Cemetery. He had arranged to be buried facing his Boardwalk Apartment building on Montrose.[11] The Boardwalk is elegant and modernist, but most of his designs for homes and museums tend to be more playful—even his design for the Holocaust Museum in Skokie includes "light" touches intended as insults to Nazis. His wife, Margaret McMurry, is an architect as well; her name appears on the marker, but she is still living as of this writing.

Nearby is a small monument for **Theodore Tieken (1911–1990)** and **Elizabeth Babson Tieken (1916–2002)**. Theodore was president of the Chicago Historical Society, and Elizabeth was an amateur archaeologist who assisted on digs throughout the middle east; in 1961 she and her daughter were reported to be the first women to enter the cave where the Dead Sea Scrolls were found.[12]

. . .

Returning to the path, you will see a small marker, set perpendicular to the road, featuring a bust of a man with a large book.

Mariano (Matt) "Scorto" Rizzo: Crime and Poetry

> "Supremely confident, Scorto smiled and onward trekked, his failing frame by a surge of bliss sustained, his dimming vision kept bright by a beam from paradise, his hearing sealed from the accustomed sounds of the nether world, harkened to the faint but haunting strains of an idyllic refrain."
> —Matt "Scorto" Rizzo, "The Crucial Hint"

One of the most wonderfully evocative monuments in Graceland, the memorial to **Matt Rizzo (1913–1987)** features a relief sculpture of him surrounded by the names of great authors, in English and in braille, along with the epitaph the poet Keats famously requested for his own headstone: "Here lies one whose name is writ in water." Rizzo's story is even more interesting than the marker would suggest.

When Charlie Rizzo moved into the tiny apartment his estranged father, Matt, called home in 1961, the elder Rizzo had only one bed, and, being blind and living alone, had never bothered to install lights. But sharing a bed wasn't difficult, because Matt seldom slept. After working as an insurance salesman by day, he would be up most of the night drinking coffee, smoking a seemingly endless stream of Lucky Strike cigarettes, and writing philosophical treatises and dense commentaries on literature and "the secret language of the poet." On tape recordings, Matt sounds like an erudite Oxford professor recorded in the days of wax cylinders.

Though Matt always told people he'd been blinded in a hunting accident, he eventually let Charlie in on the truth: in 1935, he and his friends had tried to rob Nicholas Schmidt's liquor store on West Irving Park, and he'd been shot in the face with buckshot. The wound not only kept him from getting away, it cost him his vision.[13] Newly blind, he would spend much of his twenties in prison.

By a strange coincidence, the man who would change his life was one of the most feared criminals of Rizzo's youth.

In 1924, Nathan Leopold and Richard Loeb, two highly educated young men, had been sentenced to life plus ninety-nine years for what was called the "Crime of the Century." Together, they'd murdered 14-year-old Bobby Franks and dumped his body near Wolf Lake, apparently just for the thrill of it. Clarence Darrow's brilliant defense (and their status as minors) kept their sentences to "life plus ninety-nine years" in prison, not the gallows.[14]

Leopold's family was able to pay for him to have a private cell, but after Loeb was murdered by another prisoner, officials decided that Leopold shouldn't be left alone for a while, so young Rizzo became his cell mate. Leopold had studied several languages before his incarceration and had used his time in prison to study several more. He learned braille so he could teach it to Rizzo.[15]

Rizzo always suspected that Leopold was really interested in learning braille mainly so that he could keep reading after lights out, and he may also have been simply padding his resume; he mentioned Rizzo in his autobiography, *Life Plus 99 Years*, and used the story of teaching a blind kid to read again in his parole hearings.[16]

But whatever Leopold's real motive was, the impact on Rizzo was profound. He became a voracious reader, devouring the classics, pontificating on the "secret language of the poet," and eventually writing lengthy works of his own, many featuring a character named "Scorto" who served as his personal avatar. He had dropped out of school in eighth grade, but something he read in those ancient tomes in prison awakened something inside of him. His son, Charlie, told NPR that his father's work was "an attempt to describe the revelation that so many philosophers and writers attempted to describe in their own, and the work was born of his own revelation."[17]

Several excerpts of Rizzo's writings were included in *The Hunting Accident: A True Story of Crime and Poetry*, a graphic novel about his life by David L. Carlson and Landis Blair. His papers are archived at the Newberry Library.

• • •

Proceeding south, there will be a boulder from Waupaca, Wisconsin[18] (the same place where the granite from the Chapel was quarried)[19] marked as the resting place of **Henry Field (1841–1890)**, and his infant daughter, **Gladys Field (1888)**. The Field and Lathrop (page 171) plots were originally connected; Henry was married to J. H. and Mariana Lathrop's daughter, Florence (after his death she remarried and was buried in Washington, D.C.).

South of the boulder is a sculpture of a seated figure before a reflecting pool. The sculpture, *Memory*, is by Daniel Chester French, who also sculpted the Lincoln Memorial in Washington D.C., and the Statue of the Republic in Chicago. It marks the family plot of Henry Field's brother, Marshall.

The Field Plot

"The customer is always right."
—Often attributed to Marshall Field. Lloyd Wendt and
Herman Kogan, *Give the Lady What She Wants!*

With his famous department store, **Marshall Field (1804–1906)** became the "merchant prince" of Chicago and a fixture in gilded-age society.[20]

His first wife, **Nanny Douglas Field (1840–1896)**, was well loved in their South Prairie Avenue neighborhood; Grace Meeker (page 112) described her as "a fairy godmother to all the children in the neighborhood."[21]

The Fields were generally quiet by society standards (Marshall himself was notoriously reserved), but when they threw parties, they went all out: in 1886, in honor of the 17th birthday of **Marshall Field Jr.** (1868–1905), they hosted a "Mikado Ball" that Chicagoans talked about for years. Eastern papers said at the time that the decorations alone cost $10,000, and years later it was widely said that the overall expenses came to $75,000.[22] These reports may have been adjusting for inflation; contemporary local reports claimed that "The real expense was in point of fact five thousand! And quite enough is that sum, too, for a single party."[23]

This *was* still quite a lot—well more than a decade's salary to Field's lower-level store employees, and nearly 50 years' pay for the cash boys, who made $2 per week.[24] Field would justify his low wages by claiming that if his employees only saved 15 cents per week, in a few years they would have saved thousands of dollars. (Fifteen cents per week would not add up to two thousand dollars for over 250 years.)

Marshall's second wife, **Delia Spencer Field (1853–1937)**, had been a Prairie Avenue neighbor. Marshall and Delia reportedly fell for each other when both were still married to other people—in some accounts, their affair began twenty years before Nanny Field's death in 1896. It was an open secret in the Prairie Avenue society scene. Delia's husband, Arthur Caton, was even said to approve. Grace Murray Meeker (page 112) told her son that the affair was well known, but "We didn't find it odd; we never thought about it at all."[25] Rather than pursuing a complicated divorce, Marshall and Delia waited until both of their spouses had died to hold their own semi-private wedding in England in 1905.[26]

Months after the wedding, Field Jr. was found bleeding from a gunshot wound in his own Prairie Avenue mansion, a few doors down from his father's. Officially, the story was that he'd shot himself accidentally while cleaning a pistol, and the elder Field made it known that any paper who suggested otherwise would lose his advertising. William Randolph Hearst's *Chicago Evening American*, however, already didn't get any advertising from Field, and were hardly shy about alluding to the persistent rumors that he'd really been shot at The Everleigh Club, which was only a few blocks away, or that it had been a suicide. He died in the hospital days later.[27]

The shock likely hastened the elder Field's own death. On New Year's day, barely a month after his son was buried, Field was playing golf with Robert Todd Lincoln when he became ill; the sickness developed into pneumonia and proved fatal.[28] Delia remained in the Field Mansion for some years and then moved to D.C. where she leased a house known as the Pink Palace, where her parties became the stuff of legend.[29]

Field Jr.'s wife, **Albertine Huck Field Drummond (1872–1915)**, was the daughter of brewer Louis Huck (page 247) and later married Maldwin Drummond, a British captain. Her 1909 decision to sell the Field Jr. Mansion could be considered a milestone in the decline of the old Millionaire's Row on Prairie Avenue (though, against all odds, the Field Jr. Mansion survives, now converted into townhouses).

Albertine's new house in England became a home for wounded soldiers when World War I broke out, but in the midst of the conflict, September 1915, she took ill and died; she was buried in the Field plot a few months later.[30]

> "I happen to have been left a great deal of money. If I can't make myself worthy of three square meals a day, I don't deserve them."
> —Marshall Field III, *New York Daily News*

After his father and grandfather died, papers began referring to **Marshall Field III (1893–1956)** as "the most interesting boy in the world,"[31] as the twelve-year-old was now heir to one of the world's largest fortunes. Field III was raised primarily in England and then served in World War I as a young adult. His younger brother, Henry, lived a bit of a wilder life before dying in 1917; he is buried in Virginia.

Marshall III lived the "Great Gatsby" lifestyle in Long Island while working as an investment banker during the 1920s, but later launched campaigns to help refugee children in the 1940s and founded the *Chicago Sun* newspaper in 1941.[32] In part of the ever-evolving battle between newspapers run by Chicago's wealthy families, and the changing politics of their generations, Field III intended the paper to be a liberal counterpart to the *Tribune*, then under the ownership of the archconservative Colonel Robert McCormick. Previously, Field III had bought *PM*, a New York paper so devoted to independent journalism that it refused to take advertising.[33]

When Field III died in 1956, the *New York Times* said he "was a millionaire like none other, who devoted himself to liberal causes and a philanthropist who aided race relations."[34] His son, **Marshall IV (1916–1965)**, took over the ownership of the *Sun* (by then the *Sun-Times*) and then bought the *Chicago Daily News* in 1959. His own son, Ted Field, sold his stake in the papers to become a film producer, a career that began with the film *Revenge of the Nerds*.

A later interment in the plot was **Ruth Pruyn Field (1908–1994)**, the widow of Marshall III, who worked alongside him in founding *PM* and the *Sun*. Outliving her husband by nearly forty years, she spent most of her later life running the Field Foundation, which she used as a charity focused on causes related to children's welfare and racial justice.[35]

■ ■ ■

Beyond the Field plot is a large expanse, extending clear through to the next road. These plots are for Cyrus McCormick and his descendants.

The McCormick Wilderness

"My friends are without a preacher, unable to support the present abolitionist [Rev.] Stuart of the North Church."
—Letter from Cyrus McCormick to W. S. Plumer, 1864

Though inventor Robert McCormick worked for years to develop a mechanical reaper that would automate the harvesting of crops, the first successful model was marketed by his son, **Cyrus McCormick (1808–1884)**, with the help of Jo Anderson, a man the family enslaved. The invention greatly increased the amount of grain that could be harvested on any given farm, and early biographies proclaimed that McCormick had delivered the world from famine. Some of this was hyperbole (and ignored the contributions of others who'd invented similar devices that simply didn't sell as well), but it's absolutely true that mechanical reapers revolutionized agriculture, and, in turn, much of 19th-century society.

McCormick had little luck with the invention at first—labor-saving devices were hard to sell in Virginia, where labor was considered a job for enslaved people. Upon moving the family to Illinois, though, the invention took off, and McCormick established one of Chicago's largest fortunes.

It would later be claimed—particularly by the McCormick company[36]—that McCormick's reaper won the war for the Union by freeing up farm laborers to fight, but that was somewhat ironic: McCormick wasn't in favor of secession but also didn't really want the South to lose. In 1860 he'd purchased the *Chicago Herald* and used it to spread frothing-at-the-mouth white supremacist sentiment written by his political editor, E. W. McComas. Officially his European trip in the early 1860s was to promote his business overseas, but his brother, William (page 244), wrote that he really wanted "to flee away from this land of blood and death, where we are downtrodden by abolitionism."[37] He later exchanged letters with Robert E. Lee.[38]

Cyrus McCormick, Library of Congress.

He remained friendly with Jo Anderson, staying in touch with him for the rest of his life, and even buying him a house in 1869.[39] According to the only interview Anderson ever gave, the two had grown up together, and as teenagers would sneak out to see their respective girlfriends together (though this may have just been Anderson telling people what he thought they wanted to hear; certainly no biographer has believed that teenaged Cyrus ever had a girlfriend to visit).[40]

Cyrus died in 1884. In the large plot with him is his wife, **Nettie Fowler McCormick (1835–1923)**, who was 21 when she married him (he was 47) and she outlived him by nearly 40 years, taking a major role in managing the business after his death. One of their sons, Stanley, is buried alongside his wife, Katharine Dexter McCormick, in her family's plot (page 66). Two of their other children are buried in this portion of the plot; one is a daughter, **Mary Virginia McCormick (1861–1941)**, who, like Stanley, spent most of her life in confinement due to what would likely now be diagnosed as schizophrenia.[41]

Their other child in this section of the plot, **Harold Fowler McCormick (1872–1941)**, was the first husband of Edith Rockefeller McCormick (page 159). In 1921 he and Edith were estimated to have donated five million dollars to the Chicago Grand Opera.[42] By that time, though, Harold had

Harold and Ganna, Library of Congress.

become romantically involved with Ganna Walska, an opera singer of questionable talent; his promotion of her career is presumed to have been an inspiration for the film *Citizen Kane*. Harold didn't go so far as to build her an opera house, but he hyped Ganna's 1920 Chicago debut tremendously, even after she pulled out of the performance at the last minute and fled the city. McCormick said "the opera wasn't ready, that's all," but rumors swirled that Walska simply wasn't a very good singer, and none of the teachers and treatments Harold paid for could make her one.[43]

Harold and Ganna divorced their respective spouses and married each other in the early 1920s, but Ganna spent most of their nine-year marriage in Paris while Harold tended to the family business in Chicago. He continued to promote Ganna's opera career, and she performed throughout the 1920s to mediocre reviews. The two divorced in 1931; Harold died a decade later after a long illness.

> "Why should I be able to spend this afternoon this way, or so many as I please, in touch with any thought I please from all over the world? Not by an achievement of my own. Why should I therefore have the privilege of doing and having whatever I please, while so many who could do more than I, could make use of it?"
> —Anita McCormick Blaine, Gilbert A. Harrison, *A Timeless Affair:*

If you proceed through the "wilderness" to the other side of the bushes, there are more small markers. A few are in front of the unadorned boulder that functions as the only large monument for the family, but most are in the large lot just south of the boulder.

Arthur Meeker Jr. (page 112) wrote that **Anita McCormick Blaine (1866–1954)** "was assuredly not, to put it mildly, quite like most people." A daughter of Cyrus and Nettie, Anita was widowed at 26 and devoted herself to politics, lending her name and money to fights for the eight-hour work day, improving public education, the League of Nations, civil rights, and other causes that probably made her father roll around in his section of the wilderness. Her public musings that as a rich woman she should be paying higher taxes, led then-governor Theodore Roosevelt to say, "I wish we had more people in this country like Mrs. Emmons Blaine."[44] She married **Emmons Blaine (1857–1892)**, son of presidential candidate James Blaine, in 1889. Emmons lived only three years after the wedding before dying of intestinal issues; their son **Emmons Blaine Jr. (1890–1918)** died in the influenza pandemic of 1918.

Anita's support for labor rights was somewhat surprising, not just due to her being the daughter of one of the city's most prominent and conservative industrialists but given that she was the brother of **Cyrus Hall McCormick Jr. (1858–1936)**, who is buried just north of Anita in the other portion of the "wilderness." When Cyrus Jr. took over his father's company, he was willing to shut the plant down rather than agree to an eight-hour workday. When the workers struck in 1886, Cyrus Jr. sent in Pinkerton guards, who shot several workers, leading to uprisings and rallies that included the famous Haymarket affair (see the John Altgeld entry, page 155).

Anita was the subject of a 1979 biography, *A Timeless Affair* by **Gilbert A. Harrison (1915–2008)**, who is buried near her. The owner of the magazine *The New Republic*, Harrison was married to Anita's granddaughter, public education advocate **Anna Blaine Harrison (1918–1977)**.[45]

■ ■ ■

Return back across the "wilderness" and head south down the road. Proceeding past the plot for lumber dealer **Jesse Spalding (1828–1904)**, go to the fork in the road and take a right. Nearby will be the **C. W. Sanford (1835–1871)** monument, the corners of which are marked by statues, three of which are presently headless. Sanford, like his Graceland neighbor Kranz (page 88), was a candy maker, at one time owning the largest candy factory west of New York.[46]

Just to the right of Sanford is the Hoge monument, a tall obelisk surrounded by individual markers.

Jane Hoge

"On the road to Alexandria, we passed Arlington, the former dwelling place of the rebel General Lee; the deluded man. . . . The proud old manor-house had been made the headquarters of the Union army and the freedmen alternately, and its lawns the burial place of the nation's dead—a signal rebuke of inexcusable treachery. The point of special interest to us in Alexandria was the house in which Col. Ellsworth was murdered."

—Jane Hoge, *The Boys in Blue*

In the early spring of 1865, **Jane Hoge (1811–1890)** met with Abraham Lincoln. She had been working to relieve the sufferings of the Civil War soldiers, including taking several trips to the front lines. To raise money for veterans, Graceland founder Thomas Bryan was planning a great Sanitary Fair that summer. Hoge asked Lincoln to attend, and he said that he would, if at all possible. With the Civil War clearly winding down, taking a trip back to his home state may have seemed awfully appealing to the president. By the time the fair began, though, Lincoln had been murdered, and the war was over. The fair became something of a victory lap for the Union, displaying relics and featuring speeches from Grant and Sherman.[47]

Jane Hoge

Stories of Hoge can be found in her friend Mary Livermore's book *My Story of the War* and her own exhaustive war memoir, *The Boys in Blue*. In the introduction, Rev. Thomas Eddy (page 215) wrote, "Mrs. Hoge is one of those women called into active duty by the war whose memory will remain."[48]

When reformer Frances Willard called Chicago "a paradise of exceptional women" in 1890, she was specifically talking about Hoge. "(Jane) could have commanded armies," Willard wrote. "If a man had wrought for the Union as Mrs. Hoge did, his name would have become illustrious."[49]

A bit behind Sanford and Hoge was the original burial place of one of Chicago's most noted early eccentrics, Seth Paine, who is now in an unmarked spot elsewhere in the cemetery.

Seth Paine: The Chicago Wizard

"I would not even admit a live hog to my parlor, much
  less a dead one to my stomach."
  —Seth Paine, "A Western Character"

A provincial newspaper once called **Seth Paine (c1816–1872)** "a queer chicken."[50] Arriving in town as a teenager in 1834, the Vermont-born Paine first made a name for himself as a vocal abolitionist, but he was mostly remembered for his eccentricities. Reminiscing on his career, the *Tribune* wrote that "All the 'isms' stuck to him as naturally as burrs to a sheep's back."[51] Besides abolitionism, he advocated feminism, vegetarianism, spiritualism, and more.

Perhaps his most famous venture in his lifetime was the Bank of Chicago, which he opened in the early 1850s. Spiritualism—the practice of speaking to the dead via séances and mediums—was sweeping the nation at the time, and Paine operated the bank on Spiritualist principles, employing a medium to consult the spirits of George Washington and Alexander Hamilton on banking matters. In some accounts, Paine began dressing robes and growing a long beard. He must have been quite a sight—a sort of abolitionist wizard wandering the streets of Chicago.[52]

A few times he tried moving out of the city, once complaining that there were too many hogs in town (he was an ardent vegetarian), but he always came back. In his various sojourns, he helped found the suburb of Lake Zurich, where there is still an elementary school named after him. There, he built a "Stable of Humanity," a sort of early homeless shelter or commune; hidden rooms uncovered at the site in 1941 are sometimes said to have been used to hide fugitive slaves on their way to Canada (at the time of his death several obituaries said he was one of the city's most effective Underground Railroad operatives).[53] Though his activities with the Railroad aren't well documented, one colleague wrote that Paine was one of its "leading spirits."[54]

During the war, he joined Pinkerton's Secret Service in the Virginia Peninsula, and was noted for efforts to "clean out" the Washington, D.C. jails by helping the "contraband slaves" who were languishing there escape—possibly with the help of fellow Pinkerton agent Kate Warn (page 79), who was

A group of Pinkerton secret service agents at Antietam; Paine is likely the man on the far right. Library of Congress.

known to visit the jail regularly.[55] Lincoln freed "contrabands" in the jail in 1862; some credit Paine with helping to make it happen.[56]

After the war Paine devoted all of his personal fortune and energy to building and managing a Woman's Home at Jackson and Halsted (he had long been a vocal advocate for womens' rights). He died at the Woman's Home of tuberculosis in 1872 and was initially buried in this area of the cemetery. (Gurdon Hubbard [page 230] was a pallbearer.)[57]

But it appears that no one owned the plot at the time, and when someone bought it in 1880, Paine was moved to another unclaimed spot in the section, and then moved again in 1890. He is now in a small unmarked space in section R along the north wall, near the northwest corner of the cemetery, to the right of the small red "Hoerlle" marker. Cemetery records spell his name as "Payne."[58]

. . .

In the middle of the section, you'll see a row of mausoleums set into a hillside.

The Hillside Vaults

The Hillside Vaults

"There are only two animals that do not make that mistake [of incorrect nose-blowing]. One is the horse and the other is the hobo. In neither case does the act begin with injurious back pressure nor end with the ostentatious musical fanfare."

—Dr. Henry Byford, in Evans, "How to Keep Well"

The vaults set into the hill in Section E were some of the first mausoleums in the cemetery, and presumably part of a very early landscape design. The one on the far right was sold to noted silversmith **Augustus F. Otto (1799–1890)** in 1861.

The vault on the far left is faded, but the name above the door was once "Dunham." The occupants of the vault, the family of banker and merchant **John H. Dunham (1817–1893)**, were removed and buried in the Lakeside section in 1906.

In the middle of the hillside vaults is the family tomb of **Dr. William Heath Byford (1817–1890)** who, along with Dr. Mary Harris Thompson, founded the Women's Hospital Medical College in 1870. Among the several others in the vault are his son **Dr. Henry Byford (1853–1938)** who sometimes made the news for his efforts to promote proper nose-blowing technique—he insisted that one should use what he referred to as "hobo style." "[Hobos] blow blasts through the nose like horses," he explained, "but their technique consists of pressing on one nostril, aiming the other at the rise of the road and turning on the power." This, he insisted, was the healthiest way to do it.[59] It is now more commonly known as "farmer style."

At some point the Byford vault was combined with the one to its right, so the lone door for the two middle vaults denotes it as the resting place of **Horace White (1834–1916)**. White's section of the crypt contains around ten people, mostly children who died in infancy.

Horace White

> "I happened to be on the platform with Mr. Lincoln, as a reporter, when this speech was delivered. . . . [H]e said to me that he had been urged by his friends in Springfield not to use the words 'this government cannot endure permanently half slave and half free,' because the phrase would . . . probably cause his defeat in the election, but that his mind was made up and he was determined to use those very words, because they were true and because the time had come to say so."
> —Horace White, 1914 address on Lincoln-Douglas debates

White came to Chicago at 19 and served as assistant editor of the *Chicago Evening Journal*. Raised by a religious father who disapproved of dancing and card-playing, he'd gone through a rebellious phase at Beloit college, eventually getting expelled for gambling. The betting spirit never quite left him, and he wasn't above using his position as a journalist to pump up the value of lands he'd invested in—at a salary of five dollars a week, which was only paid at all when the *Journal* could manage it, he couldn't afford *not* to have a lucrative side hustle or two.[60]

Horace was still in his early 20s when violence erupted in the Kansas territory over whether it would enter the Union as a slave state or a free state, and 22-year-old White became secretary of the National Kansas Committee, which sent aid and arms to antislavery forces there.[61] Later, when he was summoned to testify before the committee investigating John Brown's raid at Harper's Ferry, White testified that he had met Brown three times as secretary of the committee, and admitted they'd sent him some weapons for use in Kansas.[62]

White traveled with Lincoln during his famous 1858 debates with Senator Douglas, later claiming that he'd pushed Lincoln to start "training for the presidency." He remembered nights of traveling with the future president, sharing rooms in country inns and taverns, listening to him telling jokes and stories for hours. But for all of Lincoln's humor, White noted, "In all my journeyings with him I never heard any person call

Horace White, Library of Congress.

him 'Abe,' not even his partner, Herndon. There was an impalpable garment of dignity about him which forbade such familiarity."[63]

White served as the *Tribune*'s Washington correspondent during the Civil War. His first letter, written on Thanksgiving 1861, lamented the fact that there were, at the moment, a large number of enslaved people languishing in prison in Washington. "Why these forsaken creatures are held in the city dungeon I do not know," he wrote. "There is a just God, before whom slavery stands as a stupendous crime. Does anyone say slavery is not the cause, the very *sole* cause, of the war? Such a person is either a secessionist at heart, and would exult in his country's downfall, or he is a lunatic and ought to be furnished at once with the conveniences which society provides for that class of unfortunates. Why should not Congress bestir itself once more about the slavery question, and make an end of it?"[64]

After the war White served as editor in chief of the *Tribune* for nearly a decade. In later life he was an editor for the *New York Evening Post*, as well as a noted financial expert, and gave speeches on his time with Lincoln. When he died in 1916, President Wilson called it "a loss which the whole country must feel."[65]

■ ■ ■

A bit south of the vaults, behind the Finney marker, find a square marker for **Harriet Hubbard Ayer (1852–1903)**, a journalist, activist, and founder of a cosmetic empire.

Harriet, as painted by Eastman Johnson, National Gallery of Art.

Harriet's daughter, **Gertrude Ayer (1871),** lived for two months after the Great Chicago Fire, and was said to have died due to the smoke she inhaled. Harriet, who had been prescribed morphine during her baby's illness, traveled to Paris to mourn, and there she became interested in fashion.

Returning to the United States, Harriet moved to New York, where she founded a cosmetics company. Following a series of scandals and divorces, she was ordered to be institutionalized and spoke out about conditions in asylums after escaping. Her activisim attracted the notice of the *New York World*, which hired her as a beauty columnist, where she gave advice on dieting, exercise, etiquette, relationships, and more. In the 1950s, there was even a line of dolls named for her. Though pioneering in a way, claims such as "good women are happier and better if they keep their good looks"[66] can seem, at best, old-fashioned today. A recent biography says, "Although (Harriet) did not belong to the emergent feminist movements of her day, she epitomized the independent woman."[67]

The small marker next to Harriet's, which bears no name, is for Gertrude.

■ ■ ■

Moving back to the road and just a bit further west, you'll pass the enormous Allerton monument on the right, marking the grave of **Samuel Allerton (1828–1918),** one of the founders of the Union Stockyards. With him are his wives **Pamilla Allerton (1840–1880)** and **Agnes Allerton (1858–1924)**, who also happened to be sisters (Samuel married Agnes after Pamilla's death).[68]

The Harris-Goodall monument

Gossip columnist Madame X (page 110) called Samuel and Pamela's son, Robert, Chicago's most eligible bachelor. Robert (1873–1967) remained single but lived for years with a man named John Gregg and legally adopted him in 1959. Though the exact nature of their relationship is hard to gauge today, they're sometimes referred to as the first legally recognized same-sex couple. Though ownership of the plot passed to Robert, and then to John, they have no markers; their ashes were scattered in Hawaii.[69]

A bit behind the Allerton plot is a smaller stone marker with an urn in the front, a headstone for **Charles W. Harris (1918–1989)** and **Jack G. Goodall (1922–1987)**, which features a quote from the opera *Tosca*. Translated, it reads, "I lived for art, I loved for love, I never hurt a living soul!" Goodall worked for the Lyric Opera for 33 years; a performance of *Tosca* was given in his honor after his death.[70] He and Harris were longtime partners; it may be the earliest shared marker for a same-sex couple in the cemetery.

■ ■ ■

Head back to the path and move to the west past Allerton. On the right, in the corner of section N, you'll see a large obelisk for the families of railroad contractors **Royal Hill (1821–1881)** and **John McKechney (1845–1915)**, whose families were united by the marriage of their children.

Nearby is a large marker for **Judge Thomas Drummond (1809–1890)** and his daughter, **Mary Drummond (1846–1926)**, who wrote a charming piece about life in 19th-century Chicago for Caroline Kirkland's *Chicago Yesterdays*. In it she quoted her father's reminiscences of Chicago in the 1830s, when the inhabitants were "shockingly profane (but) great card players."[71] She remembered with amusement that she loved a hat with pink ribbons worn by Juliette Kinzie (page 49) so much as a little girl that "I tried to induce my mother, a much younger woman, not yet forty, to wear pink ribbons!"[72] She also recalled Abraham Lincoln visiting their house, and her father inducing the tall president-elect to walk under the chandelier to see if his head would touch it. She did not specify whether or not he *did*, making it one of those mysteries we'll probably never solve. As a lawyer, Lincoln had represented clients before Judge Drummond in more than twenty cases.

In the shadow of the 1860 election, three men from Ottawa, IL, were tried before Judge Drummond for helping Jim Gray, an enslaved man, escape. Though E. C. Larned (page 192) and Isaac Newton Arnold (page 190) made an impassioned defense, the jury returned a guilty verdict. Drummond, taking the men's side personally, gave them extremely short sentences and allowed one, John Hossack, to make a long speech that was reprinted in the papers.[73] L. C. P. Freer (page 59) arranged to pay the mens' fines, and Philo Carpenter (page 30) had already seen to it that Gray made his escape to Canada.

■ ■ ■

Just behind the McKechney obelisk is a small gray stone, flush with the ground, for one of the city's most notable 20th-century lawyers

Jewel Lafontant-Mankarious: The Jewel of Chicago

> "I always felt that being a lawyer was the greatest thing you could be."
> —Jewel Lafontant-Mankarious, "Chicago Voices"

A republican activist and lawyer, **Jewel Lafontant-Mankarious (1922–1997)**[74] once recalled that her father didn't believe she should date until she was 21. He told her, "There will be days when you will be invited everywhere." She replied, "But, Dad, there won't be another senior prom!"[75]

Her father was certainly right that one day she'd be wanted everywhere:

Lafontant-Mankarious with President and Mrs. Ford at the White House. National Archives 30805899.

she became one of the most prominent lawyers in the United States. She was considered as a nominee to the Supreme Court by President Nixon, possibly the first Black woman even to make the shortlist. Under President George H. W. Bush she served as "ambassador at large" and coordinator of refugee affairs.

After earning a degree in political science at Oberlin, Lafontant-Mankarious earned a law degree at the University of Chicago. While there, she helped found CORE (Congress of Racial Equality) and organized sit-ins, which, she pointed out later, were "years before Martin Luther King Jr.'s sit-ins."[76]

Later, she served on 17 corporate boards; on most she was the only woman *and* the only person of color. She was known as a "bridge builder" who won respect from both sides of the political aisle; though she was a republican, speakers at her funeral included prominent democrats such as Jesse Jackson and Valerie Jarrett.[77]

■ ■ ■

Just beyond Lafontant is a small, white rusticated obelisk, marking the center of the Arnold family plot.

Isaac Newton Arnold: The Endgame of the Fight against Slavery

"Nov 30, 1883. My birthday; seventy years old. Three-score and ten! Death must be at no great distance. I wish to live only so long as I may be, to some extent, useful, and not when I shall be a burden. May my remaining days be useful and innocent."
—Journal of I. N. Arnold

Among the many things that could be called a crowning achievement in the career of **Isaac Newton Arnold (1815–1884)**, perhaps the most notable was something that failed: Arnold was the first congressman to introduce a resolution to outlaw slavery completely.[78]

Isaac Newton Arnold came to Chicago at 20 and formed a law practice with Mahlon D. Ogden (page 228). When Ogden's brother, William, became the city's first mayor in 1837, 21-year-old Arnold became the city clerk. He left office early to focus on his growing law business, but politics would continue to call him throughout his life.[79] In 1856 he was part of the "Kansas Committee" that sent armed soldiers to Kansas to fight against the "border ruffians" who were attempting to make the territory a slave state by force.[80]

He was elected to congress in 1860, part of the same electoral wave that put Lincoln in the White House. There, he introduced the bill that outlawed slavery in new territories in 1862, passed a bill making foreign-born soldiers citizens upon their discharge,[81] and then introduced his famous bill that would have outlawed slavery outright in January 1864. The bill was a few months ahead of its time and didn't pass, but it helped lay groundwork for the 13th amendment the following year.[82]

After leaving office, Arnold wrote one of the first major biographies of Lincoln, peppering it with previously unknown personal anecdotes from his time in office. Toward the end of his life, he was president of the Chicago Historical Society. He was best remembered for his work with Lincoln and slavery, but obituaries pointed out that his work in city planning in the 1840s had been a major factor in the transformation of the city from a mudhole into a metropolis.[83]

Many of Arnold's family members were moved to the plot in 1873. It's very unusual for any letters or notes about removals to survive, but Arnold recorded the event in his diary with this heart-rending entry:

"April 18, 1873—Today attended the sad removal of the remains of some of my family, who were interred in the city cemetery: **Catherine E. Arnold**, died Oct 20, 1839, aged twenty-four years; died at the old Lake

Isaac Newton Arnold, Abraham Lincoln Presidential Library.

House in Chicago. Our son, **Edward Mason Arnold**, died March 1844, at my old house, northeast corner of Ontario and Dearborn streets, aged four years and seven months. **George Arnold**, my son by my present wife, died 1845, aged seven months. **Frances Isabella Arnold**, died 1846, aged five months. **Lizzie Mason Arnold**, died 1854, aged one month. It was sad to disturb their repose, but they will sleep as placidly in Graceland; alas, can they not whisper one word of the hereafter? Where are they? Do they know anything of us? Are they conscious that they are not forgotten? As one stands by the grave, how unavoidable the wish that we had done more to make them happy."[84]

Barely a week after the removals, Arnold's teenage son, **Arthur M. Arnold (1858–1873)**, drowned in the Rock River while testing a sailboat he'd built. Isaac and Arthur were only still in Illinois at the time because the *RMS Atlantic*, a White Star Line ocean liner they'd planned to take to Europe, had sunk earlier that month while en route to North America from Liverpool.[85]

. . .

Right behind the Arnold plot is a set of stones for the Larned family; E. C. Larned was Arnold's law partner.

E. C. Larned: Crusading Lawyer

"[South Carolina] was the pestilent nest in which the brood of rattlesnakes had been hatched. There, where this foul wickedness was conceived and brought forth, let the hand of swift, sure and terrible retribution fall heaviest. Let Charleston be blotted out; let the ground be plowed over the place where the false and traitorous city once stood."

—E. C. Larned, "Mr. Larned's Letter"

Lawyer **Edwin Channing Larned (1820–1884)** worked on several cases defending escaping enslaved people and those who assisted them. He was particularly noted for helping George Manierre in his defense of Moses Johnson (page 14), and an 1850 speech he gave against the Fugitive Slave Law was published and studied for years.[86] An 1860 speech on the same subject during the Hossack trial (page 188) was similarly memorable.[87] [88]

In Spring, 1861, Larned was appointed U.S. District Attorney by the newly elected Lincoln, and promptly used his authority to dismiss pending charges against people in fugitive slave cases.[89] He was visiting Washington when Col. Ellsworth became the first Union casualty (see George Fergus' entry, page 17), and was one of the men who accompanied Ellsworth's body to his parents' home in upstate New York.[90]

At the time, he suggested an immediate show of force to show "the full power of the North;" a letter he wrote to the *Tribune* (quoted earlier) seems almost shocking in its brutality today, but captures the rage and grief felt in the Union in the first months of the war, following the fall of Fort Sumter and the murder of Ellsworth.[91]

Following the war, Larned resumed his law practice, worked in the Chicago Relief and Aid Society after the Great Fire of 1871, and defended the morality of theaters.

Among those in the plot with E. C. are his wife, **Ann Frances Larned (1820–1899)**, his mother **Lucinda Larned (1787–1850)**, and a cenotaph for a grandson, **Edwin C. Larned (1887–1918)**, who was killed in World War I and buried in France.[92]

■ ■ ■

Go to the row of tombstones behind Larned's own, which is the plot of his brother-in-law, steel magnate **Joseph T. Ryerson (1812–1833)**, who married E. C.'s sister, **Ellen Larned Ryerson (1827–1881)**, and worked with E. C. in plans to make bread more affordable to the poor.[93] Next to them are cenotaphs for two children not buried here.

E. C. Larned

Arthur Larned Ryerson: Lost on the SS *Titanic*

"In what smug, complacent security we face each day— those of us who are wrapped and cradled in all the comforts of safeguards of our twentieth-century civilization! Then comes such a disaster as that of the *Titanic* and the foundations of our faith in our imperturbable security totter."

—Madame X (Caroline Kirkland), *Chicago Tribune*, 1912

In teenage Julia Newberry's diary from 1869 (page 19), she wrote that a couple of the Larned boys were "snips," but that she liked their cousin, **Arthur Ryerson (1851–1912)**, well enough. From her, this was high praise.[94]

Arthur served as president of St. Luke's Hospital before moving his family to Philadelphia early in the 20th century. He and his wife, Emily, were in Europe when they got word that their adult son had died in a Pennsylvania car accident and booked passage to the funeral on the fastest ship available: *Titanic*.

When word came that the ship was sinking, Arthur calmly helped his three children into their life vests and then brought them up to the deck, where his wife heard him joking with other passengers about the fact that the band was still playing. When the family began to board the life boats, Arthur stayed behind, following the "women and children first" maxim. A guard tried to stop his son from boarding, but Arthur said, "Of course that boy can go with his mother; he's only thirteen,"[95] a scene later dramatized in the film *A Night to Remember*. The 1997 *Titanic* film had Leonardo DiCaprio's character "borrowing" A. L. Ryerson's coat.

Emily Ryerson and the children survived the famous shipwreck (Emily remarried and is buried elsewhere). Arthur's body was not recovered, but his Chicago relatives put this cenotaph for him in the family plot, next to one for his sister **Eleanor Ryerson (1858–1917)**, who moved to Boston and lived quietly with a woman named Ann Whitman from about 1896 until her death, at which time she was buried in Massachusetts.[96]

Another, more mysterious *Titanic* cenotaph is in the Bellevue section (page 113).

■ ■ ■

Return to the route, heading west. On the left, behind the Canda-Humphries-Payson marker, is a red marker for the Goettler family.

Lt. Harold Goettler and the Lost Battalion

> "When this war is ended and peace has once more descended on the land, the Historical society will have to put an addition to the building to house the records of what Chicago is doing for this great struggle."
> —Madame X (Caroline Kirkland), "Lent Is Coming to Make Us All Fast Some More"

Airplanes were still brand new in 1918; the Wright Brothers had given their first successful demonstrations a little over a decade before. To sign up for the Air Service was incredibly dangerous—but also probably exciting in a way we can hardly imagine now, in an age when flying has become commonplace.

Harold Goettler (1890–1918), a star tackle on the University of Chicago's 1913 championship team, enlisted in the service in 1918 and was assigned to fly DH-4 planes on artillery spotting missions. On October 6 of 1918, only a few weeks after his first mission, he volunteered to search for the famous "Lost Battalion" of American troops that had been stranded in the Argonne Forest of France, surrounded by German forces, for five days. He successfully located the batallion and dropped parcels of provisions to them, but a lack of parachutes and precision for the drop made it clear that he'd need to fly even lower, despite the fact that he was already being fired on by German guns. On a second mission the plane was shot down.[97]

The battalion was rescued the next day, and Germany surrendered just over a month later. Goettler was posthumously awarded the Distinguished Service Cross in 1920, and the Congressional Medal of Honor in 1923. His papers, which are along the lines of college scrapbooks and a student diary, are available from special collections at the University of Chicago library.

■ ■ ■

Follow the road further west. On the left as the road begins to curve will be a marker for **Alexander N. Fullerton (c1805–1880)**, namesake of Fullerton Street. A lawyer-turned-real estate man, Fullerton went to revisit his boyhood home in Chester, Vermont, in 1880, and ended up dying in the room opposite the one in which he was born.[98]

Harold Goettler, U.S. Armed Forces.

Nearby is the marker for the amusingly named **Almond Walker (1805–1854)**, a merchant who began selling guns, boots, and leather in the old Fort Dearborn in 1834.[99]

■ ■ ■

Just ahead will be the triangle marked by the tall, gothic Eddy monument. This is Station five (page 215).

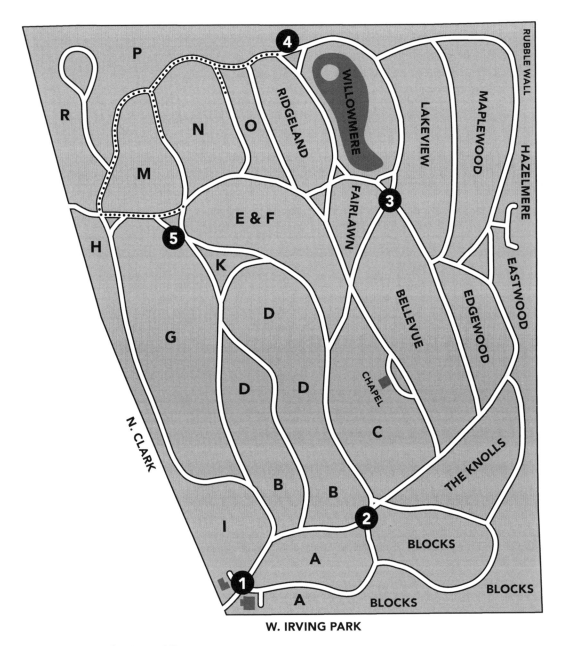

Map for Route 4-B

ROUTE 4-B

Proceeding West past Getty, on the right will be the black granite marker for investor **Matthew J. Swatek (1850–1928)**, known on some maps as the "Black Masonic Sun" grave. It actually features symbols from several different fraternal orders; Swatek joined a lot of them. Just past Swatek will be the lovely statue marking the plot of cigar box maker **Gottlieb Merz (1838–1913)**.

On the left, you'll come to an obelisk marking the family plot of **Perry H. Smith (1828–1885)**, a railroad tycoon whose mansion was said to have three faucets—one for hot water, one for cold water, and one for champagne.[1] In 1874 the Smith family was robbed by "Handy Andy,"[2] a gentlemanly young burglar who, upon breaking into a mansion, would relax in the library, writing literary criticism into the margins of their books, before making off with some of their valuables. Books inscribed by Handy Andy became collectable themselves.[3]

Take a left down Dell Avenue, passing the imposing throne-like monument to brewer **Frederick Wacker (1830–1884)** and his wife, **Catherine Wacker (1836–1884)**, who were the parents of city planner Charles Wacker (page 153).

Proceeding south, you'll see multiple memorials to the Keith brothers on the right. At most times, Graceland has allowed only one large monument per family plot, with smaller markers for individual graves. As such, it's slightly jarring to see adjacent large monuments to the Keith brothers, as well as one to their parents, **Betsy and Martin Keith (1799–1868 and 1800–1876)** right nearby. It is actually four separate family plots. Brothers **Osborn Keith (1831–1904)**, **Edson Keith (1838–1896)**, and **Elbridge Keith (1840–1905)** formed a fur and hat company that became one of the largest in the Midwest.[4] Just as their plots are together, the three had mansions on the same block of South Prairie Avenue; Edson and Elbridge were next-door neighbors, with Osborn a few doors down. Edson's granddaughter, **Katherine Keith Adler (1893–1930)**, was an author; her husband, **David Adler (1882–1949)**, was an architect who got his start working with Howard Van Doren Shaw (page 239).

Behind Elbridge is his grandson, **Allen Keith (1901–1921)**, who died of injuries sustained rescuing people from a fire that broke out in a New Haven movie theater. One of the last things he said, "I think I was the last man out, Mother," is carved on the back of his stone.

. . .

Walk into Section N, between Elbridge and Edson Keith. Just before the marker for **Henry Schucht (1826–1908)** are parrallel rows of small graves for the Powell and Allen families.

Brev. Gen. William Henry Powell and the Medal of Honor

> "The Sinking Creek Valley raid. . . . is but an additional and striking illustration of what a few brave, loyal, and determined men can accomplish, and but the evidenced verification of the oft-repeated trite phrase 'that like begets like.' And that an army of soldiers are but a photographic, or characteristic, facsimile of its commanders."
>
> —Gen. William H. Powell, "The Sinking Creek Valley Raid"

While a chorus of Union prisoners of war were singing in the notorious Libby Prison one evening, they received a note from another prisoner, **William Henry Powell (1825–1904)**, asking if they could please sing a bit louder so that he could hear them better. Badly wounded, awaiting trial for murdering a confederate officer, and suffering from typhoid fever, Powell was isolated in a dark, rat-infested cell. Even if he hadn't been ill, the confederates would have preferred to keep him away from other prisoners; Powell was known as one of the most bloodthirsty officers in the Union Army. Some of his actions are still controversial.[5]

But the raid that won him the Congressional Medal of Honor was performed without spilling a drop of blood.

The Welsh-born Powell moved to the United States as a child in 1830 and grew up mostly in western Virginia. When the Civil War broke out, he was living in Wheeling, and formed his own company, the 2nd Regiment of Loyal Virginia Volunteer Cavalry, a Union regiment in what was officially a Confederate State (though Wheeling and the western portion would soon break off to form the new Union state of West Virginia).[6]

In November, 1862, Powell led an advance guard through a snowstorm toward a Confederate camp near Sinking Creek in Greenbriar County, Virginia.

Though the rest of the Cavalry was far behind, Powell decided that his small band could capture the 500-strong camp alone. So as not to make enough noise to alarm another camp that was two miles away, he ordered the men not to fire, if possible.[7]

When Powell's men rode in, all the unready-rebels could do was try to grab at the Union soldiers' legs. "To such daring and dignified assaults," Powell wrote, "we simply responded politely by tapping them on the top of their heads with our revolvers. After thus dealing with them but for a moment, I demanded the surrender of the camp, on the condition of the protection of their lives . . . Thus I captured the camp of the 14th rebel regiment Virginia Cavalry, 500 strong . . . with Lt. Davidson and about 20 men . . . without the loss of a life, or the firing of a gun or revolver."[8]

Without a trace of modesty, Powell called it "one of the most brilliant, daring and successful feats of the late war for the Union, and of the age,"[9] and took care to note that it was evidence that soldiers were merely a reflection of their commander. In 1890 Powell was awarded the Medal of Honor.

Even as he was promoted to ranks that should have kept him out of the front lines, Powell continued to lead cavalry attacks. In 1863 he was shot in the back, captured, and eventually placed in the notorious Libby Prison, where he survived his bout with typhoid fever. After his release, he sang "Battle Hymn of the Republic" so powerfully in a meeting held at the House of Representatives that Lincoln, standing ten feet away, is said to have sent a note requesting an encore.[10]

In the row of graves across from his is a marker for his daughter, **Lucy Powell Allen (1850–1949)**, whose gravestone reads "She Fought for World Peace." An obituary notes that she was active with an organization known as The Peoples' Mandate to End War.[11]

· · ·

Walking south through the section, near the large Shortall monument is a standout gray headstone for whiskey dealers **Christ Jensen (1851–1911)** and **Elise Jensen (1854–1924)** and others in the Jensen-Jansen family. The inscription reads "To new spheres of pure activity," a quote from Goethe's *Faust*.

Near them is a flat marker for **Robert Lee "Parisian Bob" Caruthers (1864–1911)**, an early professional baseball player who was a star pitcher for such early teams as the St. Louis Browns and Brooklyn Trolley Dodgers. He was said to have earned his nickname by demanding a huge salary—some sources said $5000 a season—in 1885. Caruthers had a winning percentage that few later pitchers ever approached. But he played in the outfield as often as he pitched, and his marker recognizes him as the "most versatile major league player prior to Babe Ruth."[12]

Nellie Verne Walker's Frailey-Watson monument

• • •

Return to Dell Avenue, doubling back past the Wacker throne and taking a left back onto Northern Ave. On the left will be the mausoleum of **Simon Rottner (1850–1907)**, a baker and restauranteur. On the right will be a heartbreaking statue of a woman in mourning.

The Frailey-Watson Monument

"I didn't want to get married. I never met a man who could compete in the interest I had in my work."
—Nellie Verne Walker, sculptor, Ethel Hanft and Paula Manley, *Outstanding Iowa Women*

July 13, 1879, was a particularly awful day for the Frailey family. **Mary Frailey Watson (1857–1950)** lost her sister, **Nellie Frailey (1859–1879)**, to tuberculosis, and her son, **Willie Watson**, to cholera infantum on the same day at the home of her parents.[13]

Mary had married **James Watson (1858–1923)**, who was president of a fruit company. Likely seeing that the end was near for Nellie or Willie, or both, Mary's father and James had purchased the Graceland lot together a couple of weeks before.[14]

Mary went on to join several women's clubs and arts committees, and through these she met Nellie Verne Walker, a sculptor who had taken one of Mary's groups on a gallery tour in 1907. She eventually hired her to sculpt the monument that marks the family plot.[15]

. . .

Between the statue and the north wall are two Civil War graves—one is marked by an upright stone for **Riley Swart (1842–1933)**, who served in the 18th Wisconsin Infantry.

The other, soon to be marked, is for the only Black soldier from Illinois' own 29th United States Colored Troops regiment known to be buried at Graceland.

William Randall

"This war, I fear, has used me up."
—William Randall, Mary Randall's widow's pension file

Born in Quincy, Illinois, **William R. Randall (c1819–1877)** came to Chicago during the War and was said to be very proud of his abilities as a wood cutter, which had allowed him to provide for his family. But he interrupted his work to go to war, leaving his wife **Mary Jane Randall (c1833–1900)**[16] at home with their children, including a baby, **Parthemia "Jenny" Randall (1863–1888)**, who was only about six weeks old.

William was relatively old when he joined the 29th U.S. Colored Troops Regiment in early 1864, and served mainly as a hospital attendant, likely due to his own ill health. However, he wasn't spared the difficulties of long marches, particularly the brutal trek from Fort Harrison to Petersburg, during which he had to be rescued after a fall into the Rappahannock River. More than one friend said that the war left him "badly used up," and, though too proud to seek a disability pension, the jobs he took on after the war—ranging from cooking to hauling coal—proved to be more than he could physically withstand.[17]

"Work was as central to Randall's being as his desire for freedom," wrote Christopher Robert Reed in *Black Chicago's First Century*. "After the regiment was demobilized in November 1865, Randall had returned home 'a sickly looking man (who) did not seem to have strength to do any kind of labor.' (Yet) when comrades in arms and friends counseled a request for a disability pension, he ignored them." While working his final job, he became ill on a street car and was sent home.[18]

By the mid-1870s, Randall was largely invalid, in constant pain and cared for by Mary, who was a professional nurse. "Sometimes he would be in such misery that he could do nothing for weeks at a time," she said. "I have seen him in such misery that his fellow comrades would have to sit with him."[19] Three of their children, **Mary, Alexander and Ida Randall**, died of tuberculosis while William was struggling.[20] He succumbed to kidney disease in 1877.[21]

• • •

Slightly further west on Northern Ave, there will be a large stone on the right for **Col. Ludwig Brown (1846–1911)**. Behind it and to the left will be the Ernst family plot, behind which is a large empty space. This space is the Jacobson plot.

Ole "Young Waffles" Jacobson, the newsboy

> "Those who are desirous of studying human nature in embryo in all its phases should spend one day in Newsboys' Alley. The noblest and the lowest traits of man may be found there. . . . They fight, and play, and trade, and swear, and gamble. Italians, Jews, Turks, Swedes, Negroes, Germans, Poles, Russians, (and) Americans all mix together indiscriminately."
>
> —"Chicago's Newsboys," *Ironwood Times*

Newsboys' Alley was a stretch of Calhoun Place running from LaSalle to Wells, behind the offices of multiple newspapers and featuring rooms with benches where boys were allowed to sleep. The newsboys who gathered there developed a culture all their own.[22] Nearly every newsboy had a nickname, and the greater number of these were cruel and offensive—"Squint," "Limpy," "Blockhead,"[23] and the like. The newsboys may have been the most diverse community in the city, but, being a society of largely unsupervised children, they were not exactly polite.[24]

Theodore Jacobson probably didn't object when he was given the name "Waffles" in reference to his smallpox-scarred face. And after Theodore's premature death, his brother, **Ole Jacobson (1869*–1894)**, apparently didn't object to being called "Young Waffles" when he took over his brother Theodore's place in the alley.[25]

What little is known of Ole's life is nearly all tragic. The unmarked family plot contains several of his brothers and sisters, almost none of whom lived to the age of five. His father, a sailor, disappears from the records in the 1880s. His mother, **Anna Jacobson (c1832–1889)**, was killed in a train accident in 1889, which the papers said left her children orphans. Ole had an adult sister, **Amelia Jacobson (c1862–1891)**, but Amelia died of a laudanum overdose in 1891.[26]

By the mid-1890s, "Young Waffles" was into his twenties, and reportedly working as a fisherman, but still a familiar figure in Newsboys Alley, where he was something of an older-brother figure to many of the boys. He was often known to float a buck or two to younger boys who lost all their earnings in the endless craps games played there, telling them "Stick to work, boy, and then you can give to the other kids."[27]

Ole was killed in a terrible storm that claimed the lives of more than twenty people in May of 1894; George Fergus (page 17) told the *Inter-Ocean* that it was the worst storm he'd seen since 1854.[28] Accounts of exactly what happened to Waffles differ a bit, but the most complete account comes from a report in the *Chicago Record*. According to their story, there was an old shanty on a government breakwater. Ole had been sleeping there, and when the storm broke out he was there with a few boys—possibly newsboys that he'd taken on a fishing trip. As waves battered the shack, the boys were able to tie themselves to posts and survive, though the waves nearly beat them to death and when the storm subsided they nearly starved, as no one was left to untie them. Ole had been carried off by the waves; his drowned body washed ashore after the storm.[29]

According to a rather improbable tidbit in the *Tribune*, a deed to the family plot in Graceland was found in his pocket. A funeral was arranged and attended by over 100 newsboys, current and former, many of whom followed the carriage all the way to the cemetery. There, each boy threw a handful of dirt onto the coffin with the words "Dust to dust."[30]

The plot was never used again and has never been marked.

■ ■ ■

Take the next left down Graceland Ave. Several feet south on the left will be a dark obelisk for lumber dealer **Nelson Ludington (1818–1883)** and a lighter gray stone for **Samuel Curran (1872–1935)**, who was vice president of Royal Baking Powder. Walk in between the Ludington and Curran markers and in about 15 feet you will find a small marker, flush with the ground, for Mexican-American artist Jesus Torres.

Jesus Torres: Artist Who Made the Traditional Look Modern

"People ask me if the animals and birds I use in designs are the ones I see on the street. But I don't draw them like I see them—that would not be pleasing. I draw them the way they look best to me."

—Jesus Torres, "Tin Can Emerges as Work of Art after Pounding"

When **Jesus Torres (1898–1949)** took a ride on the new Golden State Limited train car he'd decorated in 1947, a *Tribune* profile noted that he was essentially retracing the route he'd taken on foot more than 20 years before, when he'd paid 50 cents to swim across the Rio Grande to Texas from his native Mexico.[31]

His first few years in the United States, Torres worked as an itinerant field hand and factory worker, eventually landing in the Chicago stockyards. Once he was established in town, he signed up for English classes at Hull House, and then for the art courses that were offered there, as well. Small sculptures he made from clay began to sell to Hull House faculty before they were even put in the kiln.[32]

His artistic skills quickly led to new jobs. He was adept in both metal and woodwork, designing interior decorations that mixed classic Mexican styles into the art deco stylings of the day. During the Depression he spent three years laying mosaics, carving woodwork, building staircases, and painting murals in the Radio Club, a nightclub at 433 N. Wells, photos of which show an Aztec motif that seems simultaneously modern and traditional. When the club expanded to Palatine, Torres' hand-tooled wood and copper interior artwork was part of its advertising.[33] The work led to Torres being asked to design more night clubs and hotels around the Midwest. By then, some of his metal work was being used in window displays at Sachs Fifth Avenue in New York.[34]

He was respected enough in the artistic community to begin giving lectures on copper, brass, and wood carving at the Art Institute, and his work designing furniture and artwork for Pullman railway cars began to bring him nationwide fame. Unfortunately, he passed away in June 1948, at the age of 50, just as his career was on the rise. A group of Chicago artists started a fund to support his widow, **Francisca Torres (1903–1994)**, who survived him by more than 40 years.[35]

. . .

Double back North up Graceland Ave and take a left, passing the obelisk to the Sol family on the left-hand side. **Silverio Sol (1903–1991)** was a postal clerk, an officer of the Filipino American Council of Chicago, and a founding member of the Filipino Golf Association.[36]

Follow the road as it curves. On the right, beside the red Buschmeyer stone, is a very small white marker, often hidden under grass and leaves, for what appears to be a small lot, but which holds dozens of graves.

The Foundling's Home Plot

"Those having babies of which they wish to dispose, whether they are children of sin or poverty, have but to leave them in a basket at the home and they will be cared for. No questions will be asked."
—George Shipman, "Tea to Mark 78 Years' Aid to Foundlings"

Follow Northern Avenue along as it curves south. In the middle of the curve on the right-hand side, beyond the Buschmeyer and Young markers, is a small plot in Section P, all grass except for an illegible marker flush with the ground. This plot was used by the Foundling's Home and appears to have been donated for their use.

In 1871, Dr. George Shipman learned that the coroner examined the bodies of abandoned babies nearly every day and founded a home where they could be left anonymously and cared for. But many arrived sick already, and between 1871 and 1880, more than two hundred infants who died in the home were buried in this plot. A few entries in the burial records simply say "twelve children" or "three children," but most were individual interments with a cause of death noted and a first and last name for the baby—almost always generically English-sounding first and last names picked by the workers, such as **Maud Johnson, Samuel Price**, and **Paul Potter** (though whoever named **Agnes Riddle** must have been feeling inspired). A couple were given famous names; there are babies named **Frederick Douglass** and **Benjamin Franklin** in the plot. Only a few were over a year old, with the oldest, **Mary Mubrey**, being three.[37]

Changes in policy at the home in the 1880s—notably discouraging anonymous drop-offs, providing for single mothers, and making sure not to have more babies than available wet-nurses could handle, greatly reduced the mortality rate, and changes in social mores in the 20th century reduced the need for the home.[38]

. . .

Continue down the road. On the right, near the point where Northern Ave converges with Cedar, will be the reddish stone marker for George and Amy Dewey, who likely knew Ole "Young Waffles" Jacobson (page 202) well. **George J. Dewey (1829–1901)** was the police liaison to the newsboys community.[39]

Behind Dewey is a small, long-broken marker for **Oliver Jacobs (1853–1893)**, his brother. Inventor Sarah Goode is in an unmarked spot next to him.

Sarah Goode, Inventor

"Beds for the people! Beds for the Million! Special attention is called to the French Flat Folding Bed, the Only Perfect Automatic Folding Bed in the Market. These Beds are Automatic in Movement, Weigh Less than any other Bed, Cost Less than any other Bed, and is Easier to Handle than any other Bed. Agents wanted everywhere. . . . S. E. Goode, Prop."[40]
—Advertisement, 1884

In the early 21st century, nearly a century after her death, articles began circulating listing **Sarah Elisabeth Jacobs Goode (1863–1905)** as the first Black woman to receive a U.S. Patent. This was a little hasty; a few earlier patents given to Black women have since been discovered. But she was *one* of the first, and almost certainly the first in Chicago.

Surviving records of Goode's life are sometimes contradictory, making it difficult to put together an accurate biography; most articles about her have mixed scattered facts with vague (often incorrect) guesswork. Two photographs often said to be of her circulate, but one is certainly misattributed (it shows an older white woman who was also named Sarah Goode), and the other likely is, as well. Sources variously give her birth date as 1855 or 1863. Records state that she was born in Toledo, Ohio, but she always told the census takers that she was born in Spain. Some speculate that she was born enslaved and her parents were lying about her birthplace, but this is strictly speculation.

Sarah and her parents came to Chicago after the Civil War, and here she married a Virginian, Archibald Goode. As of the 1880 census, the couple lived in the loop; he was listed as a "stair maker" while she kept house.[41] By 1900, they were living near 32nd and Prairie.[42]

At some point between those years, Sarah got involved in the furniture business, and seems to have invented at least two sorts of folding beds.

In 1885, she received her U.S. Patent for a "cabinet bed" that folded into a desk. It was her first patent, but possibly not her first invention; a year before, she was marketing what appears to have been a slightly different folding bed,

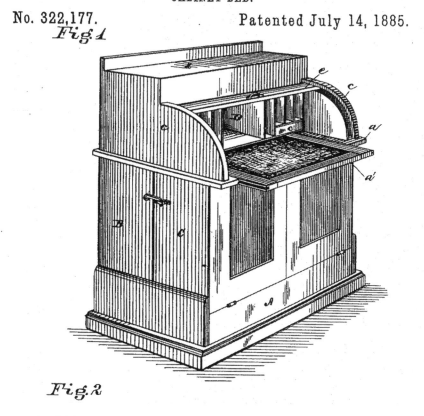

(No Model.)   3 Sheets—Sheet 1.

S. E. GOODE.
CABINET BED.
No. 322,177.   Patented July 14, 1885.
Fig.1

Fig.2

Goode's folding bed design, U.S. Patent Office.

even going so far as to exhibit it at the Milwaukee Exposition. A *Chicago Tribune* article listing the highlights of the expo wrote that "The French Flat Folding-Bed exhibited by S. E. Goode in the east gallery of the Exposition is a fine article. Its merits are, it weighs less, costs less, is more simple, and is easier to handle than any other bed."[43]

That same month, the French Flat Folding Bed was listed in a newspaper ad for Goodes' shop, Chicago Furniture House. The advertisement (which, strangely, has only been found in Cleveland newspapers) makes the shop seem like a large, booming concern, but the French Flat Folding Bed didn't bring Goode as much business as she'd hoped, and she and Archibald were plagued by bad luck. They borrowed heavily to launch the business, and a string of lawsuits show that they struggled to pay the bills.[44] On several occasions their stock was repossessed; Marshall Field and Co. repossessed a large set of goods in 1885.[45]

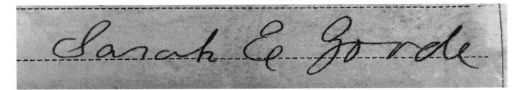

Goode's signature. Field and Co.'s wholesale sales to small businesses were far more lucrative than their retail sales in the 1880s, and Goode's $96 loan was likely for furniture to sell in her own shop, just blocks from Field's flagship store. The fact that she was able to get credit at all—particularly without her husband co-signing—in her era was remarkable.

The troubles weren't all their fault; the Goodes' State Street store operated in the first floor and basement of the Bennett Medical College of Eclectic Medicine on South State Street and a break in the upstairs pipes flooded the store, damaging thousands of dollars in stock. The school then sued them for over three hundred dollars in unpaid rent. The Goodes successfully fought until the school agreed to drop the suit in 1886,[46] but they seem to have closed the store around then. Archibald went back into construction, and apparently quite successfully; a 1904 *Broad Ax* article called him "the most successful Afro-American contractor in Chicago."[47]

Sarah died in 1905; according to the interment book, she died of heart trouble.[48] Archibald died in 1920 and is buried in Lincoln Cemetery on the south side of the city. In the plot with Sarah are two of her infant children, **Sarah Goode (1886)** and **Robert Goode (1888)**.

In 2012, the Sarah E. Goode STEM Academy in Chicago was named for Sarah.

■ ■ ■

As you head south from Sarah Goode's grave, the road will meet Cedar Ave. Just past Cedar, a gray monument marked "Willard" will be a few rows in on the right.

Julius and Samuel Willard, Convicted for Underground Railroad Work

"On the next Sunday evening in the Old-School Pres-
byterian Church, a group of the worshippers put their
heads together and discust the question whether it
would not be a good thing to mob the Willards and
inflict tar and fethers or some form of personal punishment. My informant said that he was in the group when
the proposal was made: he spoke against it and the
matter dropt at once. He thot we were not in danger:
. . . violence was at a discount."

—Samuel Willard, "My First Adventure with a Fugitive
Slave"(Spelling preserved; the Willards were vocal
advocates of simplified spelling.)

One night in Jacksonville, IL, in 1841, there was a knock on the door of shopkeeper **Julius Willard (1793–1884).** His wife, **Almyra Cady Willard (1798–
1873)**, answered to find a young woman named Lucinda who said she was
looking for work; she was enslaved by a wealthy family who was staying in
town for the summer and wanted to hire her out so they could use her wages
for "pin money." Almyra told Lucinda that since she'd been voluntarily taken
to a free state, she was now free, and brought her to a lawyer who managed
to make her emancipation legal in exchange for two years of kitchen service.
"The case," Julius' son Sam wrote, "was an easy one."[49]

Two years later, Lucinda brought another enslaved woman, Judy Green, to
the Willards. Judy had also been brought into town by her enslavers and had
decided to run away. Since her enslavers were only passing through briefly,
not staying in the state, the same rules did not apply.

Julius and Almyra's son, **Samuel Willard (1821–1913)**, a college student
at the time, was home alone when Lucinda and Judy arrived. He later wrote
that he was at a loss as to what he should do; he and his father were active in
the antislavery cause in Jacksonville and had been present when a pro-slavery
mob murdered abolitionist newspaper editor Elijah Lovejoy,[50] but outside of
the incident with Lucinda, this wasn't the sort of thing that happened much
in Jacksonville. "We had never had any connection with the 'Under-ground
Rail-Road,'" Willard wrote, "and did not know where there was a so-called
'station' of it."[51]

And so, he did what most people who helped enslaved people escape
did: improvise. He snuck Judy to the home of a man he knew was abolitionist
and then went home to confer with his parents while she hid there. Julius set
out with Judy the next morning, hoping to get her to safety.

But a party had already formed to stop them. Samuel was arrested the next morning, and attempted, in his confinement, to arrange to have someone get word to his father that he was being pursued, so that he could safely help Green find a place to hide before he was inevitably arrested, too. But Judy and Julius were captured together.

McConnell, the lawyer who'd arranged Lucinda's freedom, appeared *against* the Willards in court this time. When the case was coming up in Springfield, a friend suggested they hire a local lawyer named Abraham Lincoln, but their counsel at the time dismissed the idea at once, because "he had not any reputation, and we wanted a man of note."[52]

The Willards were convicted and ordered to pay a small fine. Appeals led by James H. Collins (page 61) went on for two years, and Samuel believed the judge was deliberately dragging it out hoping the prosecutors would get fed up and drop the matter, but in 1845 Samuel decided to change his plea to guilty simply to get the ordeal over with. He was fined one dollar and ordered to pay twenty more in court costs, and the Willards got on with their lives.

Samuel became a doctor and served as a surgeon for the 97th IL during the Civil War; he was left partially paralyzed from a disease he contracted at Vicksburg. He moved to Chicago in 1870, where he taught high school history for nearly thirty years.[53] For the crime of harboring an enslaved person, Julius and Samuel received a pardon from the governor in 2014.[54]

■ ■ ■

Proceed south and take a left (east) at the crossroads, passing the mausoleum of **Henry Piper (1840–1914)**, who ran a bakery in Old Town alongside what is now called Piper's Alley in his honor.

On the left-hand side, a bit further east, there will be a dark memorial to banker **Nathan Platt (1835–1918)**, behind which will soon be a new mausoleum for financier and preservationist **Richard Driehaus (1942–2021)**. Often described as "just a big kid" who threw parties to rival the Mikado Ball, Driehaus had a James Bond–themed party for his 77th birthday in 2019. Diana Ross provided entertainment.

A bit further east on the left is a worn, cream-colored monument to Justin Butterfield, the most sarcastic lawyer in early Chicago.

The Butterfield-Sawyer-Garrett Plot

"I blasted my political prospects by opposing the War of 1812, and ever since that I have been in favor of war, pestilence and famine!"

—Justin Butterfield, when asked if he opposed the Mexican American War. John Wilson, *Memoir of Justin Butterfield*

Once, while walking on the dirty sidewalk, lawyer **Justin Butterfield (1790–1855)** came upon Mr. Phelps, a colleague who kept no quarters of his own, but drummed up business on the sidewalk outside of the courthouse. It was a muddy day, and Butterfield looked at the streets and said, "Phelps, why don't you sweep out your office?"[55]

It was the kind of remark that his friends would remember for years as classic Butterfieldian wit. Once, when the sun shone through a window onto the bald head of an opposing lawyer, Butterfield said, "The light shineth upon the darkness, and the darkness comprehendeth it not!"[56] In a debate with a supporter of Martin Van Buren during the 1840 presidential campaign, the Van Buren supporter insisted that

Justin Butterfield, Library of Congress.

the economy had been good lately, and Butterfield, who was for William Henry Harrison, replied that "I believe in my soul that if it rained fire and brimstone, as it did at Sodom and Gomorrah . . . these lying loco-focos would exclaim 'what a refreshing shower!'"[57]

Justin Butterfield came to Chicago in 1835 and started a law practice with James H. Collins (page 61). In 1843, he defended Joseph Smith, founder of the Mormon religion, in court, securing Smith's freedom at a time when he was a fugitive. Isaac Newton Arnold (page 190) said Butterfield was, "One of the ablest, if not the very ablest lawyer we have ever had at the Chicago bar. He was strong, logical, full of vigor and resources . . . he wielded the weapons of sarcasm and irony with crushing power."[58]

In 1849, Butterfield was appointed Commissioner of the General Land Office by President Taylor, disappointing his friend Abraham Lincoln, who had wanted the job but didn't have the same connections (Butterfield was a friend of Daniel Webster). In that office, he helped organize the Illinois Central railroad, which would later be instrumental in helping the Union win the war.[59]

Butterfield held the office for three years before paralysis forced him to resign; he finished his life as an invalid in Chicago. A few years after his death, his heirs sold a bit of his land to Thomas Bryan, and it became the first part of what was to become Graceland Cemetery. Justin was moved to this spot from City Cemetery in 1871.[60]

His three daughters, known as "The Beautiful Butterfield Girls," were among the stars of Chicago society. Two of the daughters, **Ada Butterfield Gellatly (1834–1896)** and **Elizabeth Butterfield Sawyer (1828–1904)**, are buried in the plot. Elizabeth and her own daughter, **Ada Sawyer Garrett (1856–1938)** (often said to be the namesake of Ada Street), divided much of the family property into what is now Logan Square.

Ada was known as "the belle of the north side" in her youth,[61] but became a recluse after the death of her husband, railroad company official **T. Mauro Garrett (1855–1903)**. A savvy businesswoman, she spent the next two decades quietly turning her husband's fortune into a much larger one. In 1927, though, her friends found her living in a dingy downtown hotel room, dressed in rags and half starved, though she possessed a fortune estimated at around six million dollars.[62]

She was found insane and made a ward of the state, which she remained until her death in 1938. She left behind a decades-old will full of bequests to charities that no longer existed and people who had long since passed away.[63]

■ ■ ■

Across the road from the Butterfield plot will be a triangle featuring the gothic Eddy monument; this is Station five.

The Gothic Eddy monument

STATION FIVE

THE EDDY TRIANGLE

Station five is the triangle bearing a gothic-inspired obelisk marking the family plot of Reverend Thomas Mears Eddy, one of the most prominent ministers and journalists of the mid–19th century.

Reverend Thomas Mears Eddy

"We must harbor no traitors in our midst. Chicago is a cool place in the summer, but we will make it so hot for them that they will find it convenient to go South. I can only think of one place for them. We must whistle 'Yankee Doodle' in Richmond some fine day."
—Rev. Thomas Eddy, "Evening Meeting"

Raised in Ohio, **Thomas Mears Eddy (1823–1874)** recalled that the biggest entertainment in his small town was "spelling matches." "Sometimes," he wrote, "rival schools would meet and spell against each other for hours. I have often walked from three to four miles in the 'dark of the moon,' through deep mud, to such a contest."[1]

Eddy had entered the ministry before he was 20, and spent a few years as a traveling preacher on the circuit around the Ohio River. When poor health forced him to give up this rough and tumble life, he became editor of the *Northwest Christian Advocate*, a newspaper that he turned into a leading source of anti-slavery sentiment in the Midwest.

He came to Chicago in 1856 and quickly established himself as one of the most prominent ministers in town. In 1869, he left Chicago to manage the Metropolitan Church in Washington, D.C., where his congregants would include President Grant. He passed away five years later, and before the end of the 1870s had been the subject of an exhaustive biography, *The Life of Rev Thomas M. Eddy* by Charles Sims.

■ ■ ■

For Route 5-A, turn to page 219.
For Route 5-B, turn to page 247.

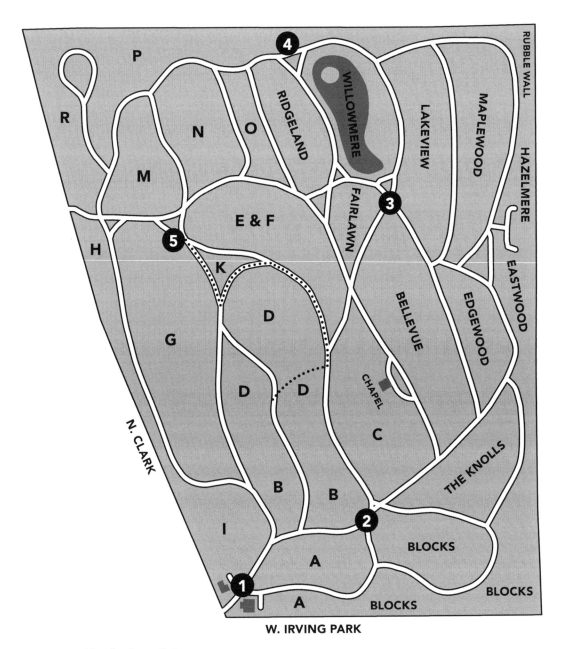

P

R

N

O

RIDGELAND

WILLOWMERE

LAKEVIEW

MAPLEWOOD

RUBBLE WALL

HAZELMERE

M

E & F

FAIRLAWN

H

EASTWOOD

K

D

BELLEVUE

EDGEWOOD

G

D

D

CHAPEL

C

N. CLARK

B

B

THE KNOLLS

I

A

BLOCKS

BLOCKS

BLOCKS

A

BLOCKS

W. IRVING PARK

Map for Route 5-A

Behind the Eddy triangle, and a bit to the left, is the very large Rietz vault, purchased in 1868 by brothers **Charles, Frederick, and August Rietz (1824–1890, 1834–1913, 1829–1901)**. After decades of mergers, the Wisconsin salt mine they owned eventually became the Morton Salt company.

Among those interred in the mausoleum in later years was **Owen H. Fay (1858–1922)**, who was married to **Anna Rietz Fay (c1875–1954)**. Fay ran a livery company with a team of around 200 horse-drawn carriages at the turn of the 20th century, by which time he'd already started to add new "horse-less" carriages to his fleet. According to *The Horseless Age*, an automobile trade magazine, he added the first electric cab to Chicago's streets in 1899.[1] The magazine predicted that passengers would enjoy "the pleasing novelty of being whizzed through the city with no apparent motive power."[2]

. . .

Just to the left of the Rietz vault is the tall obelisk for the Harrison family.

The Harrison Plot

> "In my boyhood days Ashland Avenue was known as Reuben Street. When 'Hey! Rube!' came into its greatest vogue as a term of ridicule and reproach, the name of the street, upon petition of its sorely tried residents, was changed. . . . There were seven houses on Reuben Street when I was a boy. One of these was 'the chicken woman's' at the southwest corner of Reuben and Monroe streets. If I close my eyes today, even after all these years . . . the hissing of her geese, the quacking of her ducks and the clatter of her chickens still ring in my ears."
>
> —Carter H. Harrison Jr., *Chicago Yesterdays*

Carter H. Harrison (1825–1893) and **Carter H. Harrison Jr. (1860–1953)** (who was properly Carter H Harrison IV, though he often went by Carter H.

Carter Harrison Sr., Library of Congress.

Harrison II) were part of a political dynasty that spans centuries. Carter Sr. had an uncle who signed the Declaration of Independence, and shared ancestors with presidents William Henry Harrison and Benjamin Harrison. Between the two of them, the Carters Harrison served ten terms as mayor of Chicago.

The elder Carter first served as mayor from 1878–87, supporting labor unions even in the midst of the Haymarket affair, when unions were often seen as undemocratic. Critics accused him of being soft on crime; when he ran for mayor again in 1893, the *Chicago Journal* wrote that "with Carter Harrison in the mayoralty chair, Chicago would be the widest-open town in the universe . . . (for) murderers, thieves, safe-blowers, highwaymen, pickpockets and all species of criminals."[3]

Harrison was elected again in spite of this reputation, but he was assassinated by a crank six months into the term. Just as the copperhead *Chicago Times* had stopped most of their Lincoln criticism when he was assassinated, the *Journal* then wrote that in the midst of the shocking news of Harrison's death, "We, his fellow citizens, began to realize how much this hearty, boisterous, hopeful nature was part of our life, bone of our bone, spirit of our spirit."[4]

His son, Carter H. Harrison Jr., was elected to the first of five terms as mayor four years later, though he faced similar charges of being soft on crime. A year into his first term, *Harper's* wrote that "When Carter H. Harrison (Jr.) was running for mayor of Chicago it was charged by almost the entire newspaper press of the city that his election would mean that the city would be 'wide open' (for crime). After he was elected and had assumed office, the understanding became general that Chicago really *was* wide open, and that, in the vernacular, 'everything went.'"[5]

Certainly there were some scandals and indications that he could have done a better job regulating the city; after the Iroquois Theatre fire (page 84) several papers called for his arrest. His tenure also oversaw the golden age of the old red light District.

Whatever else can be said of him, though, his reminiscences about the old days, compiled in *Chicago Yesterdays* by Caroline Kirkland (page 110), are among the most delightful memoirs of childhood in Gilded Age Chicago, recalling days of ice skating across frozen prairies all the way to Riverside (while steering clear of bullies who would later serve under him in the police force), watching croquet games with a spy glass from the cupola of his house, and pressing his ear to the keyhole while his parents and their friends sang songs like "Upidee Upida" at parties.[6]

Included in his reminiscences is the story of how a cousin died while visiting the family in 1864 during a snowstorm that was so bad that the *Tribune* didn't go to press, the roads disappeared under waist-deep drifts, and the snow was blowing so fast that horses couldn't go through. The temperatures dipped to around -25F.[7] In this deep freeze, the elder Mr. Harrison needed to trudge five blocks to find a woman to dress the body.[8] This cousin was presumably **Isabel Bradford Barbee (1825–1864)**, whose date of death is given in cemetery records as January 1, 1864, the night of the storm. She was moved from City Cemetery to the Graceland plot in 1871.[9]

To the left of Isabel Barbee's small marker, just outside the Harrison family plot, note the delightful stone of sales manager and boxing judge George A. Meshes II (1928–1986), which features a large dollar sign and the suggestive epitaph "I Would Do It Again."[10]

Edith Ogden Harrison

"Oh, those never-to-be-forgotten days of the early nineties! Then came the years of dullness when the flowing bowl was forbidden and we never dreamed that we would ever have a real New Year again. Now all that is possible once more, and the charming celebrations have been resumed; but I often wish on that day that the sleigh bells with their jingling music might replace the quiet approach of the silenced motor."
—Edith Ogden Harrison, *Strange to Say*

Carter Jr.'s wife, **Edith Ogden Harrison (1862–1955)**, wrote a number of hugely popular books of fairy tales during her husband's tenure in office, and collaborated on one with her friend, author L. Frank Baum. She was the city's

Edith Ogden Harrison, Library of Congress.

official hostess for the 1933 Century of Progress Exposition. Though she came from a wealthy background, and eventually knew nine presidents personally, she wrote in her old age that "Birth, after all, is only an accident. If one does not appreciate that being born to certain advantages only makes one's responsibility greater, then birth amounts to nothing."[11]

Even in her late 80s, she still practiced superstitions she'd learned from voodoo practitioners and household servants that she'd known as a child in old New Orleans, in the heyday of priestess Marie Laveau. She had occasionally snuck along with her family's servants to voodoo ceremonies herself.[12]

• • •

Directly behind the Harrison obelisk is a worn mausoleum on which the name "Lane" is faintly visible.

Lavinia Lane's Mausoleum of Mystery

"With a blood-curdling scream the woman (Lavinia Lane) dashed at (the judge) again, but he kept her at bay long enough to open the door and receive assistance from the outside. The troublesome visitor then went away after breaking another window."
—*Chicago Daily News*

Built for **Lavinia E. Lane (c1815–1905)**, the weather-beaten Lane vault is perhaps the only mausoleum in the cemetery that was built specifically for a woman and contains no adult men.

The lives of the occupants, though, are shrouded in mystery.

A widow, Lavinia Lane purchased the plot in March of 1868, and only days later four bodies were moved there from City Cemetery—19-year-old

The Lane Mausoleum

Cordelia Thompson (c1834–1854), who'd died in childbirth, **Martha Lock-wood (c1819–1859)**, who'd died of dropsy, and an infant child of each.[13] A cousin of Lavinia,[14] **Minnie Lane (c1854–1877)**, was later interred there when she died of tuberculosis. Lavinia herself was the final interment. Vital records for anyone in the mausoleum are elusive, but going strictly by their ages, Cordelia and Martha may have been Lavinia's daughter and sister.

Even Lavinia's correct name is a bit of a mystery. Her name is given as "Alvina Lane" in her death record and on the Graceland interment records; while it's *presumably* a typo for the Lavinia E. Lane who purchased the plot, it's not impossible that it's a whole other person.

The best documented story of Lavinia is that in 1883, she burst into the office of Judge Van H. Higgins, where she loudly and obscenely claimed that the judge owed her money.[15] The 60-year-old Higgins replied, "I will not allow you to use such language in my office," and a physical struggle between the two ensued. Several windows were broken in the melee before Lavinia could be removed from the premises.[16]

In the aftermath of the fight, the *Chicago Daily News* labeled Lavinia "A Woman on the Warpath" and "An Erratic Female."[17] Strange rumors began to circulate about her, including a tale that she had recently exhumed the body of a child and boiled its bones.[18] The judge admitted he'd known Lane in Galena, where he'd lived in the early 1850s,[19] but denied that he owed her money, and said that he believed that her attacks were part of a blackmail scheme.[20]

From a modern vantage point it's hard to tell if she was suffering from something along the lines of schizophrenia, or if the judge simply claimed she was lying (and perhaps spread the story of her boiling bones himself) to get out of paying her the debt. Though he worked alongside Lincoln in "The Sand Bar Case, the future president's last major case as a lawyer, stories about Higgins are not always flattering; a speech by Emery A. Storrs (page 116) once called him "unjust, oppressive, inhuman, and cruel."[21]

Lane launched a lawsuit against Higgins days later, but surviving paperwork furnishes few other clues, except to clarify that she said the judge had borrowed around twenty-five hundred dollars from her in 1867, and now, sixteen years later, she was demanding eight thousand.[22] She disappeared from the news, but lived more than twenty more years, dying of tuberculosis at the age of 90 in 1905.

• • •

Proceed south down the path. On the left, a monument to the Gloede family is hidden in a cluster of bushes.

The Hidden Gloede Boulder

"Our home and place of business had more than 200 refugees (from the Great Chicago Fire) . . . a few years later only one of these refugees came back, a man bringing my mother a small bell made from a piece of the Court house bell, which was destroyed at that time, 1871. My mother, after having this bell more than 50 years, presented it to me because I was born in that year, and strange as it may seem, I started getting a hobby on Bells. (I) have a wonderful collection."
—Ida Gloede, Reminiscenccs of Ida Gloede

German-born **William H. Gloede (c1838–1908)** was a government forester for King William, overseeing thousands of acres. He brought his family, including 12-year-old **Richard F. Gloede (1870–1938)**, to the United States in the 1880s.

Richard took after his father. After opening a flower shop in Chicago, he built several greenhouses where he grew rare flowers and plants with his wife, **Ida Gloede (1871–1946)**. Sometimes they'd even grow their own hybrid fruits, including a cross between a strawberry and raspberry that they called a "wonder berry."[23]

In 1907 they built their home and conservatory near the present cite of Northwestern University's football stadium. It was something of a tourist attraction; besides featuring exotic plants, they had several historical trees, including the remains of the "Potawatomie Tree," a tree said to be 600 years old, and large enough that more than 22 people could stand in the hollowed-out trunk.[24] In 1893, Richard worked on the landscaping for the Japanese garden at the World's Fair.[25]

Appropriately enough for a couple who built a "hidden garden," their burial place is hidden, as well. The boulder marked "Gloede's" is hidden in a ring of shrubs, and the mausoleum containing William, Richard, Ida, and their son **Randolph Gloede (1907–1926)** is underground beneath it.

■ ■ ■

Follow the road south; on the right you'll see the gray monument to **Fred Busse (1866–1914)**, who served as mayor from 1907–1911. Behind him is a row of small, multi-colored vaults.

The Vault Section

The Vault Section

In early maps of the cemetery, there was an oval-shaped portion of Section G that was set aside to be devoid of burial plots; an 1860 map refers to it as a "grotto." A map from the late 1870s also denotes a "grotto" area, though the drawing included on the map shows trees and grass, not the stony structure one normally associates with a grotto.

For reasons that were not recorded, at some point it was decided to convert the grotto into what became mapped as the "Vaults" section, with colorful mausoleums set into a hillside, described in landmark paperwork as "polychromatic tumuli." Visually, they look like a miniature version of the townhouses and apartments that line the nearby streets.

The first vault space was sold in January 1881, to Frederick Wagner, and the second sold barely a week later to George Eldridge. The rest were sold over the next twelve years.

Some of the interments:

Emil Gross (1858–1921) was a professional baseball player in the 1800s; he was the star catcher for the Providence Grays and was the catcher in 1880 when John Montgomery Ward pitched baseball's second perfect game (only five days after the first, though the feat wouldn't be repeated again for nearly twenty-five years). Shortly after the formation of the National League, he was blacklisted for a year due to "insubordination" by league head William Hulbert (page 233).

David J Powers (c1815–1909) was the head of the Union Wire Mattress Company. He is interred with his wife, **Eliza Powers (c1818–1888)**.

George D. Eldridge (1864–1923) was an insurance man, **Louis Weik (c1832–1926)** a bricklayer, and **Reinhard Hageman (1843–1894)** a confectioner.

The William Boldenweck family was originally in one of the vaults, but in 1912 they were moved to the current Boldenweck mausoleum in the Knolls section[26] (page 96) and Vault 5 was sold to **Stephen W. Menclewski (1868–1927)** and **Augusta E. Johnson Menclewski (1863–1955)**, a married couple who were both physicians. They lived and practiced near W. Augusta and N. Noble Streets, an area then known as "Little Poland." In 1902 Stephen was sued by a woman who claimed she'd married him and paid for his medical education only to have him use his newfound knowledge of poisons to attempt to kill her. Dr. Menclewski denied ever having been married to the woman at all (he had married Augusta barely a week before the case was announced),[27] and won the case.[28]

■ ■ ■

Return to the path and take the sharp left at the fork in front of the Seaton obelisk. Proceeding northeast around the bend away from the Vaults, on the right will be the large plot marked "Hurlbut."

The Strange Deaths of Barton Edsall and Colonel Hurlbut

> "The community were startled yesterday by the intelligence that a prominent merchant, Mr. Barton Edsall, had been found dead in his own doorway . . . A sufficient reward should be offered for the detection and arrest of the possible assassin, to secure the services of the best talent in ferreting out the awful mystery."
> —"The Edsall Tragedy," *Chicago Tribune*

For a few days, the mysterious death of **Barton Edsall (1830–1871)** was *the* topic of conversation in Chicago. Edsall, a wholesale druggist, had been complaining of a toothache when he wandered out of bed very early one morning. Shortly thereafter, his wife heard a gunshot. Edsall was found lying in the entryway of his Gold Coast mansion, bleeding from a bullet wound and no longer lucid enough to explain what happened. Another bullet was lodged in the side of the door. A gun, his own, was nearby and had been fired, but it couldn't be determined whether he had shot himself, or whether the shot that hit him had come from some other gun.[29] He was dead before dawn.

Had Edsall killed himself, perhaps driven mad by the toothache? Or could the pills he'd been taking for pain have caused temporary insanity? There had been some burglaries in the neighborhood lately—could he have been shot by someone who was trying to break in? And Edsall had recently fired the pistol at a rat—could he have attempted to shoot at another one but accidentally shot himself instead?[30]

The story had all the elements of a perfect mystery. There was strong evidence in favor of every possible scenario, and papers published every word of the coroner's inquest, in which Mrs. Edsall, the maid, several doctors, a gunsmith, a few neighbors, and several others were interviewed.[31]

Finally, on October 8, he was laid to rest at Graceland; though the cause of death wasn't totally certain, it was given as "accidental" in the interment book. Newspapers went to press that morning vowing that they'd keep investigating—that they would not forget about Barton Edsall.[32]

But that night came the Great Chicago Fire, destroying 16,000 buildings, including Edsall's house. (A few newspapers said that Belle Edsall, his wife, had been killed in the blaze, but this turned out to be an unfounded rumor. A few years later Belle married a man named James C. Spencer.)[33]

Barton's sister **Emma Edsall Hurlbut (1836–1917)** was married to Barton's business partner, **Horace A. Hurlbut (1831–1893)**, who had purchased the plot in 1865 upon the death of his brother, **Col. Frederick Judson Hurlbut (1828–1865)**.

Colonel Hurlbut survived the Battle of Shiloh and commanded a brigade under General Sherman on the March to the Sea. In April of 1865, he returned to Chicago on furlough just in time to hear word of Lee's surrender and then of Lincoln's assassination. On May 1st he was listed in newspapers among the soldiers taking a prominent role in Lincoln's Chicago funeral procession.[34]

On May 8, though, it was reported that the Colonel had disappeared on April 29th, and had not been seen since.[35] Later that day, his body was found in the Chicago River, presumably a victim of accidental drowning.[36] Most likely the reporters who listed him in the procession were working off written plans for which he didn't show up, but it's amusing to note that, according to the available data, there was a ghost in Abraham Lincoln's Chicago funeral procession.

• • •

Head north on the curving path beyond the Hurlbut plot, passing the plot of lumber dealer **Joseph Rathborne (1844–1923)** on the right. In the large triangular section on the left will be a prominent brown marker for the Ogden family.

Mahlon D. Ogden Averts a Riot

> "Doubtless we took meals alone, but I cannot remember ever doing so. There were always several house guests . . . These visitors were of all sorts and kinds, and, to my childish eyes, very interesting and delightful, even including a young man of our same name which, he seemed to think, entitled him to stay indefinitely. My surprise was great when one day I overheard my parents discussing how they might persuade him to leave, for they had become convinced that he was really an adventurer."
> —Anna Ogden West, "Through a Child's Eyes"

In the 1840s, there was a law that a prisoner who couldn't pay for his board after being released from jail could be auctioned into indentured servitude for a month. Such auctions are only known to have happened in Chicago twice. In the first, a white local drunk named Harper was sold to a Black man, George White, who paid 25 cents. The whole auction seems to have been an attempt to embarrass Harper into cleaning up his act (incidentally, it didn't work; Harper later sold the rights to his mortal remains to Dr. Brainard [page 16] in exchange for drinking money).[37]

The second was more serious.

In 1842, a man named Dodson came to believe that a man in his employ, one Edwin Heathcock, was a fugitive enslaved person and had him arrested. Unable to provide paperwork showing he was free, Heathcock was kept in the old log jail for six weeks. When no one claimed him, he was released, but since he was unable to pay his board, he was to be sold into a month of service. Though this was hardly the same system or arrangement as a slave auction in the south, it was too close for comfort—and it would have been an easy matter for someone to buy Heathcock for the month and then take him out of state and claim him as an outright slave.[38]

The antislavery faction of the city came out to the auction outside of Chapman's Building, near Clark and Lake, in force. The sheriff, clearly embarrassed by the whole proceeding and fearing a riot, could find no bidders, and said "If nothing is bid, I shall have to return him to the County Jail."[39]

Finally, **Mahlon D. Ogden (1811–1880)**, a lawyer whose brother, William, had been the city's first mayor, poked his head out of a nearby second-story window to bid 25 cents, and the auctioneer gave the announcement of "Going, going gone."[40] Having won, Ogden approached Mr. Heathcock and said, "Go where you like."[41]

And with that, Heathcock (described at the time as "a member of the Methodist church; a moral, quiet and inoffensive man"[42]) went free, and a possible riot was averted for twenty-five cents. One early account seems critical of Ogden for even participating; a later one treats him as a hero. Both accounts, though, were written by publisher Zebina Eastman.

> What became of Heathcock is not known for sure, though a North Carolina–born man by that name joined the 102nd Colored Regiment in Detroit in 1863 and served as the company cook. Another man by that name (or possibly the same one) was married in Chicago in 1881; both were listed as being born in 1818, which makes it possible one or both were the same Edwin Heathcock who was in Chicago in 1842.[43]

Mahlon Ogden was born in upstate New York in 1811, the grandson of a Valley Forge veteran, and came to Chicago in 1836. When the Great Chicago Fire came in 1871, the Ogden home was the only house in the neighborhood to survive the fire, and the house became far more famous than Ogden was himself. He lost control of the house after the financial Panic of 1873, and Potter Palmer (page 148) moved in for a time.[44] The Newberry Library stands on the site now.

. . .

Follow the road as it curves. On the right will be the Hubbard monument.

Gurdon S. Hubbard, The Swift Walker

"Looking north, I saw the whitewashed buildings of Fort Dearborn sparkling in the sunshine, our boats with flags flying, and oars keeping time to the cheering boat song. I was spell-bound and amazed at the beautiful scene before me . . . A soldier ferried me across the river in a canoe, and thus I made my first entry in Chicago, October 1, 1818."
—Gurdon Hubbard, *Autobiography of Gurdon Saltonstall Hubbard*

When teenager **Gurdon Hubbard (1802–1886)** first came to Chicago in 1818, he was an indentured servant of John Jacob Astor's fur company and carried a letter of introduction to John Kinzie (page 48) written by John's son, whom he'd met while working on Mackinaw Island. He found John much more pleasant than his modern reputation might suggest and remembered the inhabitants of Chicago of the time—a mix of early settlers, soldiers, and Native Americans—as "a convivial, jolly set" who all enjoyed fox hunts together.[45]

In his travels in those days, he was adopted as a son by Chief Waba of the Kickapoo and married a woman named Watseka. He and Watseka divorced in the 1820s, but his second wife recalled that he kept many Kickapoo customs for the rest of his life.[46]

He finally settled in Chicago 1834. He was instrumental in pushing for the Illinois Michigan Canal construction, personally persuading the board to make the Chicago River, not Calumet, the mouth of the canal, a move that may have single-handedly made it possible for Chicago to become a metropolis.[47]

By the time the city was incorporated in 1837 he was almost a legendary figure among the locals; stories were told of his ability to walk seventy-five miles in one night. A path that he reputedly wore into the ground personally became State Street—a story that's at least partially true, as it was part of the fur trading route then known as "Hubbard's Trail," other portions of which eventually became the Dixie Highway.[48] He said he was sometimes known as "Pa Pa Ma Ta Be," which translated to "The Swift Walker."[49]

The Hubbard marker

He was friendly with Abraham Lincoln and was recognized by the president among the crowd watching him speak from a balcony in 1863. According to Hubbard, Lincoln invited him to the platform, and told a guard not to bother unlocking the door, as "Hubbard is used to jumping—he can scale that fence," at which point Gurdon did exactly that.[50]

Hubbard died in 1886, having been involved in nearly every stage of the growth of the young city, from its days as a trading post to the immense population boom of the 1880s, when the population approached one million. The draft of a massive autobiography was lost in the 1871 fire, but a rewrite attempt (in which he made it as far as 1829) was published after his death.

A recipe Hubbard wrote, preserved by his wife, Mary Ann Hubbard (1820–1909):

1 lb venison
1 lb turkey breast
¾ lb bear or raccoon fat

Season meat with wild onion or leek, add salt and pepper to taste. Chop or pound the meat and mix together with the fat. Make a thin crust to cover the sides and bottom of a bake pan, add meat and top with thicker crust. Cover and bake over coals for one hour for "a most delicious dish."[51]

. . .

A little to the left of Hubbard's plot is a legible marker for janitor[52] **Asa Gile (c1833–1895)**. One of the faded markers beside it appears to be for Asa's father, **David S. Gile (1793–1880)**, who is one of Graceland's tiny number of War of 1812 veterans. Gile served under Captain Jonathan Bean in New Hampshire in the Fall of 1814, toward the end of the war.[53] In Chicago he worked as a carpenter, eventually dying in the Grand Pacific Hotel, where he had lived for several years.[54]

A bit behind Gile is the large, easily spotted Muhlke monument, and behind that is a smaller one for **David C. Presser (1833–1900)**, who is the only Graceland Mexican American war vet noted in the *Roll of Honor*, a catalog of veteran burials. He served in the Navy and would have been only about 14 at the time.[55]

Returning to walk along the curving road, across from Hubbard on your left will be a particularly faded old marble memorial topped by a draped urn. The phrase "sacred to the memory of" can be vaguely discerned. It is a marker for **Tunis Ryerson (c1830–1871)**, a lumber yard owner.[56] The equally ancient-looking gothic arched gravestone to the right of Ryerson is that of **William M. True (1812–1877)**, a contractor and builder.[57]

Proceeding on the road, you will find the curbed-off family plot with markers for both **George C. Walker (1835–1905)** and his father **Charles Walker (1802–1868)**. Charles followed his brother Almond (page 195) to Chicago in the 1830s and became active in the grain business.[58]

Across from the Walkers you'll see the headstone for **William Northrup Bentley (1777–1849)**, who owned a fashionable hotel in upstate New York

Hulbert's baseball

and was the great grandfather of novelist Arthur Meeker Jr. (page 112). He died in the 1849 cholera epidemic.[59]

Just behind the Bentley plot is a small granite marker shaped like a baseball.

William Hulbert,
The Man Who Saved Baseball

> "I would rather be a lamp post in Chicago than a millionaire in any other city."
> —attributed to William Hulbert

At a time when the still-young sport of professional baseball was plagued by corruption, gambling, and dirty tricks, some called **William Hulbert (1832–1882)** "the man who saved the game." When sports giant A. G. Spalding wrote a book on the history of the national pastime, he said, "I wish to claim for William A. Hulbert that which is due to him . . . as one who did more than any other among magnates to save and maintain the game in its integrity. His name was not enrolled among the list of moral reformers. He thought this world was good enough for him—for anybody, and he enjoyed it in his own way. And yet this man stood like a stone wall, protecting the game of Base Ball in its integrity and turning back the assaults of every foe who sought to introduce elements of dishonesty, discord, or degeneration."[60]

After making his fortune in the coal and grocery industries, Hulbert was one of the founders of the Chicago White Stockings, the team that later became the Chicago Cubs. He was one of the founders of the National League in 1876; the cities on the unique headstone are the cities that were in the National League in its first season. As head of the National league he kept tight reins on player behavior, suspending several for "insubordination," including Emil Gross (page 226), who missed a season by being put on Hulbert's "blacklist."

In an era when rules changed frequently from year to year, Hulbert once told Spalding that, "The wit of man cannot devise a plan or frame a form of government that will control the game of baseball for over five years," but the rule book he drafted lasted for thirty-five before it was revised.

. . .

A little beyond Hulburt is a small gray marker for **William D. Kerfoot (1837–1919)**, a realtor who responded to the loss of his office in the Great Chicago Fire by assembling a shack to serve as a new office with a sign reading, "All gone but wife, children, and energy."

Return to the road, following it as it curves. Note the obelisk on the right for hardware dealer **Henry B. Clarke (1802–1849)**, whose 1836 house still stands, the oldest remaining in the city by some metrics. Dying in the cholera epidemic of 1849, he specifically requested not to be buried in the old City Cemetery, and was buried near his home for fifteen years before being moved here. His marker simply reads "father." Behind it will be the Coolbaugh monument.

William F. Coolbaugh

"About sunset, July 2, (1887), I observed a rainbow of unusual beauty. It lasted 15 minutes, was a double bow, and the secondary arch brightened until both were equally brilliant. During its continuance all colors were intensified. The grass and trees became of most vivid green, while flowers, especially scarlet, seemed fairly to flame."

—Illinois Coolbaugh, *Chicago Inter-Ocean*

In 1877, a *Chicago Inter-Ocean* reporter said that he'd once heard **William F. Coolbaugh** (1821–1877), a prominent banker, say that no moral person of sound mind would ever commit suicide.[61] It was, by the time of the article, an eerie memory. The night before, Coolbaugh had dressed in a nice suit and vest, with a matching overcoat and silk hat, and walked through the stormy November night to the still-unfinished monument to Stephen A. Douglas. There, he lay down as if to rest on boards supporting a cornice and shot himself in the head.[62]

The suicide stunned the city; Coolbaugh was a rich, seemingly happy man—*the* banker of Chicago, according to some.[63] Why would he have killed himself?

Immediately—and displaying a distinct lack of delicacy—reporters began interviewing his coachman, the watchman at his bank, his son-in-law, and anyone else they could find, asking them whether Coolbaugh had been a drinking man, whether he'd suffered financial setbacks, whether his wife was happy, and numerous other stunningly invasive questions. They even sought out Marshall Field (page 174) to inquire as to Coolbaugh's character.[64]

The coroner reached a verdict of "suicide during a period of temporary insanity." Initially it was believed that Coolbaugh was despondent over failing health, but the *Tribune* insisted that he must have been in financial trouble in an article entitled "Insanity as a Fine Art."[65] The 19th-century ignorance of mental health is on full and terrifying display in all of the press' exhaustive coverage of the case. Months later it came out that Coolbaugh hadn't been as rich as everyone thought—an explanation that seemed to satisfy people more than the uncomfortable idea that wealth didn't solve all of one's problems.[66]

Born in Pennsylvania in 1821, William Coolbaugh ventured west to grow up with the country. He initially moved to the pioneer town of Burlington, Iowa, where he opened a general store at which Senator Douglas once made a speech. Looking for a bigger field to put his financial ideas into play, he came to Chicago in 1862 and opened a bank.[67] He became chairman of the Douglas Monument Committee, and in that capacity he accompanied President Andrew Johnson to lay the cornerstone of the monument during the embattled president's controversial "Swing Around the Circle" speaking tour, in which Johnson tried to drum up support by calling his political rivals "traitors."[68] Two years later Coolbaugh went to visit Senator Grimes of Iowa, his old roommate, to lobby him to vote to convict Johnson in his upcoming impeachment trial. Had he succeeded, it would have cost Johnson the single vote that allowed him to stay in office.[69]

The only other occupant of Coolbaugh's plot is his youngest daughter, **Illinois Coolbaugh Van Duzer (1872–1895)**, who would have been four years old at the time of his death. From the letters and sketches she sent to magazines, we can see that she took a keen interest in science as a teenager, making sketches of frost patterns, observing the habits of caterpillars, and inquiring about how sea birds quench their thirst. According to Graceland records she died suddenly at Jackson Sanatorium in Dansville, New York, at the age of 22.[70]

William Coolbaugh, Library of Congress.

Another Coolbaugh daughter, Mary, married Chief Justice Melville Fuller (page 86), and is buried in his plot.

. . .

Just behind the Coolbaugh plot is a gracefully curved Lyon memorial bench, designed by the architectural firm of Jenney and Mundie.[71]

The Lyon bench by Jenny and Mundey.

The Lyon Family Bench

"A man who has as strong a liking for club life and association among stage people as I have has no right
to marry."
—William C. Lyon

Whenever the city launched its periodic crackdowns on the gambling dens
that seemed to be hidden behind every door in the late 1800s, gamblers
would remark that what *they* did wasn't really any different from what went on
in "The Pit," where commodities futures were traded at the Board of Trade.
They may have had a point.

There was an art and science to the futures market, but that didn't keep it
from being a high-stakes game. Traders would use all sorts of tricks—such as
spreading rumors of surplus crops—to drive the price of wheat down, buy as
much of the supply as possible, and then use any number of tricks to drive
the price back up. If a trader managed to "corner" a market, he could set his
own price and get seriously rich—as long as he didn't mind the economic
impact such tricks could have, and as long as the corner wasn't broken. In
1897 a man named John Leiter managed to control the whole deliverable

supply of wheat for a moment, but when Phillip D. Armour (page **136**) sent out "ice breaker" ships to the frozen lake to increase delivery routes the price dropped from nearly $2.00 a bushel to only 25 cents, and Leiter lost ten million dollars in a day.

There were few traders as daring as **John B. Lyon (1829–1904)**. While he didn't corner the market in his first attempt in 1868, he did manage to push the price of wheat up from 1.80 to 2.20, making himself a fortune. According to the *Tribune* retrospective, "Lyon . . . concluded he could do what he pleased with the market."[72] Four years later he and a few others made the biggest corner attempt that had ever been made, but they were still holding their supply of wheat when news of a larger harvest than expected came. The price plummeted, and Lyon was ruined.[73]

He was right back in the pit, making more trades, the next day. No deal was too big or too risky for him, only too small and too easy. He once told a friend, "If I have the same opportunity as you, I will either drive a better horse or quit the game." Though known as a friendly enough man—always "John," not "Mr. Lyon" to the other traders—manipulating the market seems to have been his singular passion.[74]

However, his granddaughter, **Cornelia Conger** (1887–1973), remembered him as a man who "was much interested in philosophy," and who "heartily disliked bigots." During the 1893 World's Fair, John and his wife, **Emily Lyon** (1832–1917), hosted Swami Vivekananda at their home when he came to speak at the Congress of World's Religions, the major interfaith conference held at the new Art Institute building. Some suggested that the Lyons should put the swami in a hotel because they were also hosting white southern guests who might object to sleeping under the same roof as an Indian man, but Emily said, "I don't care a bit if all our guests leave. This Indian is the most brilliant and interesting man who has ever been in our home, and he shall stay as long as he wishes."[75] In his Chicago talks, the Swami is sometimes credited with introducing yoga to the United States;[76] six-year-old Cornelia adored him and told stories about him for the rest of her life. She became a noted decorator.[77]

The "Lyon" memorial bench at Graceland was built in the plot in 1901,[78] a year after the death of John's son, **William C. "Billy" Lyon (1852–1900)**. Billy finished his primary education when he was so young that no university would take him; after joining his father's business at 16, he often joked that he'd gotten into the Board of Trade only because he couldn't get into college. He soon became known as "the Boy Speculator," every bit as daring and successful as his father, but after a few years he left trading to invest in railroads.[79]

Investing was simply a job to him; William loved the theater and "Bohemian life" far more than he liked business. He lived in the notorious First Ward rather than a more glamorous area and seemed to like his various social clubs better than any home or family he could imagine for himself. He once upbraided Cornelia when she waved at him through a club window because "When a gentleman is in his club, he is invisible."[80] Newspapers regularly reprinted jokes he told around the clubs, and he developed a reputation as a bon vivant. A lifelong bachelor, he died in 1900 of heart disease.

• • •

Behind the Lyon bench is a Celtic cross designed by sculptor Leonard Volk for the family of **Julia Goodwin (1865–1869)**.[81] Several feet to the left of it is a very interesting large marker for manufacturer **Franklin Brown (1824–1870)** featuring a now-worn portrait of a man and one or two infants, with the epitaph "weep for his children too young to weep for themselves," likely a paraphrase from Elizabeth Barrett Browning's "Aurora Leigh."

Return to the path. On the right, as the road overlaps slightly with Route 2-A, there will be a marker in the form of a square-cornered shaft topped by a globe, on which appear the words of Psalm 23. It marks an extended family of artists who worked in a wide variety of media.

The Shaw-Judson-McCutcheon Plot

"To think people pay me for doing this!"
—Howard Van Doren Shaw, "Ragdale Restored"

Architect **Howard Van Doren Shaw (1869–1926)** designed buildings such as the first planned shopping center, as well as the Goodman tomb at Graceland (page 147). The large marker topped by a globe was designed by him;[82] nearby are the smaller stones marking the plots of his family. Among those interred her are his wife, poet **Francis Shaw (1872–1937)**, daughter **Evelyn Shaw McCutcheon (1813–1977)**, and Evelyn's husband, **John McCutcheon (1870–1949)**, who for many years was the cartoonist for the *Chicago Tribune*. A Pulitzer Prize winner, John was also an occasional member of the famous Whitechapel Club, a group of newspaper men who met in a clubhouse that was decorated with skeletons, murder weapons, and other gruesome paraphernalia.[83] He accompanied Theodore Roosevelt on part of his 1909 safari.[84]

"The artist serves humanity by feeding its hungry spirits
in as real a sense as (a cook) feeds hungry bodies."
—Sylvia Shaw Judson, "Quaker Artists"

The Shaw monument

Another small red stone marks Shaw's other daughter, **Sylvia Shaw Judson (1897–1978)**[85] who was a professional sculptor. Her fabulous art deco relief sculpture *The Spirit of Electricity* can still be seen on the old ComEd substation on North Dearborn that couldn't be demolished when Block 37 was built.

In recent years, she's become most famous for *Bird Girl*, the haunting statue that appeared on the cover of John Berendt's novel *Midnight in the Garden of Good and Evil*. The Shaw family house and studio, Ragdale, was donated to Lake Forest as an artist's colony in 1986.[86]

. . .

Just to the left of Shaw is the large black monument to brewer **Franz Bartholomae (1839–1918)**, near which a monument is currently planned for architect **Helmut Jahn (1940–2021)**. Behind Bartholomae's monument is a shaft topped by a robed woman and bearing the name of **Edward H. Hadduck (1811–1881)**, who was a boarder in Dexter Graves' hotel (page 241) and later married Dexter's daughter, **Louisa Graves Hadduck (1815–1884)**. Edward and Louisa's daughter, Helen, married **Joseph de Koven (1833–1898)**, a banker. Their own daughter, Louise, married another banker, **Joseph T. Bowen (1854–1911)**, whose name appears on the south side of the shaft.

Louise de Koven Bowen

> "When I was told I could have a party I sometimes won-
> dered if the pleasure I got out of it was worth the wash-
> ing of the crystal chandelier."
> —Louise de Koven-Bowen, *Growing Up with a City*

Born in 1859 to a pioneer family who regaled her with stories of Chicago in the frontier days, **Louise de Koven Bowen (1859–1953)**[87] became a part of high society as a young woman; her memoir, *Growing Up with a City*, looked back with amusement on how she felt it was terribly stylish to have a footman named Cornelius, on stealing gooseberries from Eli B. Williams (page 8), and on being afraid she'd look hopelessly uncivil if she hosted a party and sent invitations through the mail instead of delivering them by hand.[88] The digestive adventures brought on by the gooseberries may have taught her a lesson about stealing, and set her off on the road to her life as a social reformer.

Her memoir also provides a wonderful eyewitness account of Lincoln Park in its early days, when it was still being transitioned from the old City Cemetery to a park. "It had been a graveyard," she wrote, "and as we drove through it we saw countless open graves with a piece here and there of a decayed coffin and every now and then on a pile of dirt a bone, evidently dropped by those removing the bodies. The whole place looked exactly as if the Judgment Day had come, the trumpets had sounded and everyone had arisen from their graves, dropping now and then a little piece of their anatomy as they fled to Graceland or Rose Hill where they again deposited themselves underground."[89]

Bowen was one of several high-society women who became early supporters of Jane Addams and Hull House, and was a founder of the Woman's Club. Besides the autobiography and a memoir of her time with Jane Addams (*Open Windows*), she wrote several books and pamphlets detailing her committees' investigations into working and playing conditions in Chicago's hotels, dance halls, cheap theaters, and department stores. In particular, *The Department Store Girl* is a fascinating glimpse into labor and social conditions for single young women, and retail workers in general, around 1910. One would not think of a department store as a den of iniquity, but after interviewing 200 young women who worked in them, Bowen found that the long hours and low pay left nearly all of them constantly tired, in poor health, and extremely vulnerable to sexual predators.[90] In 1941, Bowen became the first woman to receive the Rotary Club's gold medal for distinguished service. By the time of her death in 1953 she was considered one of the country's foremost social workers.[91]

She also may have commissioned the *Eternal Silence* statue; her signature appears frequently in the probate file for her great Uncle, Henry Graves, on whose lot the statue stands (page 42).

∎ ∎ ∎

Take a right off the road, going between the curbed-off plots of Hadduck-Bowen and **Marcus Stearns (1816–1890)**, who, like his Graceland neighbor William Coolbaugh, was a millionaire business man who ended his own life with a pistol. A jury determined he had been depressed over ill health.[92]

You will pass another curbed-off family plot, that of **Samuel Meigs Johnson (1822–1864)**. It's interesting to contrast the lengthy tributes to early Civil War casualties, such as William Webb (page 1) with an 1864 death like Johnson, whom the *Tribune* mentioned just briefly more than a month after his death:

"On the 11th of January last, the death of Captain Samuel L. Johnson, formerly a member of the Board, was announced. The usual resolutions of sympathy and condolence were tendered to the family of the deceased—another of the many brave men who have yielded up their lives in defense of the union."[93] They didn't even get Samuel's middle initial right.

. . .

On the left, the last plot before you reach the road will be that of the High family.

The High Plot

John High (c1807–1857) died in the terrible 1857 fire that also killed John Dickey (page 243); his body was laid out for an inquest at the office of Dr. Brainard (page 16).[94] John had been an influential business man in the city for twenty years, a partner of H. H. Magie (page 137), who leased Potter Palmer (page 148) the space for his first store.[95] John and his wife, **Elizabeth High (c1812–1852)**, were moved to Graceland in 1866.[96]

John's death left his and Elizabeth's five children on their own; at the time, the oldest was **George Meeker High (1840–1898)**, who had watched his father rush into the burning building and then saw his body carried out. Only 17 at the time, he became executor of his father's considerable estate, and impressed everyone with how well he handled it. Though his own official cause of death decades later was heart failure, many traced it to an incident in Boston six weeks earlier, when he had been run down by horses while riding a bicycle.[97]

George M. High's son, **George Henry High (1864–1945)**, was an internationally known photographer whose work in the 1930s was shown in salons the world over, and still commands high prices at auctions.[98]

A great granddaughter of John, **Ellen Dudley Root (1892–1941)**, was a successful theater actress and the first wife of architect John Wellborn Root Jr. (page 114). She was working for the ambulance service in France at the time of her death on New Year's Day, 1941.[99] Her simple brown marker, just off the side of the High family markers, was designed by Herman Lackner of her ex-husband's firm, Holabird and Root.[100]

. . .

Just past the High plot is the paved road. Take a left, and on your right will be two McCormick lots, on a path crossed over by Route 1-A (page 5).

Herbert Stone and the Other McCormick Plot

"After the dreary wastes of all our unimaginative preach-
ers, with their 'ethical purpose in art' . . . and Heaven
knows what clap-trap beside, a good round wholesome
lie, a splendid unbelievable fabric of events that never
happened and hardly could happen, is as refreshing as
a sea-wind through city streets in summertime."
—H. S. Stone and Hannibal Kimball on Rudyard
  Kipling, *The Chap Book*

A classmate of **Herbert Stuart Stone (1871–1915)** never forgot the day the class was assigned to write compositions about the wastebasket.[101] Most students wrote essays describing the basket, but Herbert, whose father founded the *Chicago Daily News*, wrote a monologue from the basket's point of view—in it, the basket told how it enjoyed reading the essays that were thrown into it, and, though it hated to disagree with the teacher, it thought some of them were pretty good. "We had described the basket as a thing," the classmate wrote, "Herbert Stone had given it life."[102] As an adult, Herbert became a publisher, founding the magazine *House Beautiful* and serving as the American publisher to authors such as George Bernard Shaw.

He was in the smoking room of the *RMS Lusitania* when it was hit by a torpedo and drowned when the ship sank;[103] his body was recovered in Ireland and buried here three months later, in a plot marked by a monument bearing the name of his wife's grandfather, a man he never met.

Herbert was married to **Mary Grigsby McCormick Stone (1877–1955)**, a granddaughter of **William S. McCormick (1815–1865)**. A brother of Cyrus (page 176), William had helped build the family business in Chicago after moving from Virginia.[104]

Though nominally in favor of the Union and against secession, the first generation of Chicago McCormick brothers favored compromise with the south, and William and his wife, **Mary Ann Grigsby McCormick (1828–1878)**, quit going to church in Chicago because of all the abolitionist sermons.[105] He suffered from poor health throughout the early 1860s and died months after the Civil War ended. A biography of his brother states that in his last moments, William begged his brothers to "realize the folly of money-making and 'forbear one another in love.'"[106] A son of William, Ambassador **Robert Sanderson McCormick (1849–1919)** married **Katherine Medill McCormick (1853–1932)** and is buried with her in the Medill plot (page 138).

But the third brother, **Leander McCormick (1819–1900)**, buried in the plot of mostly newer markers to the right of William's monument, claimed that it was truly their father who invented the reaper, and, while Cyrus was charged with marketing it, the funds were supposed to have been divided equally among the three brothers. Leander devoted his life to proving it, even after Cyrus died. It's likely telling that William and Leander are buried far across the cemetery from Cyrus, though there's room in his "wilderness" for dozens more burials.[107]

Elsewhere in the plot are Leander's grandson, **Robert Hall McCormick III (1878–1963)**, a lawyer and real estate developer, and great-grandson son, who went by **Robert Hall McCormick Jr. (1914–1997)**. The two were credited with conceiving the ultramodern glass wall apartments at 860 North Lake Shore Drive in the late 1940s. There were troubles with regulating temperature and light early on, but Robert Jr. felt that it was well worth it for the "terribly exciting" views of storms over Lake Michigan.[108]

Among the more recently interred descendants is **Robert Hall McCormick VI (1944–2012)**, a real estate broker; in contrast to some of his namesake ancestors, he was described in his obituary as "an outspoken liberal . . . who had a knack for making convincing arguments in political discourse with his conservative pals."[109]

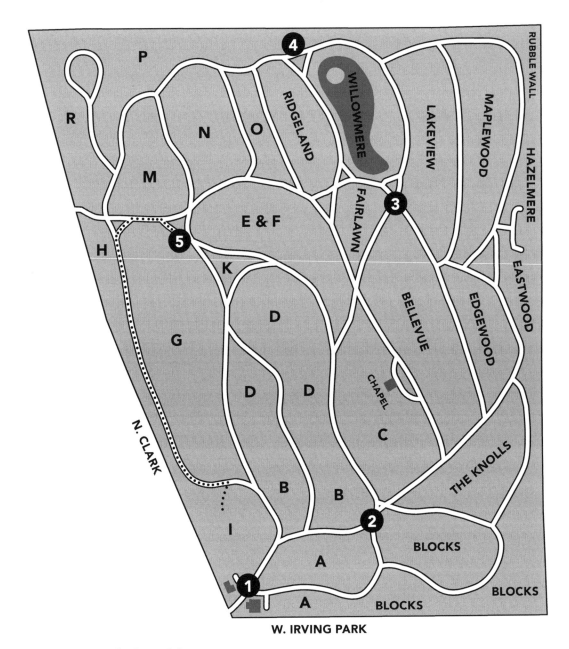

Map for Route 5-B

Walk past the Eddy triangle and down the road toward the West wall. Just past the red and white marker for brewer **Frederick Lehmann (c1820–1872)** will be the mausoleum marked Huck, ornamented with lions' heads.

The Huck Mausoleum

> "The funeral [of Clara Kenkel Huck] took place at the late home of the deceased, No. 292 Indiana Street . . . Upon the piano, that has so often lent its accompaniment to the glorious voice that is hushed for earthly hearers, rested a cover of crepe . . . above this was an easel bearing a large photograph of Mrs Huck, taken the morning after her death. It showed a face of great beauty in sweet repose, the expression angelic, ethereal, as if she still heard the faint echoes of the swan song from Lohengrin and 'Home Sweet Home,' the numbers she sang the day of her death."
>
> —"Mortuary, Clara Kenkel-Huck," *Chicago Daily Inter-Ocean*

Louis C. Huck (1842–1905), son of fellow brewer John A. Huck (page 10), may not be in his own mausoleum. In 1947, his second wife, Paula Reif Huck (born 1863), had his remains, and those of their daughter, removed.[1] Records indicate that the ashes of the daughter, **Paula Huck Gould (1894–1931)**, were returned to the vault, but if Louis' were, the records don't indicate it.

His first wife, **Clara Kenkel Huck (1850–1888)**, had been a very popular opera singer, noted for a soprano voice with an unusual timber. On tour, she was known to play 11 different characters in one night.[2] She gave up her career when she married Louis at the age of 16, but continued to appear onstage in all of the biggest Chicago venues for occasional performances[3] until her death from heart trouble in 1888.[4] She died in Germany, but her remains were brought home and placed in an ornate sarcophagus so large that a special funeral car had to be designed to carry it.[5]

The Huck Mausoleum

Of Clara and Louis' three youngest daughters, one married a German baron, another an Italian marquis, and one, Albertine, married Marshall Field Jr. (page 174).

Five children of Clara and Louis who died in infancy are in the tomb, as well as one adult son, **Henry E. Huck (1874–1921)**. After Clara's death, Louis married Albertine's good friend Paula Reif.[6] Louis' son with Paula, **Louis C. Huck Jr. (1896–1952)**, made millions in manufacturing and invented four-wheel automobile brakes and a blind rivet that was used in B-24 bombers during World War II.[7] Louis Jr.'s stone outside the vault contains a space for his wife, Dorothy, with a blank date of death; she died in 1988 and was interred in Michigan.[8]

Paula was still alive and living in Italy when Louis Jr. died in 1952,[9] but records as to what became of her, or the final disposition of her husband's ashes, could not be determined.

■ ■ ■

Take a left to head south down Western Avenue, parallel to the western wall.

On the left side of the road, several feet down, look for the tall red marker for **Adolph Weidenbaum (1815–1891)**. Several feet behind it, to the right of a small gray marker for **Patrick J Weldon (1850–1937)**, is an unmarked space for John Q. and Rachel Grant.

John Q. Grant and Rachel Grant

> "Sunday Rev. Archibald James Carey was on his high horses. He railed at his flock of sheep for permitting their names to appear on the rolls or in the Bulletin each week without paying their class dues. J. Q. Grant, who always has the courage to give expression to his honest convictions, arose and took a hand in the wordy combat. He showed or proved that he himself and many others had paid their dues without receiving the proper credit, and when he got through Rev. Archibald was as quiet as a church mouse."
> —*The Broad Ax*, no title, Dec. 5, 1903

John Q. Grant (1842–1913) and **Rachel Collins Grant (1846–1917)** were born in the 1840s in Kentucky and North Carolina, respectively. John was born enslaved according to his obituary,[10] and Rachel likely was as well, though her parents appear to have escaped to the relative freedom of Chicago when she was only a baby.[11]

John is said to have come to Chicago after the Civil War,[12] though some records indicate he was involved with Quinn Chapel, the city's first prominent

Black church, as early as 1862. In the 1870s he was elected to the office of High Constable, a job that mostly required him to oversee repossessions, and was often noted in the press as the only Black constable in Chicago. Frequently sued and arrested himself, a *Chicago Defender* writer later said that Grant "well understood not only the law of service, but how to evade the law of service if the occasion required."[13]

Scanning John's mentions in newspapers of his era shows an entreprenurial and ambitious spirit: in between stints as a constable, he is variously listed as the owner of the Southern Hotel at 22nd and Wabash, a pawn broker, a collection agent, and a number of other jobs, and he seems to have been a member of both the Freemasons and the Odd Fellows. In 1912, *The Broad Axe* reported that he had died and then issued a correction, stating that "he is alive and improving and is not thinking about dying at the present time."[14] He passed away six months later.

After the original Quinn Chapel was destroyed in the Great Chicago Fire, the church met for several years in a new building at West Van Buren and South Federal before the still-standing chapel at 2401 S. Wabash was built in 1891. When the Van Buren Street location was demolished in 1916, the son of Joseph Hudlun (page 255) arranged to find a time capsule that had been set in the cornerstone when it was first built, just after the Great Chicago Fire. Inside was Rachel's hymnal, still bearing her maiden name of Rachel Collins. At the time, she was still alive and said to be the oldest member of the church.[15]

■ ■ ■

Further south on Western Avenue, the Wolfer marker is particularly striking: the gray obelisk features an inset relief sculpture on which most of the features have been worn smooth by the elements. It's presumably the face of **Josephine Wolfer (c1882–1886)**, a saloon-keeper's daughter who died of diptheria at the age of 4.[16]

Behind Wolfer, and a bit to the right, is a small monument featuring a book on top of a pillow; the signature on the book reproduces the autograph of author Florence McLandburgh.

Florence McLandburgh:
Early Science Fiction Author

"What we desire is the abolition of the huge and terrific engines of death man has invented. This is the blot on civilization . . . We women should not be silenced in this controversy."

—Florence McLandburgh, "Let the Women Be Heard"

In 1925, **Florence Mclandburgh (1850–1934)** wrote a letter to the *Akron Beacon Journal* questioning whether it was a virtue to fear God, or anything else, when fear led us to build weapons of war.[17] In response, a reader wrote that he assumed Florence was "a gifted young woman, (but a) product of modern education," who had not yet realized the softening virtue of religion.[18] An amused friend wrote back that Florence was, in fact, nearly 80. "To see her now," she wrote, "a sprightly old lady with white curls, you might accuse her of being young, or even rebellious, but you certainly could never accuse her of not having had her sufficient set-tos with religion."[19]

In her youth, Florence was a pioneering author of "gothic science fiction," and published a book entitled *The Automaton Ear and Other Stories* in 1876. Written when she was sick and feeble due to no disease that doctors could identify, the title story was about a professor who invents a device that allows him to hear sounds from the distant past—it is now considered a pioneering work in the "time viewer" subset of science fiction stories.[20] The book was praised by Henry Wadsworth Longfellow as "very powerfully written, and excites the organ of wonder very strongly, almost too strongly sometimes."[21]

Decades later, during World War I, she wrote patriotic poetry under the name McLandburgh Wilson, though in one of her frequent (and fascinating) letters to the newspapers in the 1920s, she claimed that "nobody won the war."[22]

By 1920 she was living in Akron, Ohio, where a reporter found her eager to reminisce about the Great Chicago Fire, the McCormick Ball, and actor Edwin Booth. She had been sickly all her life (it was implied that her health forced her to stop writing when she was still in her 20s), but thanks to a local doctor she was now "a chirrupy, dainty, fragile old lady."[23]

■ ■ ■

Further into the grass past McLandburgh and to the right, find the Foute headstone, behind which is a marker for several people in the Rhines family, including the city's most notorious "slave catcher."

Henry Rhines:
The Abolitionists' Enemy

"As for us, rather than to be a public officer who had aided in the re-enslavement of any man (as Rhines has just done), we would choose to spend our days in a slave gang on a southern plantation."
—"A Claimed Fugitive Given Up," *Western Citizen*

In 1840, **Henry Rhines (1808–1852)** was one of three sheriff's deputies in the city, and that year he made his mark on local history by being the man who arrested and interrogated John Stone for the murder of Lucretia Thompson. Stone would be the first man hanged in Chicago.[24]

But most of his career in Chicago made him more infamous than famous; by 1844, when he ran for city marshall, he was already so well known for his eagerness to arrest (or, properly, kidnap) people suspected of being escaped enslaved people that his opponents branded him a "notorious negro catcher."[25] One undated account has him arresting the whole family of a man named Nicholas Jones and robbing his wife before sending them south.[26] In 1846, he was the man described in the press as the "degraded, drunken wretch" who arrested the men whom lawyers Freer, Larned, and Collins helped escape (page 59).[27] At one point, when he tried to stop the *Great Western*, from sailing off with several escapees, Captain Walker said, "You must be a damned scoundrel," and sailed away as Philo Carpenter (page 30), L. C. P. Freer (page 59), James Collins (page 61), and others cheered from the shore.[28]

Rhines was always quick to threaten to shoot people who didn't obey his commands and is known to have followed through on the threat once: in 1847, he was indicted for shooting a barkeeper who tried to throw him out.[29] The barkeeper Timothy Dunn died the next month.[30] A month after that, Rhines was reported to have escaped from the jail,[31] and a few weeks later was captured in New Orleans.[32] The whole issue must have blown over in the end; though no article explaining how Rhines escaped murder charges has been found, in 1851 he was listed as one of the men who helped bring in Moses Johnson for the landmark case won by George Manierre (page 13).[33] Rhines died the next year and was moved to Graceland in 1869.[34]

His son, **Henry "Dump" Rhines (1844–1904)**, was one of the most famous billiard players in the country.[35] Dump's brother, **Volney Rhines (1839–1906)**, managed a billiard hall on East Adams Street himself toward the end of his life.[36]

. . .

Return to the road and proceed south, following it as it curves to the left. Just before it curves again to the right will be the Fargo obelisk, the grave of **Charles Henry Fargo (1897–1932)**, an army reserve officer who was flying over the south side of Chicago when his plane's engine failed. Fargo and his co-pilot could have parachuted to safety, but that would have meant abandoning the plane, and risk having it crash into a street or building. They opted instead to crash it into a vacant lot, minimizing the damage but sacrificing their own lives.[37]

Walk past Fargo's marker into the grass of Section I. Several yards past Fargo, look for the red granite prairie-style monument topped by a bronze urn with a green patina.

Ernst Schmidt: The Radical Doctor

"The name of the wrongfully executed shines radiantly through the ages, upheld by the pity and veneration of mankind, a solemn warning for those who desecrate the name and the spirit of justice."
—Dr. Ernst Schmidt, "Marks Their Grave"

In 1848, many Germans had to flee the country after failed liberal uprisings. One of these "forty-eighters," **Dr. Ernst Schmidt (1830–1900)**, came to Chicago, where he served on the boards of multiple hospitals and became the most respected radical in town.

He became active in politics immediately upon his arrival, particularly in the abolition movement, which led him to get involved in the Underground Railroad,[38] and to make a speech at memorial services for John Brown.[39] During the Civil War he served as a lieutenant colonel in the 2nd Missouri Infantry, and after the war, when many old-time abolitionists were getting involved in the temperance (anti-drinking) movement, Schmidt was elected president of an *anti*-temperance group.[40]

The prairie-style monument was designed by an architect often listed (though sometimes not) as one of Schmidt's sons, Richard E. Schmidt, who also designed the Schoenhofen pyramid (page 119).[41] [42]

■ ■ ■

Turn right at Schmidt, proceeding further west toward the brick wall, and you'll soon see the small bluish gray stone memorial marked "Dickens" on your left.

Augustus Dickens, Charles Dickens'
Scapegrace Brother

"Augustus Dickens . . . liked his friends but was quite sarcastic about men he disliked. He remarked on one occasion, 'Say, Bernard, I don't wish that man would die, but I do wish God would remove him from my path.'"
—Frederick Barnard, neighbor of Augustus Dickens, "When Boz Lived in Chicago"

When Charles Dickens returned to the United States in 1867 for a reading tour, Chicagoans assumed he would be coming to town. After all, his brother, **Augustus Dickens (1827–1866)**, had just died in Chicago a year before. Surely Charles would want to comfort the widow, meet her children, and visit the gravesite at Graceland. When he announced that he wasn't coming this far west, local papers called him every name in the book.[43]

Really, though, making a Chicago trip would have been terribly difficult for him. Though Dickens was willing enough to consider a trip that he sent his advance agent, George Dolby, to examine halls and scout locations for a reading, his poor health would have made the long train ride inadvisable. And, though no one in Chicago yet knew it, there was *another* Mrs. Augustus Dickens still living, abandoned, back in London. Visiting the Mrs. Augustus Dickens in Chicago could have led to a scandal.

Bertha Phillips (1827–1868) was the daughter of either a prominent merchant or an English lord who presented her to Queen Victoria, depending on which source one reads. When the married Bertha became pregnant by the also-married Augustus Dickens in the 1850s, the two fled to the United States, where Augustus tried his hand at various trades before coming to Chicago, where he used his famous name to get a position with the Chicago and Alton Railway.

He and Bertha had five more children after the first, including triplets **Ophelia, Lincoln, and Violet (1865)**, who died in infancy within days of each other. The two lived on Clark Street near Burton, just below Lincoln Park. Neighbors remembered Augustus as a very funny man; he may have been a scapegrace, but neighbor Fred Barnard said that "A more genial and whole-souled man never lived." Bertha was recalled as a marvelous piano player.[44] Legend has it that Augustus appeared in theatrical adaptations of his brother's novels.

After Augustus died of tuberculosis in 1866, Bertha was rumored to be living in poverty, but anecdotes about her from friends indicate that she was able to make ends meet. However, she died of an accidental morphine overdose on Christmas Eve of 1868.

Charles, despite the possible scandal, arranged to make annual payments to provide for the surviving children, but didn't write the payments into his will, so they were stopped after his own death in 1870. Though the children all seemed friendly in their attitudes toward their uncle in a 1913 *Inter Ocean* article, one of their grandchildren, Deborah Dickens Anthony, was quoted in her obituary as saying she'd been raised to believe that "if anybody knew she was related to Charles Dickens, she'd have to sit on the porch with a bag over her head."[45] A few generations later, feelings had cooled, and the children's descendants worked with The Dickens Fellowship to have a marker placed on the long-unmarked grave in 2004.

・・・

Pass Dickens and head closer to the wall. Near the wall is a relatively prominent monument marked "Gray." Behind it is a rounded marker for Willis Montgomery and a smaller one for Joseph Hudlun, both of which say "Papa" on the top. This unassuming plot, and the seemingly empty one just north of it, are among Graceland's most thrilling mysteries.

Joseph Henry Hudlun and the Underground Railroad

"I remember (Hudlun) well. He used to drive a horse and
   buggy to work every day. Everybody knew him, just as
   they know Joe (Hudlun Jr.) today."
—Harry J. Rogers, "Janitor Joe 47 Years On Job at
   Board of Trade"

There were several stories told as to how **Joseph Henry Hudlun (1830–1894)**[46] gained his freedom. Born enslaved in Culpepper County, Virginia, some versions said that after he was taken to St. Louis, one day he simply walked onto a river boat and began working as a cook, remaining on the ship as it sailed away. He simply got off the ship when it docked in Illinois before anyone realized he wasn't supposed to be there. Other versions say that he worked as a sailor on a few trips to Liverpool and then made his way across the lakes from New York to Chicago.[47]

Though accounts of how he got to Chicago differ, it was always said that on his first day in town, he talked his way into a job sweeping floors at the original Board of Trade that was located on Water Street in 1854. In 1857 he built a house at Dearborn and Polk, once listed by the *Chicago Defender* as the first house built by a Black family in the city.[48]

The Hudlun and Montgomery markers

The house, which miraculously survived the Great Chicago Fire, had served as shelter during the Underground Railroad days; Joseph's brother, Peter, was operating a "station" in St. Louis. He would bring the escapees to Alton, where Joseph would meet them and bring them to Chicago.[49] His son, Joseph Jr., said he remembered many times in later years when his parents would be heard "chuckling in reminiscences over their adventures."[50]

Joseph's wife, Anne Hudlun, was a Chicago woman he'd known in Virginia. They turned their home into a shelter after the Great Chicago Fire for several families, including the Atkinsons (page 68), earning Anna the nickname "The Fire Angel." (She died in 1914 and is buried at Mt. Greenwood.)[51]

Joseph worked his job at the Board of Trade for 39 years; ringing the bell that opened and closed business in addition to his other duties. He saved valuable papers from the vault during the 1871 fire, and, in 1893, tackled a gunman who was firing into the Pit.[52] His son remembered him reminding Phillip Armour (page 136) to wear his overcoat.[53]

He came to be an expert on commodities and could tell every story of attempts at "corners" from his decades of work, but he never got involved in speculating himself. Instead, he made more than most of the traders ever did by sweeping up the leftover grain and seed samples every night and selling them to feed stores and stables. At the time of his death in 1894, it was reported that he'd amassed as much as $80,000—well over a million in today's money.

A portrait of Joseph was hung in the "Hall of Celebrities" at the Board of Trade for decades;[54] his son, Joseph Jr., took over his position there upon his death and held the job for half a century more.[55] Interred with him is a teenage daughter **Sarah Jane Hudlun (1857–1872)** and an infant daughter **Anna Hudlun (1858)**.[56]

In a strange twist, though, the headstone for Joseph is *not* in the plot he purchased. His plot is the one directly north of his marker, marked by a base to which no monument was added. Records indicate that this base was intended for a Hudlun monument, but apparently never used, which opens the mystery of why his marker is in the adjacent Gray family plot.

The obelisk near Hudlun gives the names of **Robert W. Gray (c 1830–1892)**, his wife **Martha Gray (1841–1916)**, and Martha's mother, **Mary Ann Stevens (c1815–1887)**. As Black women born in pre-war Missouri,[57] Mary Ann and Martha were likely born enslaved. Records show that Mary Ann was initially buried in Joseph Hudlun's plot and moved to this spot when Martha purchased it upon Robert's death, so it's to be assumed that they must have been close to the Hudluns—the most obvious scenario that springs to mind is that they were among the enslaved people he helped escape from St. Louis.

Others in the plot include **Louise Ellston (c1846–1908)**, a Black woman whose place of birth was unknown to whoever filled out her death certificate but is the only person in the plot who could possibly match the "sister" marker that is present. She was likely Martha's sister and came to Chicago with Martha and Mary Ann; the Kentucky-born **Frank J. Ellston (c1846–1902)** whose grave is marked would have been her husband.

Biographical details on the Stevens-Gray family are scarce, but Martha appeared several times in the social registers of Black newspapers, one of which notes that she'd attended Mardi Gras in 1914. She would have been in her 70s by then.[58]

Behind the Gray marker, next to Hudlun's, is another small rounded gravestone, topped with the word "Papa," for **Willis Montgomery (c1829–1894)**. What little information on Montgomery exists is remarkably error-prone: the cause of his 1894 death is listed as "unintelligible" in the Graceland internment book;[59] the 1880 census-taker enumerated Montgomery at his barber shop near Kinzie and Water Streets, not his home (a note on the form says "keeps his shop here but don't live here,") and in the spot for his mother's birthplace a note says "Can't tell."[60] The best newspaper item about him is a brief reference to him having a barber shop of his own in Evanston in 1876, which made the news only for having caught fire.[61]

Though many vital records say that Montgomery was born in Harrodsburgh, Kentucky, around 1829, his gravestone mistakenly gives the date as 1859. As a Black man born in Kentucky in the 1820s, it's likely that he was born enslaved (as was his wife, Kentucky-born **Ada Montgomery (1828–1913)**, who is buried with him). His death certificate notes that 1859 was the year he came to Chicago.

The last interment in the plot, **Charles Williams (1863–1934)**, was a Black man born during the war in Virginia. In Chicago he worked as a waiter and was a member of the John Jones lodge; he died in a Masonic home in Rock Island.[62]

Of course, the connection between the Hudlun, Montgomery, Gray, and Williams families are in the realm of speculation, but that they were families Hudlun had helped escape on the Underground Railroad is perhaps the simplest explanation to the mystery.

Some "last words" attributed to Graceland residents:

NETTIE MCCORMICK: "How lovely! How lovely! How lovely!"[63]

BOB FITZSIMMONS: "Keep fighting and remember: good fighters never lose."

JOE HILL (cremated at Graceland): "Don't mourn for me—organize!"

JOHN ALTGELD: "Any political institution, if it is to endure, must be plumb with the line of justice."

GEORGE MANIERRE: "Plaintiff. . . . defendant . . ."[64]

JOSEPH MEDILL: "What is the news?"

KATHERINE MEDILL MCCORMICK: "My god, what a bottom." (She was looking at an attendant who was walking away.)[65]

CYRUS MCCORMICK: "Work! Work! Work!" (or, in other sources, "It's all right, it's all right. I only want heaven").[66]

CAPT. PETER WOOD: "I thank God for my sickness; I am ready to go, thy will be done, O Lord; God bless you all."[67]

CARTER HARRISON: "Give me water. Where is Annie?"

PAMILLA ALLERTON: "Talk, do not look sober. Be cheerful. Be happy."[68]

CAP STREETER: "Now, don't go feeling bad, Ma. We'll get ours back yet. I'll fight 'em."

REV. THOMAS MEARS EDDY: "Tell the rich men to lay down their gold for God."[69]

Appendix

Famous Chicago Names

Notes

The Origins of Graceland Cemetery

1. "The President's Funeral." *Chicago Tribune*, Apr 26, 1865.

2. "Lieut. Gen. Grant." *Chicago Tribune*, Jun 11, 1865.

3. "An Exhibit from Rome." *New York Times*, Feb 13, 1892.

4. Selzer, Adam. *HH Holmes: The True History of the White City Devil.* Skyhorse Publishing, 2017.

5. Letter of Dr. Rosa, 1822, quoted in *Documents of the Assembly of the State of New York*, Vol Three. Albany, Carrol and Cook, 1846.

6. Walker, George Alfred. *Gatherings from Graveyards.* London, Long and Co., 1839.

7. "Doctors All Agree." *Chicago Tribune.* Mar 23, 1890.

8. "City Built on Graves." *Chicago Tribune.* Aug 8, 1897.

9. Bryan, Thomas. "Our Two Cemeteries." *Chicago Tribune*, Dec 8, 1862.

10. Vernon, Christopher. *Graceland Cemetery: A Design History.* University of Massachusetts Press, 2012.

11. No title. *Park and Cemetery*, Jan 1906.

12. Vernon. *Graceland Cemetery.*

13. Krupp, Emma. "Check Out Before and After Pictures of Graceland Cemetery." https://www.timeout.com/chicago/news/check-out-before-and-after-photos-of-graceland-cemetery-newly-reopened-after-last-months-derecho-091820.

Station One

1. No title. *Chicago Times*, Apr 17, 1862.

2. "Our Two Cemeteries." *Chicago Tribune*, Dec 5, 1862.

3. "The Court House Bell." *Chicago Tribune*, Jan 14, 1872.

4. "The Historical Chair." *Chicago Tribune*, Sep 6, 1860.

5. "Old Abe's Proclamation—Its Clandestine Sale." *Chicago Times*, Nov 19, 1863.

6. No title. *Chicago Times*, Apr 17, 1862.

7. "Burials on the Soldiers' Lot at Rose Hill Cemetery." *Chicago Tribune*, Apr 21, 1862.

8. Graceland Cemetery Records, Section I-A.

9. "Death of Col Webb—Resolutions of Respect." *Chicago Tribune*, Jan 1, 1862.

10. G. W. G. "The 42nd Illinois in Winter Quarters." *Chicago Tribune*, Jan 23, 1862.

Route 1A

1. *Proceedings of the Bunker Hill Monument Association.* Boston, Bunker Hill Monument Association, 1895.

2. "Ninety and Nine." *Chicago Tribune*, Oct 24, 1876.

3. Theodore Gridley pension records.

4. "Almost a Century." *Chicago Tribune*, Jan 5, 1876.

5. Ibid.

6. Graceland Cemetery Records, Section A, Lot 9.

7. Baumgartner, Kabria. *In Pursuit of Knowledge: Black Women and Educational Activism in Antebellum America.* New York University Press, 2019.

8. Graceland Cemetery Records, Section A, Lot 9.

9. Graceland Interment Book Volume 2.

10. "Afternoon Telegrams." *Burlington Free Press*, Oct 16, 1871.

11. "Fatal Incidents." *Chicago Tribune*, Oct 10, 1871; he was unnamed in the report but later writers connected the story to Dewey.

12. Obituary. *Chicago Tribune*, Apr 3, 1945.

13. "The Late Captain Aiken." *Chicago Tribune*, Aug 18, 1864.

14. "From the White House." *Chicago Tribune*, Jun 14, 1864.

15. "The War in Virginia." *Chicago Tribune*, Aug 8, 1864.

16. "The Lost City." *Chicago Tribune*, Jan 5, 1873.

17. U.S. Census Bureau. United States Census 1860.

18. Graceland Cemetery Records, Section B, Lot 3.

19. "Has a Bad Memory." *Chicago Daily Inter-Ocean*, Apr 20, 1889.

20. Maher, Genevieve, "When the Gold Coast Was a Brewery." *Chicago Tribune*, Aug 18, 1963.

21. Ibid.

22. Ibid.

23. "The Fire of Monday." *Chicago Tribune*, Oct 21, 1857.

24. "Terrible Conflagration." *Chicago Tribune*, Oct 20, 1857.

25. "The Fire Department." *Chicago Tribune*, Oct 20, 1857.

26. "She Was a Lincoln Pall Bearer." *Topeka State Journal* (and others), Jan 19, 1917.

27. Advertisement. *Chicago Tribune*, Jan 19, 1884.

28. Letter of C. F. Hoffman, Jan 10, 1834, reprinted in *Carlisle Weekly Herald*, May 13, 1834.

29. *Chicago Democrat*, Jan 11, 1834, as paraphrased in *Illinois Weekly State Journal*, Feb 8, 1834.

30. *Album of Genealogy and Biography, Cook County, IL.* Calumet Book and Engraving Co., 1896.

31. *A History of the City of Chicago: Its Men and Its Institutions.* Chicago, 1900.

32. *Album of Genealogy and Biography.* 1896.

33. *A History of the City of Chicago: Its Men and Its Institutions.* The Inter Ocean, Chicago, 1900.

34. "Cap Morrison Swears He'll Stick to Ward." *Chicago Tribune*, Sep 16, 1916.

35. ""-!!**!!_*!—* !!!-**-!!!**!!" *Chicago Tribune*, Oct 6, 1916.

36. "Friends of Old Shun Morrison after His Death." *Chicago Tribune*, Dec 16, 1929.

37. "Easy Money!" *Chicago Tribune*, Aug 25, 1916.

38. "Millionless Millionaire Morrison Dies." *Chicago Tribune*, Dec 15, 1929.

39. "To Correspondents." *New York Mirror*, May 11, 1833.

40. Hawkins, C. M. Eulogy on George Manierre, privately published.

41. Manierre, George. "A History of the Manierre Family in Early Chicago." *Journal of the Illinois State Historical Society*, 1911.

42. "The Fugitive Slave Case in Chicago." *Buffalo Morning Express*, Jun 11, 1851.

43. "Fugitive Slave Case Trial." *Buffalo Morning Express*, Jun 7, 1851.

44. Blackett, R. J. M. *The Captive's Quest for Freedom.* Cambridge University Press, 2018.

45. *Industrial Chicago: The Bench and Bar.* Chicago, Goodspeed Publishing Co., 1896.

46. Miller, Florence Lowden. "The Pullmans of Prairie Avenue." *Chicago History*, Spring 1971.

47. *Catalog of the Fourth Exhibition, Pittsburgh Architectural Club*, 1907.

48. Matile, Roger. "John Frink and Martin Walker: Stagecoach Kinds of the Old Northwest." *Journal of the Illinois State Historical Society*, No. 95, No. 2, Summer 2002, 119–131.

49. Graceland Cemetery Records, Section B, Lot 16.

50. "Abbreviated Telegrams." *Rock Island Argus*, Apr 14, 1891.

51. Andreas, A. T. *History of Chicago.* Chicago, A. T. Andreas Publisher, 1884, 461.

52. "Rush Medical College." *Gem of the Prairie*, Feb 19, 1848.

53. Reilly, Frank W. "Leaves from the Notebook of a Resurrectionist." *Chicago Tribune*, Dec 29, 1878.

54. "Death of Dr. Brainard." *Chicago Tribune*, Oct 11, 1866.

55. "Great Meeting in Chicago." *Buffalo Weekly Republican,* July 18, 1848.

56. "The Popular Uprising." *Chicago Tribune*, Jan 13, 1863.

57. "Death of Dr. Brainard." *Chicago Tribune,* Oct 11, 1866.

58. Graceland Interment Book Volume 1.

59. Goodheart, Adam. *1861: The Civil War Awakening.* Random House, 2011.

60. Ibid.

61. Ibid.

62. Miller, H. H. "The Famous Tour." *Chicago Tribune*, Feb 16, 1896.

63. Ibid.

64. "First Officer Shot." *Overbrook Herald* (Overbrook, KS), May 31, 1895.

65. Goodheart, Adam. *1861: The Civil War Awakening.*

66. "The Famous Tour." *Chicago Tribune*, Feb 16, 1896.

67. "Pioneer at the Case." *Chicago Daily Inter-Ocean*, Aug 5, 1895.

68. "Robert Fergus Cut Down." *Chicago Tribune*, Jun 24, 1897.

69. Ibid.

70. "Passing of the Fergus Firm." *Chicago Daily Inter-Ocean*, Feb 4, 1900.

71. Ibid.

72. Julie Newberry's Diary.

73. Ibid.

74. Templeton, Lucy. "Books—Old and New." *Knoxville News Sentinel*, Jun 4, 1933.

75. Schroeter, Joan G. "Death and the Maidens: The Newberry Girls and the Marriage Question." *Journal of the Illinois State Historical Society*, Spring 2000.

76. Newberry, Julia. *Julia Newberry's Diary.*

77. Kirkland, Caroline. *Chicago Yesterdays Daughaday*, 1919, 124.

78. "The Late W. L. Newberry." *Chicago Daily Inter-Ocean*, Dec 29, 1885.

79. "Preserved in Medford Rum." *St Paul Globe*, Dec 26, 1885.

80. "The Late W. L. Newberry." 1885.

81. Morris, Dwight, to *Chicago Tribune*, published Jan 22, 1886.

82. Konkol, Mark. "Ghost Story Back from the Dead." *Chicago Sun Times*, Oct 30, 2009.

83. U.S. Census Bureau, United States Census 1850.

84. U.S. Census Bureau, United States Census 1860.

85. *Record of Service of Michigan Volunteers in the Civil War*, Ihling Bros, 1900.

86. Civil War Pensions index.

87. Marriage record. David R. Rothrock and Jane McClure, May 28, 1872.

88. Testimony of "Jennie" Rothrock. *Briggs v Briggs.*

89. *Briggs v. Briggs* divorce records.

90. Ibid.

91. Ibid.

92. Ibid.

93. Advertisement. *San Francisco Examiner*, Apr 6, 1877.

94. *Briggs v. Briggs* divorce records.

95. Ibid.

96. Graceland Cemetery Records, Section D, Lot 475.

97. *Briggs v Briggs* divorce records.

98. Inez Briggs death certificate.

99. Graceland Cemetery Records, Section D, Lot 475.

100. Display ad. *The Reporter*, Apr 1903.

101. Graceland Cemetery Records, Section D, Lot 475.

102. "Death of Tuthill King." *Chicago Tribune*, Mar 17, 1886.

103. "The Tuthill King Estate." *Chicago Tribune*, Jun 18, 1886.

104. "Personal Mention." *Railway Age Monthly*, Jun 1880.

105. "Burying the Dead." *Chicago Tribune*, Jul 18, 1864.

106. Graceland Cemetery Records, Section B, Lot 450.

107. "Aid for the Wounded." *Chicago Tribune*, Apr 10, 1862.

108. "Chicago Literary Union." *Chicago Tribune*, Apr 29, 1862.

109. "Last of Earth." *Chicago Tribune*, May 19, 1862.

110. "Burying the Dead." 1864.

111. "B. H. Campbell Found." *Chicago Daily Inter-Ocean*, Jan 29, 1891.

112. No title. *Chicago Times*, Nov 23, 1863.

113. "It Is Done." *Chicago Times*, Jan 2, 1863.

114. "The Florence Nightingales of the North." *Chicago Tribune*, Mar 19, 1863.

115. "The Soldiers Home Meeting." *Chicago Tribune*, Aug 29, 1863.

116. "The Soldiers Home." *Chicago Times*, Aug 24, 1863.

117. "The Times Attack on Mrs. E. E. Hosme." *Chicago Tribune*, Aug 24, 1863.

118. Hosmer, Ann. *Reminiscences of Sanitary Work and Incidents Connected with the War for the Union*. Unpublished, Chicago History Museum Manuscripts Collection.

119. Ibid.

120. Obituary. *Chicago Tribune*, Jan 14, 1867.

121. Letter from MaryJo Hoag, Smith file.

122. Obituary. *Hyde Park Herald*, Feb 23, 2005.

123. "Women Help Slug Police." *Chicago Tribune*, Jan 18, 1915.

124. "Mary Wilmarth, Chicago Leader 50 Years, Dies." *Chicago Tribune*, Aug 29, 1919.

125. Ibid.

126. *History of Medicine and Surgery and Physicians and Surgeons of Chicago*. Biographical Publishing Corp., 1922.

127. "Fifty Years Ago." *Chicago Tribune*, Dec 24, 1882.

128. Hammond, H. L. Memorial Sketch of Philo Carpenter. Read before the Chicago Historical Society, Jul 17, 1888.

129. Ibid.

130. Ibid.

131. "Topographical Legend." *Chicago Daily Inner-Ocean*, Apr 22, 1883.

132. Hammond. *Memorial Sketch of Philo Carpenter*.

133. "Another -Gallant Soldier Gone." *Chicago Tribune*, Jul 9, 1863.

134. Ibid.

135. Ibid.

136. Ibid.

137. "At Graceland." *Chicago Tribune*, May 31, 1869. As of this article, there was no monument for Scott.

138. Currey, Josiah Seymour. *Chicago: Its History and Its Builders*. S. J. Clarke Publishing, 1918.

139. Vernon, Christopher. *Graceland Cemetery: A Design History*, University of Massachusetts Press, 2012.

140. Graceland Interment Book Volume 1.

Route 1-B

1. "Jacob Rehm's Career." *Chicago Tribune*, Apr 4, 1886.

2. Adams, Isaac. *Life of Emery A. Storrs*. Hubbard Bros, 1886.

3. "Let Down Easy: Jake Rehm, Chief of the Whiskey Thieves, Sentenced Yesterday." *Chicago Daily Inter-Ocean*, Jul 8, 1876.

4. Grant, Ulysses S. *The Papers of Ulysses S. Grant, Jan 1–Oct 21, 1876*. Southern Illinois University Press, 2005.

5. "Jacob Rehm's Career." *Chicago Tribune*, Apr 4, 1886.

6. "Frauds on Shipping." *The Queen's Messenger*, Apr 1, 1869.

7. "Plan 'Sings' as Jazz Antidote among Youth." *Chicago Tribune*, Jun 9, 1924.

8. "Again the Horse Show." *Chicago Daily Inter-Ocean*, Nov 2, 1890.

9. Interment book and other sources say 1849; various documents in the pension file say 1847.

10. *Massachusetts Soldiers and Sailors of the Revolutionary War, Vol 10*. Also reports from muster rolls preserved in the widow's pension file.

11. Declaration for Widow, Feb 6, 1857. Preserved in pension file.

12. Byron, M. G. *Genealogy of the Merrick Family of Massachusetts*.

13. The original interment book lists his burial place as "country."

14. Graceland Cemetery Interment Book Vol 1.

15. Graceland Cemetery Records, Section A, Lot 286.

16. Delphia Merrick widow's pension files.

17. Merrick, Charles. Clinton to U.S. State Department, Feb 1893. Preserved in widow's pension file.

18. "Obituary. Major Charles C. Merrick," *Chicago Daily Inter-Ocean*, Jul 4, 1893. Charles served in the 51st Illinois during the Civil War; he's buried in Malcolm, IA.

19. Graceland Cemetery Records, Section A, Lot 286.

20. "1776 Veteran Buried Here Is Little Known." *Chicago Tribune*, Jul 4, 1959.

21. David Kennison pension file.

22. "An Aged Orator." *Emancipator and Republican*, Aug 16, 1848.

23. "Great meeting in Chicago." *Buffalo Weekly Republican*, Jul 18, 1848.

24. "God's Severity." *Chicago Daily Inter-Ocean*, March 18, 1889.

25. "Dr. Wm Fawcett Is Dead." *Chicago Tribune*, Jun 12, 1901.

26. Turak, Theodore. *William Le Baron Jenney: A Pioneer of Modern Architecture*. Umi Research Press, 1986.

27. Graceland Cemetery Records, Section S, Lot 11.

28. "Difficulties in Reaching Chicago in 1831," *Chicago Daily Inter-Ocean*, Oct 1, 1905.

29. No title. *Chicago Democrat*, Feb 18, 1834, quoted in Kirkland, Joseph, *The Story of Chicago*. Chicago, Dibble Publishing Co., 1892.

30. Graceland Cemetery Records, Section S, Lot 3.

31. Ibid.

32. "Graves Gives $50,000 Memorial to Horse." *Chicago Daily Inter-Ocean*, Sept 2, 1907.

33. Henry Graves Probate.

34. Ibid.

35. Sample, Omar. "Improving the Cemetery Monument." *Art and Progress*, Nov 1911.

36. "Organized with a Purpose." *The Butte Daily Post*, Sept 2, 1907.

37. "Fall at Graceland, Chicago." *The Modern Cemetery*, Jan 1895.

38. "Died of Heart Disease." *Chicago Republican*, Jul 25, 1867.

39. "A Brutal Police Officer." *Chicago Tribune*, Jul 26, 1867.

40. "Died of Heart Disease," 1867.

41. Graceland Interment Book Volume I.

42. No title. *Chicago Tribune*, Jul 72, 1867.

43. Bennet, Fremont O. *The Chicago Anarchists and the Haymarket Massacre*. Chicago, Blakely Printing Co., 1887.

44. No title. *Des Moines Register*, Mar 18, 1873.

45. Graceland Interment Book Volume 2.

46. Jones, David A. *From Slave to State Legislature: John W. E. Thomas, Illinois' First African American Lawmaker*. Southern Illinois University Press, 2012.

47. "City Brevities." *Chicago Daily Inter-Ocean*, Aug 28, 1878.

48. Storey, Wilbur. "The President's Revocation of General Hunter's Order." *Chicago Times*, May 21, 1862.

49. "The Price of Slaves in Maryland." *The Daily Evening Express* (Lancaster, PA), Aug 22, 1863.

50. William Gill pension.

51. Sutton's name appears on the military records of several members of the 116th.

52. Military records for Gill and Jackson, preserved on fold3.com.

53. Sears, Richard D. *Camp Nelson, Kentucky: A Civil War History*. University Press of Kentucky: Lexington, KY, 2002. Sears' book is an exhaustive collection of primary source accounts of Camp Nelson and an incredibly invaluable resource on the 116th.

54. Gill and Jackson records in "Compiled Military Service Records of Volunteer Union Volunteers Who Served The United States Colored Troops."

55. U.S. Census Bureau, United States Census 1910.

56. Ibid.

57. "Policeman Coughlin Is Shot." *Chicago Tribune*, Aug 10, 1900.

58. "Shoots into Theater Crowd." *Chicago Record*, Aug 10, 1900.

59. "Mr Horace Jackson Dead." *Chicago Defender*, Mar 9, 1912.

60. "Half a Million Dead." *Chicago Tribune*, May 5, 1895.

61. Dailing, Paul. "The Long Death of Jean LaLime." *Chicago Reader*, Oct 18, 2018.

62. Ibid.

63. Letter quoted in Haydon, James Ryan, 1932.

64. Dailing. "The Long Death of Jean LaLime."

65. Palmer, Peter et al. *The ESPN Pro Baseball Encyclopedia.* Sterling Publishing Co., 2007.

66. Obituary. *Chicago Tribune*, Jun 23, 1865.

67. Keating, Ann Durking. *The World of Juliette Kinzie: Chicago Before the Fire.* University of Chicago Press, 2019.

68. "The Republicans in Council." *Chicago Tribune*, Oct 3, 1860.

69. "The News." *Chicago Times*, May 17, 1862.

70. "A Startling Event" and "The Emperor of the Asses." *Chicago Times*, May 17, 1862.

71. "Important Proclamation." *Chicago Tribune*, May 20, 1862.

72. Kinzie, Arthur M. "The First Black Regiment." *The Outlook* Vol 59, 1898.

73. "From Gen Hunter's Command." *Chicago Tribune*, Jul 4, 1862.

74. "Debate in the House." *Burlington Free Press*, Jul 8, 1862.

75. "Black Soldiers." *Chicago Tribune*, Jul 16, 1862.

76. Robertson, Mary D. "Northern Rebel: The Journal of Nellie Kinzie Gordon, Savannah, 1862." *The Georgia Historical Quarterly* Vol 70, No. 3 (Fall 1986).

Station Two

1. "Francis C. Sherman, Esq." *Chicago Journal*, Apr 16, 1862.

2. *Biographical Sketches of the Leading Men of Chicago.* Chicago, Wilson and St. Clair Publishers, 1868.

3. Cemetery Sales Records.

4. Aldrich, C. Knight. *Quest for a Star: The Letters and Diaries of Francis Trowbridge Sherman.* University of Tennessee Press, 1999.

Route 2-A

1. "Reeves, Office Building Thief, Dies in Prison." *Chicago Tribune*, Apr 18, 1938.

2. Chase, Dudley. "Address on the Occasion of the Funeral of Daniel Elston, Esq." Privately published, Chicago History Museum.

3. "Queer Old City Files Found Show Odd Oath of Office." *Chicago Tribune*, Jan 15, 1908.

4. "Old Time Facts and Fancies." *Chicago Daily News*, Aug 24, 1892.

5. "County Court." *Chicago Tribune*, Jan 26, 1870.

6. "Burying the Dead." *Chicago Tribune*, Jul 18, 1864.

7. *Marquis' Guide Book of Chicago*. Chicago, A. N. Marquis and Co., 1885.

8. Graceland Cemetery Records, Section B, Lot 300.

9. *New York Tribune*, quoted here from reprint "A Slave Hunt." *Boston Liberator*, Dec 11, 1846.

10. "Arrest of the Fugitives in Chicago." *American Freeman*, Nov 10, 1846.

11. "The People in Committee of the Whole!" *Western Citizen*, Nov 3, 1846.

12. "Man Hunting in Chicago." *Chicago Tribune*, Apr 4, 1861.

13. Freer, L. C. P. "The Old Liberty Guard." *Chicago Tribune*, Apr 5, 1861.

14. "The Old Liberty Guard." *Chicago Tribune*, Apr 6, 1861.

15. "Slavery in Chicago," 1891.

16. "Letter from 'An Old Timer.'" *Chicago Daily News*, Feb 27, 1894.

17. Andreas, A. T. *History of Chicago*. Chicago, A. T. Andreas Publisher, 1884, 422.

18. Ibid. 64, 161.

19. Lusk, D. W. *Politics and Politicians of Illinois*. Springfield, H. W. Rokker, 1887.

20. "Our Recent Western Tour." *Frederick Douglass' Paper*, Mar 25, 1859.

21. Gale, Edwin O. *Reminiscences of Early Chicago and Vicinity*. Revell Publishing, 1902.

22. "Indictment." *The Liberator* (Boston), Nov 17, 1843.

23. "The People in Committee of the Whole." *Western Citizen*, Nov 3, 1846.

24. "The Voice of Chicago!" *Western Citizen*, Nov 10, 1846.

25. James H. Collins to George W. Clark, Nov 7, 1846. Zebina Eastman Papers, Chicago Historical Society.

26. "Death of James H. Collins." *Buffalo Daily Republic*, Jul 12, 1854.

27. Graceland Cemetery Records, Section C, Lot 224.

28. *Chicago Daily American*, Sept 2, 1840, reprinted in *Chicago Tribune*, May 31, 1948.

29. History of Madison County, Illinois, Unigraphic, 1882

30. Ibid.

31. *New York Tribune* account of Ann Eliza DeWolf funeral, reprinted in *Alton Weekly Telegraph*, Sept 30, 1853.

32. "The Dewolf Children." *Western Citizen*, Oct 18, 1853.

33. See Pamela Bannos' transcription of City Cemetery lot sales in the Common Council files, http://hiddentruths.northwestern.edu/lots.html.

34. Graceland Cemetery Records, Section B, Lot 417.

35. "Died." *Chicago Tribune*, Jun 5, 1862.

36. Ibid.

37. "Octogenarian." *Chicago Daily Inter-Ocean*, Apr 21, 1891.

38. "Louis Schmidt, Noted Chicago Surgeon, Dies." *Chicago Tribune*, Jul 13, 1957.

39. Nash, Capt. Eugene A. *A History of the 44th Regiment New York Volunteer Infantry*. R. Donnelly and Sons, Chicago, 1911.

40. Ibid.

41. Ibid.

42. Ibid.

43. Graceland Cemetery Records, Section C, Lot 321.

44. "Plant These Trees; Grow Some History." *Chicago Tribune*, Dec 26, 1993.

45. Fields, Armdon. *Katharine Dexter McCormick*. Praeger, 2003. Note: spelling of her name varies between "Katharine" and "Katherine." I've used the biographer's spelling.

46. Ibid, 14.

47. Fields, *Katharine Dexter McCormick*, 2003.

48. Harrison, Gilbert A. *A Timeless Affair: The Life of Anita McCormick Blaine*. University of Chicago Press, 1979, 157.

49. Ibid, 159.

50. Meeker, Arthur Jr. *Chicago With Love*. Knopf Publishing, 1955.

51. Harrison, *A Timeless Affair*, 1979.

52. "Wife of Stanley McCormick Takes the Stand." *Chicago Tribune*, Dec 13, 1929.

53. Harrison. *A Timeless Affair*, 1979.

54. Fields. *Katharine Dexter McCormick*, 2003.

55. Monroe, Harriet. *John Wellborn Root: A Study of His Life and Work*. New York, Houghton Mifflin and Co., 1896.

56. Lyon, Jeff. "Generations: A Quiet Quest to Honor a Family's Legacy." *Chicago Tribune*, Feb 23, 1992.

57. "Chicago in 1843." *Illinois Record*, Jul 9, 1898.

58. Jones, John. *The Black Laws of Illinois*. *Chicago Tribune* Book and Job Office, Chicago, 1864.

59. Payne, Ethel. "The Amazing Story of John Jones." *Chicago Defender*, Jul 21, 1951.

60. Advertisement. *Frederick Douglass' Paper*, Oct 13, 1854 (and other dates).

61. Blanchard, Rufus. *Discovery and Conquests of the North-West*. R. Blanchard and Co., 1900.

62. "Slavery in Chicago," 1891.

63. Junger, Richard. "God and Man Helped Those Who Helped Themselves: John and Mary Jones." *Journal of Illinois History*, Summer 2008.

64. "Freedom to Be Purchased." *Weekly Wisconsin*, Aug 11, 1852.

65. Obituary. *Chicago Tribune*, May 22, 1879.

66. "The Black Laws." *Chicago Tribune*, Nov 19, 1864.

67. "An Important Interview." *Chicago Republican*, Feb 9, 1866.

68. Payne. "The Amazing Story of John Jones," 1951.

69. "Cultured Negro Ladies." *Chicago Tribune*, Oct 28, 1888.

70. Blanchard. *Discovery and Conquests*, 1900.

71. Ibid.

72. Wells, Ida B. *Crusade for Justice: The Autobiography of Ida B. Wells*. University of Chicago Press, 1970.

73. Junger, Richard. "God and Man Helped Those," 2008.

74. Ibid.

75. Jones. *"The Black Laws of Illinois,"*1864.

76. Graceland Interment Book Volume 1.

77. Letter from Mary Jones, Graceland Cemetery Records, Section C, Lot 450.

78. Bell, Howard H. "Chicago Negroes in the Reform Movement, 1847–1853." *Negro History Bulletin*, Apr 1958.

79. Henry Bradford death certificate.

80. "Meeting of the Colored People," 1850.

81. "Testimonial to the Late James Collins." *Western Citizen*, Jul 24, 1854.

82. "Frederick Douglass in Chicago." *Frederick Douglass' Paper*, Feb 18, 1859.

83. "The Contrabands from Cairo." *Chicago Tribune*, Oct 9, 1862.

84. "Colored Children in the Public Schools." *Chicago Tribune*, Oct 6, 1864.

85. Forbs, Ella. *African American Women during the Civil War.* Routledge, 2013.

86. U.S. Census Bureau. United States Census 1870, 1880.

87. Reed, Christopher Robert. *Black Chicago's First Half Century.* University of Missouri Press, 2005.

88. "L. G. Wheeler." *Chicago Tribune*, Mar 5, 1885.

89. "The Courts." *Chicago Tribune*, May 3, 1882.

90. Reed. *Black Chicago's First Half Century*, 2005.

91. Mary Jones Affidavit 1890.

92. Browning, Norma Lee. "Mary Hastings Bradley: An Unclassified Author." *Chicago Tribune*, Jul 14, 1946.

93. Phillips, Julie. *James Tiptree Jr.: The Double Life of Alice B Sheldon.* St. Martin's Press, 2015.

94. "Explorer's Last Right—no rites." *Chicago Tribune*, Oct 28, 1976.

95. Phillips. *James Tiptree Jr.*, 2015.

96. "Hunt in Chicago." *Western Citizen*, Jun 10, 1851.

97. "Slavery in Chicago." 1891.

98. "Topographical Legends." *Chicago Daily Inter-Ocean*, Apr 22, 1883.

99. "Border Ruffian Sexton Robbing Graves." *Chicago Tribune*, Nov 9, 1857.

100. Pinkerton, Allan. *Strikers, Communists, Tramps and Detectives.* New York, G. W. Carleton and Co., 1878.

101. Wakeman, Edgar. "A Detective's Early Life," widely circulated, taken here from *Indiana State Sentinel*, Sept 25, 1889.

102. Bonansinga, Jay. *Pinkerton's War.* Rowman and Littlefield, 2011.

103. "Tributes to the Departed." *Chicago Daily Inter-Ocean*, Dec 31, 1878.

104. Graceland interment book Volume I.

105. Pinkerton. *The Somnambulist and the Detective*, 1882.

106. "Mrs. Kate Warn," 1868.

107. Ibid.

108. Recko, Corey. *A Spy for the Union: The Life and Execution of Timothy Webster.* McFarland & Company, Inc., 2013.

109. "The Whicher Murder." *Des Moines Register*, Mar 26, 1874.

110. "The Missouri Tragedy." *Chicago Daily Inter-Ocean*, Mar 21, 1874.

111. Stiles, T. J. *Jesse James: Last Rebel of the Civil War*. Vintage Books, 2002.

112. "A Detective's Fate." *St. Louis Post-Dispatch*, Mar 16, 1874.

113. "Joe Whicher's Murder." *Atlanta Constitution*, Oct 7, 1883.

114. "Gad's Hill." *Chicago Tribune*, Mar 21, 1874.

115. Stiles, T. J. *Jesse James*, 2002.

116. Steward, John. *Pinkertons, Prostitutes and Spies*. McFarland, 2019,

117. "The Pinkerton Burial Place." *Watertown Republican*, Jul 16, 1884.

118. "Drugged to Death." *Chicago Daily News*, May 8, 1882.

119. U.S. Census Bureau. United States Census 1880.

120. Graceland Interment Book Volume 3.

121. "Drugged to Death," 1882.

122. "The Midwife Discharged." *Chicago Tribune*, May 14, 1882. Note: Mrs. Hinz's name is spelled in several ways. I have used "Hinz" as it appears in cemetery records.

123. "Drugged to Death," 1882.

124. "A Life Sacrifice." *Chicago Daily Inter-Ocean*, May 8, 1882.

125. No title. *Chicago Tribune*, May 9, 1882.

126. "List of Agents." *The North Star*, Jan 23, 1851 (and various other dates).

127. "Frederick Douglass in Chicago." *Frederick Douglass' Paper*, Feb 18, 1859.

128. "Universal Suffrage." *Chicago Tribune*, Dec 28, 1866.

129. "Fifteenth Amendment." *Chicago Daily Inter-Ocean*, Apr 8, 1870.

130. Forbs, Ella. *African American Women*, Routledge, 2013.

131. "Jacob F. Platt." *Chicago Daily Inter-Ocean*, Feb 18, 1888.

132. "Business Chances of Chicago's Colored Youth." *Chicago Daily Inter-Ocean*, Jul 19, 1896.

133. "Richard T. Greener." *Chicago Tribune*, Oct 16, 1883.

134. *Marquis' Guide Book of Chicago*, 1885.

135. "Curtain Bought Because Cheap." *Chicago Tribune*, Jan 2, 1904.

136. "Proper Rules as to Theater Doors." *Chicago Tribune*, Jan 4, 1904.

137. "The Known Dead." *Chicago Tribune*, Dec 31, 1903.

138. "Death Due to Iroquois." *Chicago Tribune*, Mar 3, 1904.

139. "$500,000 Hospital as Fire Memorial." *Chicago Daily Inter-Ocean*, Mar 20, 1904.

140. Bateman, Newton. *History of Cook County*. Munsell Publishing Co., 1905.

141. *Marquis' Guide Book of Chicago*, 1885.

142. Megan, Graydon. "Richard Brown, Newberry Executive." *Chicago Tribune*, Jan 30, 2019.

143. Davidson, F. E. "In Memoriam." *Journal of the Society of Western Engineers*, Nov 1916.

144. de Young, Ruth. "Recalls Days of Coach and Four Going to Races." *Chicago Tribune*, Feb 5, 1932.

145. https://twitter.com/lillianjuliaD.

146. King, Willard L. *Melville Weston Fuller*. Macmillan Co., New York, 1950.

147. No title. *Chicago Tribune*, Feb 20, 1863.

148. Ely, James. *The Fuller Court*. ABC-CLIO, 2003.

149. "Justice Fuller Dies." *Chicago Daily Inter-Ocean*, Jul 5, 1910.

150. "Fowler's Painless Dental Parlors." *Chicago Daily News*, Oct 27, 1893.

151. Knox, Janice, and Heather Olivia Belcher. *Chicago's Loop*. Arcadia, 2002.

152. "A Line o' Type or Two." *Chicago Tribune*, Apr 20, 1938.

153. "Miss Kranz, 82, Candy Shop Aid for Years, Dies." *Chicago Tribune*, Apr 12, 1952.

154. Obituary. *Chicago Tribune*, Dec 15, 1993.

155. "R. Cummings Is Dead." *Chicago Tribune*, Jul 13, 1897.

Route 2-B

1. "Son of a Chicago Pioneer Drops Dead in a Dance." *Chicago Tribune*, Nov 26, 1901.

2. "Funeral Services for Dr. R. D. MacArthur." *Chicago Tribune*, Oct 27, 1922.

3. "Big Graft Laid to John A. Linn." *Chicago Tribune*, Jan 20, 1906.

4. "Medical Frauds." *The Medical World*, Sept 1914.

5. Ibid.

6. Cassini, Oleg. *In My Own Fashion*. Simon and Schuster, 1987.

7. "Sisters Share in $7,000,000." *Leavenworth Times*, Apr 1, 1917.

8. Graceland Cemetery Records, Section B, Lot 300.

9. Mahony-Griffin, Marion. *The Magic of America*.

10. Ibid.

11. Gapp, Paul. "A Design for Honoring Unsung Architects." *Chicago Tribune*, Jan 8, 1978.

12. Decker, Brenna. "Marion Mahoney Griffin's Signature Style and Pioneering Influence." https://www.classicist.org/articles/marion-mahony-griffin/.

13. Available online through the Art Institute of Chicago, https://archive.artic.edu/magicofamerica/.

14. Starrett, Vincent. *Penny Wise and Book Foolish*. Covici Friede, 1929.

15. Finley, Larry. "The Case of Too Many Sherlocks." *Chicago Sun-Times*, Oct 27, 1986.

16. Starrett. *The Private Life of Sherlock Holmes*, 1933.

17. Graceland Cemetery Records, Section C, Lot 903.

18. Kaplan, Louis. *Laszlo Moholy-Nagy: Biographical Writings*. Duke University Press, 1995.

19. *The New Bauhaus*, dir. Alysa Nahmias, 2019.

20. "Notes from Graceland." *Modern Cemetery*, Oct 1893.

21. "It Has a Crematory." *Chicago Tribune*, Nov 25, 1893.

22. Ibid.

23. Ibid.

24. "How Chicago Looks Upon the Custom of Cremation." *Chicago Tribune*, Apr 17, 1898.

25. "Chicagoan Has Fine Collection of French Art." *Chicago Tribune*, Jun 21, 1931.

26. "Was a Native of East Montpelier." *Barre Daily Times*, Nov 4, 1910.

27. Pridmore, Jay. "Focusing on Collectors Rather than Artists." *Chicago Tribune*, Nov 19, 1987.

28. Rich, Daniel Caton. "The Mrs. L. L. Coburn Collection," booklet. Art Institute, 1932.

29. Janssen, Kim. "Trump Thinks He Owns Renoir, but Art Institute Says Real One Hangs in Chicago." *Chicago Tribune*, Oct 19, 2017.

30. "30,000 Expected to March as Area Honors Its War Dead." *Chicago Tribune*, May 28, 1966.

31. "Dead in His Own Walls." *Chicago Tribune*, May 5, 1896.

32. Porterfield, Billy. "Builder Did Double Duty to See Capitol Completed." *Austin American-Statesman*, Nov 20, 1989.

33. Ibid.

34. Cox, Mike. *Legends and Lore of the Texas Capitol*. The History Press: Charleston, SC, 2017.

35. Graceland Cemetery Records, Knolls Section, Lot 9.

36. Obituary. *Chicago Tribune*, Jan 10, 1973.

37. "Edison and the Big Fair." *Chicago Tribune*, May 13, 1891.

38. No title. *Chicago Daily News*, Jun 16, 1897.

39. "View the Carson Fight." *Chicago Tribune*, Jun 9, 1897.

40. "Bob Fitzsimmons Is Victim of Pneumonia." *Pittsburgh Post-Gazette*, Oct 23, 1917.

41. "Dies in Germany." *Chicago Tribune*, Aug 23, 1922.

42. "He's Still Generous." *Chicago Tribune*, May 1, 1948.

43. "Election Time Recalls Brilliant Career of Congressman." *Chicago Tribune*, Oct 21, 1956.

44. "Greatest Day in the History of Florence." *Florence Herald*, May 1, 1903.

45. Ibid.

46. "White House Lady Is Most Charming, Says Mrs De Priest." *Chicago Tribune*, Jul 17, 1929.

47. "Politics Linked to Hoover Tea." *Louisville Courier-Journal*, Jun 15, 1929. Some sources quote him as saying "institution" in place of "white civilization." It would have meant the same thing.

48. "De Priest Calls Legislators of Dixie Cowards." *Chicago Tribune*, Jul 2, 1929.

49. Graceland Cemetery Records, Knolls Section, Lot 15, Sublot 4.

50. Johnson, Jack. *My Life and Battles (Mes Combats)*, 1911.

51. "Johnson Given the Decision." *New Orleans Times-Picayune*, Dec 28, 1900.

52. "Fitz Is Beat in Second Round." *Philadelphia Inquirer*, Jul 18, 1907.

53. "Jack's 'Mammy' Hears the News." *Emyra Star Tribune*, Jul 5, 1910.

54. Graceland Cemetery Records, Bellevue Lot 437.

55. "Lawson's Plain Taste to Mark Rites and Tomb." *Chicago Tribune*, Aug 21, 1925.

56. Ibid.

57. Ibid.

58. *Report of the Proceedings of the Society, 1891.*

59. *The Congressional Globe*, 1866.

60. Digital Collections, Duke University Libraries. https://idn.duke.edu/ark:/87924/r4xw4853x.

61. *Report of the Proceedings of the Society, 1891.*

62. Kirkland, Caroline. *Chicago Yesterdays*. Daughaday, 1919, 127.

63. Renwick, Edward. *Recollections*, privately published; retrieved from https://issuu.com/jrenwick/docs/recollections.

64. "Golf." *New York Tribune*, Aug 20, 1902.

65. Though often listed as Jewish, it's a bit unclear. In an 1890 speech he refers to "your Martin Luther" and "We German Lutherans." "Down on the Law." *Chicago Tribune*, May 29, 1890.

66. "Death Takes Editor of *Staats-Zeitung*." *Chicago Tribune*, Mar 2, 1907.

67. Ibid.

68. Kirkland, Caroline. "News of Chicago Society." *Chicago Tribune*, Jul 11, 1920.

69. "Boyd Hill, 66, Dies; 40 Years an Architect." *Chicago Tribune*, Jan 7, 1964.

70. Meeker, Arthur Jr. *Chicago with Love*. Knopf, 1955.

71. Moffett, India. "Mrs. Meeker Recalls Parties She Attended at Field Mansion." *Chicago Tribune*, May 23, 1936.

72. Grossman, Ron. "Lost Lake Shore Drive." *Chicago Tribune*, Mar 31, 1985.

73. Meeker. *Chicago with Love.*

74. Inventory of the Arthur Meeker Jr. Papers, Newberry Library.

75. "Had a 'Hunch' Not to Go." *Chicago Tribune*, Apr 17, 1912.

76. "Owens Obsequies." *Lafayette Journal and Courier* (Lafayette, IN), Jan 20, 1931.

77. Monroe, Harriet. *John Wellborn Root: A Study of His Life and Work*. Houghton Mifflin and Co., New York, 1896.

78. Ibid.

79. "Sewed Up His Heart." *Chicago Daily Inter-Ocean*, Jul 22, 1893.

80. Ibid.

81. Williams, Daniel H. "Stab Wound of the Heart and Pericardium." *Medical Record*, Mar 27, 1897.

82. Ibid.

83. "Rare Feat in Surgery." *The Colored American*, 1902.

84. Adams, Isaac. *Life of Emery A. Storrs, His Wit and Eloquence*. Chicago, G. L. Howe, 1886.

85. Ibid.

86. "Mrs. Emery Storrs Will." *Chicago Tribune*, June 29, 1888.

Station Three

1. "No Prayer at the Grave." *Chicago Tribune*, Sept 2, 1888.
2. "Remembers the Poor." *Chicago Tribune*, Jan 11, 1893.
3. Heinen, Joseph C, and Susan Barton. *Lost German Chicago*. Arcadia Publishing, 2009.
4. "Peter Schoenhofen." *Chicago Tribune*, Aug 21, 1888.
5. "Funeral of Peter Schoenhofen." *Chicago Daily Inter-Ocean*, Jan 6, 1893.
6. Graceland Cemetery Records, Bellevue Section, Lot 16.
7. Small, Albion. *Americans and the World-Crisis*. University of Chicago Press, 1917. The oft-repeated quote is difficult to source; this 1917 work presents it as a "current sneer" around Pullman.
8. Kelly, Jack. *The Edge of Anarchy: The Railroad Barons, The Gilded Age, and the Greatest Labor Uprising in America*. St. Martin's Press, 2019.
9. Conway, J. North. *Bag of Bones*. Lyons Press, 2012.
10. "Lies in Solid Rock." *Chicago Tribune*, Oct 24, 1897.
11. Ibid.
12. "Pullman's Massive Sarcophagus." *Chicago Daily News*, Oct 25, 1897.
13. "Pullman Will Read." *Chicago Chronicle*, Oct 24, 1897.
14. "Millions in Trust." *Chicago Chronicle*, Oct 25, 1897.
15. "The George M. Pullman Memorial." *The Granite News*, May 1900.
16. Turner, W. G. "Ownership of Ancient Indian Graveyard in Dispute." *Detroit Free Press*, Mar 9, 1919.
17. Taft, Lorado. *The History of American Sculpture*. MacMillan, 1903.
18. "To Start Class in Russian." *Chicago Tribune*, Jun 2, 1900.
19. "Monument in Lincoln Park." *Chicago Daily Inter-Ocean*, May 4, 1884.

Route 3-A

1. Ott, John Nash. *My Ivory Cellar*. Twentieth Century Press, 1958.
2. "Martha Plumbs Depths of Jazz in River North." *Chicago Tribune*, Sept 18, 1921.
3. Kell, Bill. "Authentic Story of Famed Austin High Jazz Band." *The Garfieldian*, Jan 7, 1959.
4. "Prodigal Sons of Austin High Back in Honor." *Chicago Tribune*, Jun 19, 1942.
5. Dold, Bruce. "Lawrence 'Bud' Freeman, Chicago-style Jazz Legend." *Chicago Tribune*, Mar 16, 1991.
6. Freeman. *Crazeology*, 1989, 2.
7. Ibid.
8. No author. *A History of Chicago: Its Men and Institutions*. The Inter Ocean Press, 1900.
9. Personal interview with Evelyn Lee, granddaughter.
10. Royko, Mike. "It Was Wrigley, Not Some Goat, Who Cursed Cubs." *Chicago Tribune*, Mar 21, 1997.

11. "Four Recruits Join Cubs for Fall Workout." *Chicago Tribune*, Sept 15, 1953.

12. Ruth Page Front Room No. 10 (March 27, 1985). Chicago Film Archives, Video Identifier V2011–05–0565.

13. "Ruth Page." *Chicago Tribune*, Dec 2, 1974.

14. "Hello, Ruth? It's Sunday." *Chicago Tribune*, May 22, 1983.

15. Morris, Robert. "The Hidden Sides of Architect Bruce Goff." *Paper City*.

16. Fortini, Amanda. "The Man Who Made Wildly Imaginative, Gloriously Disobedient Buildings." *New York Times*, Sept 10, 2018.

17. "Opening of Renegades: Bruce Goff and the American School of Architecture." https://www.archdaily.com/899991/opening-of-renegades-bruce-goff-and-the-american-school-of-architecture-at-bizzell.

18. Fortini. "The Man Who Made Wildly, 2018.

19. Darby, Edwin. *The Fortune Builders: Chicago's Famous Families*. Garrett County Press, 2011.

20. Kriplen, Nancy. *The Eccentric Billionaire: John D. MacArthur*. Amacom, 2008.

21. Ibid.

22. Ibid.

23. "Glessner's New Mansion." *Chicago Daily News*, Jan 24, 1888.

24. Bock, Richard. *Memoirs of an American Artist*. C. C. Publishing Co., 1989.

25. Hubbard, Elbert. *Little Journeys to the Homes of Great Business Men*. Elbert Hubbard publisher, 1909.

26. "House of Armour: Aleka." *Classic Chicago Magazine*.

27. Page, Eleanor. "Russian Princess in the Stock Room." *Chicago Tribune*, Apr 5, 1976.

28. "Royal Shopgirl Is Wed to Royal Clerk with Pomp." *Chicago Tribune*, Sept 15, 1928.

29. Mabon, Mary Frost. "Golfer's Stroganoff." *Sports Illustrated*, Feb 29, 1960.

30. "Alexandra Galitzine Armour." *Chicago Tribune*, Dec 12, 2006.

31. *Reminiscences of Chicago during the Great Fire*. Chicago, R Donnelly and Sons, 1915.

32. "Legislature of South Carolina." *Charleston Daily Courier*, Dec 5, 1859.

33. "Disunion Doctrines of Modern Democrats." *National Era* (Washington, D.C.), Feb 9, 1860.

34. "The Proposed Congress of the Southern States." *The Weekly Mississippian*, Jan 25, 1860.

35. "Noted Chicagoan Dead." *Indianapolis Journal*, Mar 17, 1899.

36. Medill, William to Mary Medill, Jan 15, 1863. Reprinted in "Fredericksburg: Civil War Letters of Major Medill." *Chicago Tribune*, Aug 22, 1943.

37. Ibid.

38. Barnet, James. *Biographical Sketch of Major William H. Medill*. Chicago, J. Barnett, 1864.

39. "A Child of the Gold Coast." *St Louis Post Dispatch*, Jan 23, 1949.

40. Patterson, Eleanor. "'Why Can't They Let Me Alone?' Capone Asks." *San Francisco Examiner*, Jan 18, 1931.

41. Patterson, Eleanor. "Einstein—Glimpses of Man behind Scientist," reprinted in *San Francisco Examiner*, Feb 11, 1931.

42. Hartwell, Dickie. "No Prissy Is Cissy." *Collier's Weekly*, Nov 30, 1946.

Route 3-B

1. "The Better Class of Cemetery Monuments." *Park and Cemetery*, Jan, 1909.

2. Bradley, Van Allen. *Music for the Millions: The Kimball Piano and Organ Story*. Chicago, Henry Regnery Co., 1957.

3. Meeker, Arthur Jr. *Chicago with Love*. Knopf, 1955.

4. "New Rembrandt Owned in City," 1913.

5. "El Dorado of Art Owned by Woman Too Old to Know." *Chicago Tribune*, Feb 7, 1920.

6. "K. Schneider Does Work on Monument (for) Chicago Architect." *The Herald* (Crystal Lake, IL), Jun 6, 1929.

7. Smith, Michael Glover, and Adam Selzer. *Flickering Empire: How Chicago Invented the U.S. Film Industry*. Wallflower Press, 2015.

8. Ibid.

9. Ibid.

10. Ibid.

11. Kenneth Sawyer Goodman diary, Newberry Library.

12. Ibid.

13. Wendt, Lloyd, and Herman. *Give the Lady What She Wants!* South Bend, And Books, 1952.

14. Ibid.

15. Cassell, Frank. *Suncoast Empire: Bertha Honore Palmer, Her Family, and the Rise of Sarasota*. Rowman and Littlefield, 2017.

16. Bizzarri, Amy. *Iconic Chicago Dishes, Drinks and Desserts*. Arcadia Publishing, 2016.

17. Phyllis. "Is Mrs. Potter Palmer the Only American Woman Who Knows How to Spend a Fortune?" *Chicago Tribune*, Sept 22, 1907.

18. Maher, James. *Twilight of Splendor*. New York, Little Brown, 208.

19. "Mosaics." *Inland Architect*, October 1903.

20. "Our Classmate." *Junction City Weekly Union*, Sept 30, 1871.

21. Thompson, Slason. *Eugene Field*. Charles Scribner's Sons, 1901.

22. Ibid.

23. *Reminiscences of Chicago during the War*. Chicago, R. R. Donnelly, 1914.

24. "Barbara McClurg Potter, 1295–2012." *Chicago Tribune*, Jan 25, 2012.

25. "The Court House Bell." *Chicago Tribune*, Jan 14, 1872.

26. Porter, H. H. *A Short Autobiography*. Privately published, 1915.

27. "The Monument and Its Setting." *The Monumental News*, Apr 1916.

28. Seifert, Andrew. *Pride 2008: School of Thought, Retired Northwestern*

prof David Hull reminisces about a life in the community, https://newcity.com/2008/06/26/pride-2008-school-of-thought-retired-northwestern-prof-david-hull-reminisces-about-a-life-in-the-community/.

29. Ibid.

30. Ibid.

31. Ibid.

32. "'Abe' Lincoln's Cabin." *Chicago Tribune*, Aug 22, 1891.

33. Green, James. *Death in the Haymarket*. New York, Anchor Books, 2007.

34. "How They Won." *Chicago Daily Inter-Ocean*, Nov 11, 1892.

35. "The Anarchists Pardoned." *St. Louis Globe-Democrat*, Jun 27, 1893.

36. Altgeld, John. *The Cost of Something for Nothing*. Chicago, Hammersmark Publishing Co., 1904.

37. "Shoots Father and Son." *Chicago Tribune*, Aug 4, 1891.

38. "Bury Streeter, Keep Plug Hat to Rally Round." *Chicago Tribune*, Jan 30, 1921.

39. "Fiction as a Theme." *Chicago Tribune*, Oct 13, 1894.

40. Monroe, Harriet. *Harlow Niles Higinbotham*, a memoir with brief autobiography. Chicago, no publisher given, 1920.

41. "Mrs. McCormick Holds Opera Is City Necessity." *Chicago Tribune*, Oct 20, 1921.

42. "Rich Women as Santa." *Chicago Tribune*, Dec 24, 1911.

43. Wilson, Marjorie. "Rockefeller Millions and Psycho-Analysis Fail to Settle Conflict of Money, Love and Ambition." *San Francisco Chronicle*, Oct 16, 1921.

44. "Mrs. McCormack [sic] Says She Was Tut's Wife." *Santa Ana Register*, Feb 23, 1923.

45. Harrison, Edith Ogden. *Strange to Say*. Chicago, A. Kroch and Sons, 1949.

46. Quinby, Ione. "Illness, Money, Loss Reunite Mrs. McCormick and Kin." *Nashville Tennessean*, Aug 21, 1932.

47. "Daughter of Oil Baron Passes at Drake Hotel." *Moline Dispatch*, Aug 26, 1932.

48. "Cuts Income of Princess." *Chicago Tribune*, May 23, 1901.

49. "Stirred by Burnham, Democracy Champion." *Chicago Record-Herald*, Oct 15, 1910.

50. Ibid.

51. Graceland Cemetery Records, Willowmere Section, Lot 26.

52. Ibid.

53. Graceland Cemetery Records, Evergreen Section, Lot 1.

Station Four

1. No title. *Chicago Record*, Jan 16, 1894.

2. Corneau, Grace. "Chicago Girl Wins Fame as Musical Composer in Paris." *Chicago Tribune*, Apr 6, 1902.

3. "Mr and Miss Getty Leave for Boston." *Chicago Tribune*, Feb 13, 1915.

4. "Goes to India to Become a Buddhist." *Oakland Tribune*, Nov 28, 1909.

5. Jewett, Eleanor. "Art and Artists." *Chicago Tribune*, Aug 27, 1922.

6. Classified ad. *Chicago Tribune*, Oct 22, 1950.

7. Cinderella (alias of unknown columnist). "Society and Entertainment." *Chicago Tribune*, Jun 26, 1915.

8. "Pittsburgh Women Honored by French." *Pittsburgh Daily Post*, Mar 20, 1921.

9. Getty, Alice, to Charles Hutchinson, 1915. The Newberry Library, Newberry Midwest MS Hutchinson, Box 2, Folder 100.

10. Waterbury, Florence. "Alice Getty." *Artibus Asiae*, Vol 9, No. 4, 1946.

11. New York City Municipal Deaths, 1795–1949.

12. Waterbury. "Alice Getty," 1946.

Route 4-A

1. "Sextus N. Wilcox." *Chicago Daily Inter-Ocean*, Jun 23, 1881.

2. "Streeter Claims Titled Stepchild." *Chicago Daily Inter-Ocean*, Dec 11, 1900.

3. "Gossips Find a Social Feud." *Chicago Daily Inter-Ocean*, Oct 7, 1910.

4. "Sister Says Authoress Is Insane from Overwork, Not Drink." *St. Louis Post-Dispatch*, Oct 7, 1910.

5. No title. *Chicago Daily Inter-Ocean*, Sept 11, 1904.

6. Potter, Margaret. *The Golden Ladder.* Harper and Brothers, 1908.

7. "'Golden Ladder' Barred." *Detroit Free Press*, May 17, 1908.

8. "Society Girls Are Good Fans, Chance Avers." *Manitoba Free Press*, Feb 26, 1916.

9. "Sister Says Authoress Is Insane," Oct 7, 1910.

10. Sherlock, Barbara. "Physician Was Up to Challenge." *Chicago Tribune*, Sept 4, 2005.

11. Isaacs, Deanna. "Tigerman on the Loose." *Chicago Reader*, Nov 23, 2011.

12. Middleton, Mary. "Chicagoans' Story of Diggings in Iraq." *Chicago Tribune*, Mar 24, 1961.

13. "Bandit Blinded by Gun Wound Sent to Prison." *Chicago Tribune*, Dec 12, 1935.

14. Baatz, Simon. *For the Thrill of It.* Harper Perennial, 2009.

15. Schmich, Mary. "Words Don't Do Justice to Bond of Father, Son." *Chicago Tribune*, Jun 16, 2002.

16. Leopold, Nathan. *Life Plus 99 Years.* Doubleday, 1958.

17. Rizzo, Charlie. "Walking with My Father." *NPR*, Jun 15, 2007.

18. "Among the Dealers." *The Monumental News*, Jan 1898.

19. "Notes from Graceland." *Modern Cemetery*, Oct 1893.

20. Wendt, Lloyd and Herman Kogan. *Give the Lady What She Wants.* Rand McNally, 1952.

21. Moffett, India. "Mrs Meeker Recalls Parties." *Chicago Tribune*, May 23, 1936.

22. "After Fifty Years Prairie Avenue Stirs Again." *Chicago Tribune*, Dec 12, 1937.

23. "Chicago Society." *Chicago Daily Inter Ocean*, Mar 20, 1886.

24. Wendt and Kogan, 1952.

25. Meeker, Arthur Jr. *Chicago with Love*. Knopf, 1955.

26. "Mrs Caton Today Becomes Mrs. Field." *Chicago Daily Inter-Ocean*, Sept 5, 1905.

27. Koenigsburg, M. *King News*. F. A. Stokes Co., 1941.

28. "Name among the Members of Many Exclusive Clubs." *Chicago Daily Inter-Ocean*, Jan 17, 1906.

29. "Mrs. Delia Field, Merchant's Widow." *New York Times*, Jun 24, 1937.

30. "Mother of Young Field Dies Abroad." *Chicago Tribune*, Sept 20, 1915.

31. "Here Is Most Interesting Boy in World." *Chicago American*, Nov 29, 1905.

32. Phillips, Julie. *James Tiptree Jr.: The Double Life of Alice B Sheldon*. St. Martin's Press, 2015.

33. Wickware, Francis Sill. "Marshall Field III." *Life*, Oct 18, 1943.

34. *Caumsett: The Marshall Field III Gold Coast Estate*. Arcadia Publishing, 2016.

35. Heise, Kenan. "Ruth Field, Benefactor and Civic Leader." *Chicago Tribune*, Jan 28, 1994.

36. Ott, Daniel. "'The Reaper Is to the North': The Genesis of a Lie." *Journal of the Illinois State Historical Society* Vol. 105, No. 4 (Winter 2012).

37. W. S. to C. H. McCormick, quoted in Hutchinson, William T, *Cyrus Hall McCormick: Harvest, 1856–1884*. D Appleton-Century Co., New York, 1935.

38. Hutchinson, 1935.

39. Ibid.

40. "Hustings Court." *Richmond Dispatch*, Jan 13, 1855.

41. Harrison, Gilbert A. *A Timeless Affair: The Life of Anita McCormick Blaine*. University of Chicago Press, 1979.

42. "John D's Daughter Gets Quiet Divorce." *New York Daily News*, Dec 29, 1921.

43. "Richest Singer in World Flees on Eve of Debut." *Chicago Tribune*, Dec 20, 1920.

44. "Raps the Tax Dodgers." *Chicago Tribune*, Jun 23, 1899.

45. Harrison. *A Timeless Affair*, 1979.

46. "Bon Bons and Sugar Plums." *Chicago Tribune*, Jan 20, 1866.

47. Hoge, Jane. *The Boys in Blue*. Treat and Co., New York, 1867.

48. Eddy, Rev. Thomas. Introduction to Hoge. *The Boys in Blue*, 1867.

49. Willard, Francis. "Mrs. Jane C. Hoge." *Chicago Daily Inter Ocean*, Sept 3, 1890.

50. No title. *The Sovereign Squatter*, Aug 19, 1856.

51. "Seth Paine." *Chicago Tribune*, Jul 7, 1872.

52. "The Story of a Chicago Character." *Burlington Free Press*, Jul 29, 1872.

53. Burgess, Nancy. *Tracing the Underground Railroad in Lake Zurich*. https://www.eapl.org/sites/default/files/docs/Tracing%20the%20Underground%20Railroad%20in%20Lake%20Zurich.pdf.

54. Blanchard, Rufus. *Discovery and Conquests of the North-West*. R. Blanchard and Co., 1900.

55. "Seth Paine," 1872.

56. Rutter, David. *In Search of Seth Paine*. https://jwcdaily.com/countrymag /2020/04/01/in-search-of-seth-paine/.

57. "Funeral Obsequies." *Chicago Tribune*, Jun 10, 1872.

58. Graceland Interment Book Volume 2.

59. Evans, Dr. B. W. "How to Keep Well." *Chicago Tribune*, May 15, 1927.

60. Ritchie, Donald. *Press Gallery: Congress and the Washington Correspondents*. Harvard University Press, 2009.

61. *Biographical Sketches of the Leading Men of Chicago*. Chicago, Wilson and St. Clair Publishers, 1868.

62. No title. *Brooklyn Evening Star*, Feb 28, 1860.

63. White, Horace. *The Lincoln and Douglas Debates*. University of Chicago Press, 1914.

64. White, Horace. "Our Washington Letter." *Chicago Tribune*, Dec 4, 1861.

65. "Messages of Sympathy from President Wilson." *Chicago Tribune*, Sept 22, 1916.

66. Ayer, Harriet Hubbard. *Harriet Hubbard Ayer's Book*. New York, King-Richardson Co., 1902.

67. Blaugrund, Annette. *Dispensing Beauty in New York and Beyond: The Triumphs and Tragedies of Harriet Hubbard Ayer*. Arcadia Publishing, 2011.

68. Harrison, Mitchell C. *Prominent and Progressive Americans*. New York Tribune Press, 1902.

69. Burgin, Martha, and Maureen Holtz. "Robert Allerton: The Private Man and the Public Gifts." *The News-Gazette*, 2009.

70. "INC.lings." *Chicago Tribune*, Jan 6, 1988.

71. Drummond, Mary, in Caroline Kirkland, *Chicago Yesterdays*. Daughaday, 1919, 119.

72. Ibid., 123.

73. Ryan, John H. "A Chapter from the History of the Underground Railroad in Illinois." *Journal of the Illinois State Historical Society*, Apr 1915.

74. Lafontant-Makarious, Jewel, "Chicago Voices." *Chicago Tribune*, Jul 21, 1991.

75. Ibid.

76. Ibid.

77. "Bridge Builder, Barrier Breaker Is Remembered." *Chicago Tribune*, Jun 6, 1997.

78. *The Congressional Globe*, Jan 6, 1864, 113–117.

79. *In Memoriam, Isaac Newton Arnold*. Ontario, Fergus Printing Co., 1885.

80. Blanchard. *Discovery and Conquests of the North-West*. 1900.

81. "I. N. Arnold's Death." *Chicago Daily News*, Apr 25, 1884.

82. "Regeneration of the Nation. Speech of Hon. I. N. Arnold Delivered in Congress, Jan 6, 1864." *Chicago Tribune*, Jun 6, 1864.

83. *In Memoriam, Isaac Newton Arnold*, 1885.

84. Ibid.

85. Ibid.

86. Larned, E. C. *The New Fugitive Slave Law. Speech in Reply to Hon. S.A. Douglas*. Privately printed, 1850.

87. Larned, E. C. "The Fugitive Slave Law." *Chicago Tribune*, Mar 19, 1860.

88. *In Memoriam: Edwin C. Larned*. Chicago, A. C. McClurg and Co., 1886.

89. Blanchard. *Discovery and Conquests of the North-West*, 1900.

90. Larned. "Mr. Larned's Letter," 1861.

91. Ibid.

92. *In Memoriam: Edwin C. Larned* A.C., 1886.

93. Ibid.

94. Newberry, Julia. *Julia Newberry's Diary*.

95. Affidavit of Mrs Ryerson, http://www.titanicinquiry.org/USInq/AmInq16 Ryerson01.php.

96. Eleanor Ryerson vital records.

97. Bamford, Sgt. Hal. *Airman*. Dec 1958.

98. "Death of A. N. Fullerton." *Chicago Tribune*, Sept 29, 1880.

99. "Biographies: Charles Walker Esq." *The Chicago Magazine: The West as It Is*. Mar 1857.

Route 4-B

1. Kirkland, Caroline. *Chicago Yesterdays*. Daughaday, 1919.

2. "Handy Andy." *Chicago Tribune*, Jan 28, 1874.

3. "Stories about Burglars." *Chicago Tribune*, Dec 2, 1894.

4. Turner, Henry. *Industrial Chicago*. Chicago, Goodspeed Publishing Co., 1894.

5. McCabe, Bishop Charles. "William H. Powell." *Chicago Tribune*, Jan 10, 1905.

6. "Biographical Sketch of Brig Gen. Wm. H Powell." *Wheeling Daily Intelligencer*, Jan 25, 1865.

7. Powell. "The Sinking Creek Valley Raid," 1892.

8. Ibid.

9. Ibid.

10. McCabe, Bishop Charles. "William H. Powell." *Chicago Tribune*, Jan 10, 1905.

11. "Last Honors Paid to Lucy Allen." *Chicago Daily News*, Mar 31, 1949.

12. "Quite a Change." *St Louise Post-Dispatch*, Jan 25, 1894.

13. Interment Book.

14. Graceland Cemetery Records, Section P, Lot 425.

15. "Club Women of Chicago to Make Annual Gallery Tour." *Chicago Daily Inter-Ocean*, Feb 11, 1907.

16. In census records and later articles, Mary's birth year varies from 1830 to

1840; the date 1833 is based on her 1887 deposition in attempt to get a widow's pension, in which she said she was 54.

17. Reed, Christopher Robert. *Black Chicago's First Century*. University of Missouri Press, 2005.

18. Ibid.

19. Deposition of Mary Jane Randall widow's pension file.

20. Ibid.

21. Graceland Interment Book Vol 3.

22. "One Cripple Who Finds Life Profitable and Pleasant" *Chicago Daily Inter-Ocean*, Mar 30, 1902.

23. "Chicago's Newsboys," 1899.

24. "One Cripple Who Finds Life Profitable and Pleasant," 1902.

25. "'Waffles' Is Buried." *Chicago Tribune*, May 26, 1894.

26. Graceland Interment Book Vol 5.

27. "'Waffles' Is Buried," 1894.

28. "Forty Years Ago," *Chicago Daily Inter-Ocean*, May 20, 1894.

29. "Survived the Storm." *Chicago Record*, May 21, 1894.

30. "'Waffles' Is Buried," 1894.

31. Flavin, Genevieve. "Aztecs' Glory Finds Rebirth in Torres' Art." *Chicago Tribune*, Nov 16, 1947.

32. Ibid.

33. "Newlyweds Charmed by Silo Apartment." *Chicago Daily Herald*, Jul 29, 1965.

34. "Wood Carving and Copper Work Being Done by Jesus Torres." *Rock Island Lines News Digest*, Mar, 1947.

35. "Obituary." *Chicago Tribune*, Jun 15, 1948.

36. Quintos, C. Campos, "The Aim of the Filipino Golf Association." *The Philippine Messenger* Vol 3, No. 9, Apr 1936.

37. Lot records.

38. "Babes of the Street." *Chicago Tribune*, Jun 29, 1884.

39. "George Dewey Is Dead." *Chicago Daily Inter-Ocean*, July 4, 1901.

40. *Cleveland Gazette*, Sept 13, 1884.

41. U.S. Census Bureau. United States Census 1880.

42. U.S. Census Bureau. United States Census 1900.

43. "Local and Exposition Notes." *Chicago Tribune*, Sept 21, 1884.

44. *Marshall Field and Co. v Goode* and others; there are several mid-1880s lawsuits against the Goodes, which provide a certain amount of detail to their biographies.

45. *Marshall Field and Co. vs Sarah E. Goode*.

46. *Bennett Medical College vs. Goode*.

47. "Chips." *The Broad Ax*, Apr 9, 1904.

48. Graceland Interment Book Volume 6.

49. Willard, Samuel. "My First Adventure with a Fugitive Slave: The Story of It and How It Failed." Samuel Willard papers, Abraham Lincoln Presidential Library.

50. Willard, Samuel. "The Killing of Lovejoy: Samuel Willard's Recollections." *Chicago Tribune*, Mar 12, 1884.

51. Willard. "My First Adventure with a Fugitive Slave," Lincoln Presidential Library.

52. Ibid.

53. "Death of Dr. Samuel Willard." *Journal of the Illinois State Historical Society*, Apr 1913.

54. Keilman, John. "Three Abolitionists Convicted of Aiding Slaves among Those Pardoned by Governor Quinn." *Chicago Tribune*, Jan 1, 2015.

55. Wilson, John. *Memoir of Justin Butterfield*. Chicago Local News Co., Chicago, 1880.

56. Stevenson, Adlai Ewing. *Something of Men I Have Known*. A. C. McClurg and Co., 1909.

57. "Old Timer's Fancies" (Judge Caton). *Chicago Daily News*, Sept 4, 1894.

58. Arnold, I. N. *Recollections of Early Chicago and the Illinois Bar*. Ontario, Fergus Printing Co., 1881.

59. Wilson. *Memoir of Justin Butterfield*, 1880.

60. Vernon, Christopher. *Graceland Cemetery: A Design History.* University of Massachusetts Press, 2012.

61. "Young Bachelor Left a Million." *Chicago Tribune*, Jul 16, 1938.

62. "Woman Recluse, Reckoned Rich, Ill of Hunger." *Chicago Tribune*, Feb 25, 1927.

63. "Have Hard Time Finding Charity in Garrett Will." *Chicago Tribune*, Jul 24, 1938.

Station Five

1. Sims, Charlie. *The Life of Rev. Thomas M. Eddy.* Cincinnati, Nelson and Phillips, 1879.

Route 5-A

1. "Minor Mention." *The Horseless Age*, Jun 7, 1899.

2. No title. *Horseless Age*, May 1898.

3. "Thieves on the Run." *Chicago Evening Journal*, Mar 31, 1893.

4. "Carter Harrison's Loving Nature." *Chicago Evening Journal*, Oct 28, 1893.

5. Matthews, Franklin. "Wide Open Chicago." *Harper's Weekly*, Jan 1, 1898.

6. Kirkland, Caroline. *Chicago Yesterdays*. Daughaday, 1919.

7. "The Great Snow Storm." *Chicago Tribune*, Jan 3, 1864.

8. Kirkland. *Chicago Yesterdays*.

9. Graceland Cemetery Records, Section G, Lot 68.

10. George Meshes (obituary). *Chicago Tribune*, Jan 29, 1986.

11. Harrison, Edith Ogden. *Strange to Say*. Kroch and Sons, Chicago, 1949.

12. Ibid.

13. Graceland Cemetery Records, Section G, Lot 237.

14. "Deaths." *Chicago Tribune*, Apr 17, 1877.

15. "Mrs. Lane's Suit." *Chicago Tribune*, Nov 14, 1883.

16. "A Woman on the Warpath," 1883.

17. "An Erratic Female Sues Judge Higgins." *Chicago Daily News*, Nov 14, 1883.

18. "Judge Higgins' Queer Assailant." *Chicago Daily News*, Nov 8, 1883.

19. "Van H. Higgins Dead." *Chicago Tribune*, Apr 18, 1893.

20. "A Woman on the Warpath," 1883.

21. Adams, Isaac. *Life of Emery A. Storrs.* Philadelphia, Hubbard Bros, 1886, 128–136.

22. *Lane vs. Higgins.*

23. Bateman, Newton. *Historical Encyclopedia of Illinois.* Chicago, Munsell Publishing Co., 1926.

24. Gloede. *Reminiscences of Ida Gloede.*

25. Munsell, William. *Historical Encyclopedia of Illinois.* W. B. Conkey Co., 1948.

26. Graceland Cemetery Records, Knolls Section, Lot 13.

27. Marriage record, Oct 22, 1902.

28. "Dr. Menclewski Wins Divorce Suit." *Chicago Tribune*, Jan 13, 1903.

29. "Coroner's Inquest: In the Afternoon." *Chicago Tribune*, Oct 7, 1871.

30. "The Edsall Tragedy," 1871.

31. "The Last Tragedy." *Chicago Tribune*, Oct 8, 1871.

32. "The Edsall Tragedy." *Chicago Tribune*, Oct 8, 1871.

33. Edsall probate file.

34. "The City: The President's Funeral." *Chicago Tribune*, May 2, 1865.

35. "Mysterious Disappearance." *Chicago Tribune*, May 8, 1865.

36. "The News." *Chicago Tribune*, May 9, 1865.

37. "The Auction Block." *Chicago Tribune*, Feb 15, 1874.

38. "The First Slave Sale in Chicago." *Chicago Tribune*, Jan 18, 1874.

39. "Negro Sale in Chicago." *Western Citizen*, Nov 18, 1842.

40. "Negro Sale in Chicago." *Emancipator and Republican* (Boston), Dec 15, 1842.

41. "The First Slave Sale in Chicago." *Chicago Tribune*, Jan 18, 1874.

42. "Negro Sale in Chicago," 1842.

43. Edwin Heathcock pension file.

44. "Mahlon D. Ogden." *Chicago Tribune*, Feb 14, 1880.

45. Ibid.

46. "Pa Ma Ta Be." *Chicago Tribune*, Sept 24, 1903.

47. Lincoln, Abraham. *The Collected Works of Abraham Lincoln Vol 2.* Wildside Press, 2008.

48. "Pa Ma Ta Be," 1903.

49. Hubbard. *Autobiography of Gurdon Saltonstall*, 1891.

50. Browne, Francis Fisher. *The Every-Day Life of Abraham Lincoln.* New York, N. D. Thompson Publishing Co., 1887.

51. "Pa Ma Ta Be," 1903.

52. "A Highway Robbery." *Chicago Daily Inter-Ocean*, Aug 8, 1880.

53. David Gile pension records.

54. U.S. Census Bureau. United States Census, 1870.

55. Lewis, E. R. *Roll of Honor.* Board of Commissioners of Cook County, 1922.

56. *Reports of the Decisions of the Appellate Courts of Illinois*, 1878.

57. Lincoln. *Collected Works*, 2008.

58. "Obituary." *Chicago Tribune*, Jun 29, 1868.

59. Meeker, Arthur Jr. *Chicago with Love*. Knopf, 1955.

60. Spalding, A. G. *America's National Game*, 1911.

61. "The Banker's Death." *Chicago Daily Inter-Ocean*, Nov 15, 1877.

62. "Coolbaugh." *Chicago Tribune*, Nov 15, 1877.

63. No title. *Fort Wayne Daily Gazette*, Nov 16, 1877.

64. "The Banker's Death," 1877.

65. "Insanity as a Fine Art." *Chicago Tribune*, Nov 21, 1877.

66. "A Former Rumor." *Chicago Tribune*, Jun 2, 1878.

67. Remey, J. T. "William F. Coolbaugh." *Annals of Iowa*, Jul 1906.

68. "A. Johnson." *Chicago Tribune*, Sept 6, 1866.

69. *Iowa Journal of History and Politics* Vol 1, 1903. *State Historical Society of Iowa*. Iowa City, 1903.

70. Note in the Coolbaugh file.

71. *Inland Architect*, Vol 37.

72. "Noted Grain Man Dead in Chicago." *Chicago Tribune*, Dec 21, 1904.

73. "Corners of the Past." *Chicago Tribune*, Sept 30, 1888.

74. "Famous for Deals." *Buffalo Commercial*, Dec 27, 1904.

75. Conger, Cornelia. "'Reminiscences' of Swami Vivekananda," 1956.

76. Jackson, Victoria. "Windy City Yoga." *Yoga Journal*, Jul/Aug 1999.

77. Conger. "Reminiscences," 1956.

78. *Inland Architect*, Vol 37.

79. "William C. Lyon Is Dead." *Chicago Tribune*, Sept 25, 1900.

80. Page, Eleanor. "Gentlemen at Chicago Club Remain Invisible." *Chicago Tribune*, Mar 3, 1969.

81. Daniel C. Goodwin to George Higginson, February 1895, Daniel C. Goodwin folder, Box 84, Chicago Fire of 1871 Collection, Personal Narratives, Chicago History Museum.

82. *Monumental News*, 1921.

83. Dennis, Charles H. "Whitechapel Nights." *Chicago Daily News*, Sept 5, 1936.

84. McCutcheon, John T. "With McCutcheon in Africa." *Chicago Tribune*, Feb 27, 1910.

85. Sandman, Gary. *Quaker Artists*. Lulu Press, 2015.

86. Anderson, Jon. "Ragdale." *Chicago Tribune*, Sept 17, 1986.

87. Bowen, Louise de Koven. *Growing Up with a City*. The MacMillan Co., 1926.

88. Ibid.

89. Ibid.

90. Bowen, Louis de Koven. *The Department Store Girl.* Juvenile Protective Association of Chicago, 1911.

91. "Mrs. Bowen, 94, Dies, Rites Set for Tomorrow." *Chicago Tribune*, Nov 10, 1955.

92. "The Result of Ill- Health." *Chicago Tribune*, Apr 6, 1890.

93. "Portland Excursion." *Chicago Tribune*, Feb 27, 1864.

94. "The Great Calamity." *Chicago Tribune*, Nov 6, 1857.

95. Wendt, Lloyd, and Herman Kogan. *Give the Lady What She Wants!* South Bend, And Books, 1952.

96. Graceland Interment Book Volume 1.

97. "George M. High Passes Away." *Chicago Tribune*, Nov 29, 1898.

98. "G. H. High Dies, World Famous Photographer." *Chicago Tribune*, May 22, 1945.

99. "Mrs. Ellen Root Dies in France." *The Miami News*, Jan 2, 1941.

100. Herman Lackner interview with Judy Blum, 1995. Chicago Architects Oral History Project, Art Institute of Chicago.

101. Stone, H.S. "Notes." *The Chap-book*, July 1, 1894.

102. Steinberg, Elain Fitzsimmons and Frankenstein, Irma. *Irma: A Chicago Woman's Story.* University of Iowa Press, 2004.

103. "Vanderbilt Gave Up Life Belt." *New York Tribune*, May 15, 1915.

104. Hutchinson, 1925.

105. Ibid.

106. Ibid.

107. The Wisconsin Historical Society maintains all of the pamphlets, papers, letters, and more that survive in the McCormick-IHC collection.

108. Chase, Al. "Glass Homes Whip Sun, Wind, Rain Hazards." *Chicago Tribune*, Aug 30, 1952.

109. Reese, Ronnie. "Robert Hall McCormick 1944–2012." *Chicago Tribune*, Jun 26, 2012.

Route 5-B

1. Graceland Cemetery Records, Section G, Lot 91.

2. Advertisement. *New Orleans Times*, Dec 17, 1865.

3. "Music on the Waters." *Chicago Daily Inter-Ocean*, Jun 9, 1881.

4. Graceland Interment Book Vol 4.

5. "Mortuary: Clara Kenkel Huck," 1888.

6. "Christmas Day's Death Harvest." *Chicago Tribune*, Dec 26, 1905.

7. "Final Rites Held for Louis Huck." *Detroit Free Press*, Jul 13, 1952.

8. Dorothy Bernard West Huck death certificate.

9. "Final Rites Held for Louis Huck." 1952.

10. "Obituary." *Chicago Tribune*, Jan 29, 1913.

11. Reed, Christopher Robert. *Black Chicago's First Half Century.* University of Missouri Press, 2005.

12. "Obituary," Jan 29, 1913.

13. Fields, A. N. "Chicago's Early History Presents Brilliant Features." *Chicago Defender*, Nov 12, 1932.

14. No title. *The Broad Axe*, Jun 15, 1912.

15. "Short Interesting History of the Formation and Development of Quinn Chapel." *The Broad Axe*, Apr 8, 1916.

16. Graceland Interment Book Volume 4.

17. McLandburgh, Florence. "Is Fear a Virtue." *Akron Beacon Journal*, Feb 12, 1925.

18. Fashing, John. "Fear Is Not a Virtue." *Akron Beacon Journal*, Feb 24, 1925.

19. No title, author. *Akron Beacon Journal*, Feb 26, 1925.

20. Sims, Michael. *Frankenstein Dreams: A Connoisseur's Collection of Victorian Science Fiction.* Bloomsbury, 2017.

21. Advertisement. *Chicago Tribune*, May 15, 1876.

22. McLandburgh, Florence. "To the Editor." *Akron Beacon Journal*, Nov 22, 1923.

23. Van de Grift, Josephine. "Poor Health Fails to Check Ambitions of Girl Writer." *Akron Beacon Journal*, Jul 24, 1920.

24. "The People v John Stone." *Chicago Daily American*, May 8, 1840.

25. Goodspeed, Arthur Weston. *History of Cook County. Chicago*, Goodspeed Historical Association, 1909.

26. Andreas, A. T. *History of Chicago*, 1884.

27. *New York Tribune*, quoted here from reprint, "A Slave Hunt," *Boston Liberator*, Dec 11, 1846.

28. Eastman, Zebina. "Lake Reminiscences." *Chicago Tribune*, May 30, 1874.

29. "Man Shot." *Fond Du Lac Whig*, Oct 21, 1847.

30. No title. *The Weekly Wisconsin*, Dec 1, 1847.

31. No title. *Milwaukee Daily Sentinel*, Dec 30, 1847.

32. "Fugitive from Justice." *New Orleans Times-Picayune*, Jan 20, 1848.

33. "Excitement at Chicago—Abolitionism." *Daily State Register (Springfield, IL)*, Jun 9, 1851.

34. Graceland Cemetery Records, Section G, Lot 1.

35. No title. *Kansas State Register.* May 14, 1904.

36. Advertisement. *The Railway Conductor*, Nov 1904.

37. "Plane Falls in City, Two Die." *Chicago Tribune*, May 1, 1932.

38. "500 Will Honor Dr. Schmidt on 80th Birthday." *Chicago Tribune*, Dec 28, 1949.

39. "Ernst Schmidt Dies." *Chicago Daily News*, Aug 27, 1900.

40. "Anti-Temperance Mass Meeting." *Chicago Republican*, Aug 13 1867.

41. Schmidt, Axel. *Der Rothe Doktor von Chicago.* Germany, Peter Lang GmbH, 2003.

42. "Honor Schmidt Tomorrow on 90th Birthday." *Chicago Tribune*, Nov 13, 1955.

43. "A Hypocrite in Literature." *Chicago Tribune*, Mar 21, 1868.

44. "When Boz Lived in Chicago," May 4, 1913.

45. Rodkin, Dennis. "The Dirty Dicken." *Chicago Reader*, Jun 24, 2004.

46. Note: Joseph's last name is also given as Hudlum, Hudlin, or Hudlam; I've used Hudlun based on the gravestone.

47. "Board of Trade Men in Mourning." *Chicago Tribune*, Jun 19, 1894.

48. Fields, A. N. "Writer Tells of First Amusement Park in Chicago." *Chicago Defender*, Nov 19, 1932.

49. "Janitor Joe 47 Years on Job at Board of Trade," 1928.

50. Ibid.

51. "Death and Funeral Services of Mrs. Anna Elizabeth Hudlun." *The Broad Axe*, Nov 28, 1914.

52. "Crank with a Gun." *Chicago Tribune*, Sept 28, 1893.

53. "'Janitor Joe' Fifty Years at Board of Trade." *Chicago Daily News*, Sept 4, 1931.

54. Brown, Hallie Q. *Homespun Heroines* (entry on Anna Hudlun). Oxford University Press, 1926.

55. "Janitor Joe 47 Years on Job at Board of Trade," 1928.

56. Graceland Cemetery Records, Section I, Lot 336.

57. U.S. Census Bureau. United States Census 1880.

58. No title. *The Broad Axe*, Mar 14, 1914.

59. Graceland Interment Book Volume 5.

60. Willis Montgomery death certificate.

61. "Evanston." *Chicago Daily Inter-Ocean*, May, 13, 1876.

62. "Obituary: Charles Williams." *Moline Dispatch*, Jan 29, 1934.

63. Roderick, Stella Virginia. *Nettie Fowler McCormick*. New Hampshire, Richard R. Smith, 1956.

64. Testimonial of Respect of the Bar of Chicago to the Memory of Hon. George Manierre, privately printed, 1863.

65. McKinney, Megan. *The Magnificent Medills*. Harper Collins, 2011.

66. Hutchinson, William T. *Cyrus McCormick*, 1935.

67. "The Late Captain Wood—Funeral Services." *Chicago Tribune*, Dec 21, 1865.

68. "With Our Dead." *Chicago Daily Inter-Ocean*, Sept 18, 1887.

69. "Eddy Memorial Services." *Baltimore Sun*, Oct 12, 1874.

Index

Gregg, John, 187
Gridley, Amy, 5–6, 38
Griffin, Marion Mahony, 92–93
Griffin, Walter Burley, 93
Gross, Emil, 226
Gurley, Jason, 40, 42

Hadduck, Edward, 241
Hadduck, Louisa Graves, 241
Hageman, Reinhard, 226
Hall, Elbridge, 25–26
Hall, Elizabeth Kimbark, 26
Hallberg, Lawrence (Lars), 85
Hamman, James, 89
Hammond, T. C., 98
Harris, Charles, 187
Harris, Henry, 44
Harrison, Anna Blaine, 179
Harrison, Carter, 30, 155, 219–221, 258
Harrison, Carter, Jr., 219–222
Harrison, Edith Ogden, 160
Harrison, Gilbert, 178, 179
Harrison, President William Henry, 211
Haymarket Affair, 29, 44, 155–156, 179, 220
Healy, G. P. A., xi, xii, 160
Heathcock, Edwin, 229
Heegaard, William, 114
Herman, Pee-wee, 133
Hettler, Herman, 116
High, Elizabeth, 243
High, George Henry, 243
High, George Meeker, 243
High, James, 171
High, John, 11, 243
Higinbotham, Harlow, 158
Hill, Boyd, 110
Hill, Elizabeth Dawson, 29
Hill, Joe, 95
Hill, Royal, 188
Hinz, Augusta, 81
Hjortsberg, Max, 25
Hoge, Jane, 180
Holabird, John, 108
Holabird, John, Jr., 108
Holabird, William, 108
Holabird and Roche, 2, 94, 108
Holabird and Root, 108, 114, 243
Holmes, H. H., ix
Holmes, John, 160
Holmes, Maud, 160
Honore, Benjamin, 104
Honore, Henry H., 148, 149, 151
Honoro, Laura, 104
Hosmer, Ann, 27–28
Hosmer, Charles, 28
Hosmer, Oliver, 28

Hossack, John, 188, 192
Howard, William, 25
Hoyt, William, 84–85
Hubbard, Gurdon, 182, 230–232
Hubbard, Mary Ann, 232
Huck, Clara, 247
Huck, Henry, 249
Huck, John, 10, 247
Huck, Louis, 247–249
Huck, Louis, Jr., 249
Huck, Paula Reif, 247–249
Hudlun, Joseph, 255–258
Hudlun, Joseph, Jr., 250
Hulbert, William, 226, 233–234
Hull, David Lee, 154
Hunter, Gen. David, 49–51
Hurlbut, Emma, 228
Hurlbut, Frederick, 228
Hurlbut, Horace, 228
Hutchinson, Charles, 113

Insull, Margaret, 127
Iroquois Theater Disaster, 84–85, 162, 220
Isham, Ralph, 135

Jackson, Horace, 45–47
Jackson, Jesse, 189
Jackson, President Andrew, 30
Jacob, Godfrey, 5
Jacobs, Oliver, 206
Jacobson, Amelia, 203
Jacobson, Anna, 203
Jacobson, Ole "Young Waffles," 202–203, 206
Jahn, Helmut, 241
James, Frank and Jesse, 80–81
jazz music, 36, 127, 128, 171
Jenney, Elizabeth, 40
Jenney, William Le Baron, ix, 40, 96, 108, 236
Johnson, Edna Shaw, 68
Johnson, Elizabeth "Tiny," 103
Johnson, Etta Duryea, 103
Johnson, Henrietta, 72
Johnson, Jack, 87, 88, 98, 102–104
Johnson, John, 72
Johnson, Moses, 14, 76, 192, 252
Johnson, Octavia, 72
Johnson, President Andrew, 70, 107, 116, 117, 236
Johnson, Rush, 68
Johnson, Samuel, 242–243
Judson, Sylvia Shaw, 240

Kahn, Fazlur, 129
Keats, John, 19, 172
Keith, Allen, 198

ADAM SELZER is the author of numerous books on Chicago, history, and folklore, including *H. H. Holmes: The True History of the White City Devil.*

The University of Illinois Press
is a founding member of the
Association of University Presses.

University of Illinois Press
1325 South Oak Street
Champaign, IL 61820-6903
www.press.uillinois.edu